CW00823235

Victor's Adventures in Spain:
Las Aventuras de Víctor en España:

A **SPANISH LANGUAGE** Parallel Text Study Book

Victor's Adventures in Spain:
A parallel Text Study Book

Gordon Smith-Durán

In collaboration with Cynthia Smith-Durán

LightSpeed Spanish

2014

Copyright © 2014 by LightSpeed Spanish

All rights reserved. This book or any portion thereof may not be reproduced or used in any manner whatsoever without the express written permission of the publisher except for the use of brief quotations in a book review or scholarly journal.

First Printing: 2014

ISBN ISBN 978-1-502-98591-0

LightSpeed Spanish
7 Simpasture Gate
Newton Aycliffe, Co. Durham DL5 5HH

www.lightspeedspanish.co.uk

Dedication

This goes out to all of our students and supporters who have excouraged us to continue on our quest to demystify the Spanish language and make it accessible to everyone.

.

Contents

Acknowledgements

We would like to thank all of the people who have contributed to the writing and publishing of this book. It could never have been written without the many hundreds of patient hours that our students have spent with us whilst we nattered on about the Spanish language.

To those and everyone else who has contributed in some way to this book, we thank you for all your support and encouragement.

Preface

This book is designed to be useful to students from Absolute Beginner to Intermediate and beyond. The reason we say this is that there are many levels on which you can use this book to improve your Spanish. We will explain how this can be done as you make your way through the workbook.

Victor's Adventures is a fun story that incorporates all the latest learning techniques and methods designed to help you learn at your optimum.

IMPORTANT AUDIO INFORMATION!
There are no CD's with this book. All the audios are downloaded online.

The story comes with a full audio book, read by Cynthia Smith-Durán, as well as additional Vocabulary and Idiom Builder audio resources along with an 'Into the Learning Zone' mp3, all of which can be freely downloaded from the website address:

www.lightspeedspanish.co.uk/victors-adventures

All you need do is to add this address into your browser, a password that you can find in this book and the audio files will be downloaded to your PC.

Victors Adventures is designed to walk you through some of the key grammatical structures of the Spanish language without making a massive deal of them. Grammar can be frightening to many people and for that reason we want you to be able to learn and retain the information whilst having the most fun possible.

As you set about working through this book, go at the pace that's right for you. There is no hurry and it's not a race.

The most important factor in learning at speed is that you enjoy the process. If it feels like it's becoming work, take a break. Listen to the audio instead, have a beer, just do something else and come back to it later when you're fully refreshed.

We recommend that you aim to do some learning each day. This helps information to go into your long term memory and helps your Spanish increase at a decent speed.

Finally, don't limit yourself to this book. There is a wealth of resources out there. Spread yourself about. Keep your learning varied and interesting. And remember: **use all the free resources we offer in our webpage**:

www.lightspeedspanish.co.uk

You learn so much more when you're having fun!

Your introduction to our system.

Here at LightSpeed Spanish we have designed a progressive learning system, which, by simply following along with us, will allow you to quickly build your Spanish comprehension and your ability to formulate great, well structured sentences.

This will be the first in a series of books that will assist you in developing your Spanish at a comfortable but rapid rate. This is not a complicated grammar book, but rather, it contains straightforward explanations in an easy to understand way that have been incorporated into a progressive learning pace that is sure to suit you.

Our Recommendation.

Everyone has different ways of learning and distinct learning styles. Some of our students will undoubtedly whizz through the book whilst others will be more methodical, taking one step at a time. Our only advice is that you go at the pace that's right for you and, even more importantly, that you follow the guidelines we offer you throughout the course. Naturally, this isn't a one-time-learning exercise and the beauty of this book is that you can keep coming back to it in order to increase your knowledge and confidence.

The Audio Transcript.

Each chapter has its own corresponding sound track which you will find on the transcript audio by going to: **www.lightspeedspanish.co.uk/victors-adventures**
We suggest that before you begin a specific part you listen to the spoken dialogue so that you become familiar with the sounds and pronunciation.
Remember: You don't have to consciously understand what you hear. You can trust that your mind will be making notes on how certain words are pronounced and sentences are formed.

Grammar and Vocabulary Lessons.

Accompanying each chapter is a lesson that takes you through a step by step guide of the main grammatical structures that appear as the story unfolds. It's worth studying this before moving on as it will help you gain so much more from the experience. Of course, whether you look at it before or after you read the chapter is entirely up to you.

The Vocabulary Builder audio.

Using the proven method of linking known words with new words, we have created a audio of key words and verbs from the story for you to learn. With this system, you can easily learn and, more importantly, retain a wealth of new vocabulary that will help you understand Víctor's Adventures even more easily and quickly.
We have also provided you with a quick memory guide to complement the audio on page 241.

The "Learning Zone" audio.

Using the most modern techniques to assist you in achieving your optimum learning capacity, this pack contains an audio that is specifically designed to help speed up your Spanish. In it, we guide you into the ideal "learning zone" and show you how you can get into the "zone" easily and quickly each time you begin to learn. Purely optional, this guided learning track is available for those who really want to take their learning to LightSpeed.

Breaking down verbs.

In the index on page 201 there is a section on breaking down or 'conjugating' verbs. We strongly recommend that you complete this part along with the exercises before you begin to read the story. This, too, will assist you greatly in identifying and understanding the verbs used within it.

The Best Way to Read the Story.

This is a parallel text story, and so there'll be a great temptation to read the Spanish whilst taking a sneaky peak at the English translation. Although sometimes that will be appropriate, we recommend that you cover up the English text until you finish that particular page and spend some time working out what everything means. You'll be very surprised at how much you already know! Trust your intuition.

For the More Advanced Learner.

If you are finding that translating from Spanish to English is a little too easy for you, then simply work the other way around. Read the English and translate it into Spanish. It's always more challenging that way. Remember: There are many ways to say the same thing in Spanish, so if you come up with something different to what's in the text, it could still be correct. ¡Buena suerte!

Lesson 1. Masculine and Feminine words. Palabras Masculinas y Femininas.

As you read this first chapter perhaps you can notice that it's filled with words like "el", "la", "un", "una" etc.
This is because all Spanish "naming words" (nouns) are either 'masculine or feminine'.

The Good News.

The good news is that, with the majority of Spanish nouns, you can easily know if they are masculine or feminine because of their endings.
e.g.

*Many masculine naming words end with **O***
*Many feminine naming words end with **A***

The Bad News.
The bad news is that, because there are masculine and feminine words, the Spanish language has to have four ways of saying the word "THE"

These are:

"THE" when talking about one masculine thing	*= EL*
"THE" when talking about one feminine thing	*= LA*
"THE" when talking about more than one feminine thing	*= LAS*
"THE" when talking about more than one masculine thing	*= LOS*

Then we have the words "A" and "SOME".

For example, "A dog", "Some dogs".

These are:

"A" when talking about one masculine thing	*= UN*
"A" when talking about one feminine thing	*= UNA*
"Some" when talking about some masculine things	*= UNOS*
"Some" when talking about some feminine things	*= UNAS*

Task: **Watch out for them in chapter 1. Also, watch what happens to the nouns (naming words) and adjectives (describing words) when they are plural.**

Ahora te toca a ti. / Now it's your turn.

How would you write?

1, The dog (perro)

1, *el perro*

2, The house (casa)

2, *la casa*

3, The tables (mesas)

3, *las mesas*

4, The boys (chicos)

4, *los chicos*

5, A cat (gato)

5, *un gato*

6, A cow (vaca)

6, *una vaca*

7, Some jackets (chaquetas)

7, *unas chaquetas*

8, Some glasses (vasos)

8, *unos vasos*

9, A hat (gorro) and (y) a scarf (bufanda)

9, *un gorro y una bufanda*

10, Some bags (bolsos) and some coats (abrigos)

10, *unos bolsos y unos abrigos*

Víctor y sus aventuras en España

Capítulo 1

Víctor Carlisle es un joven de veinticinco años. Vive en York, en el norte de Inglaterra. Trabaja en una oficina. Su trabajo es aburrido y Víctor no está contento. ¡Quiere vivir una aventura!

Un día llega a casa de sus padres con noticias inesperadas:

Víctor -Papá, mamá, quiero hablar con vosotros. No estoy feliz en mi trabajo. No es interesante y estoy cansado de estar en Inglaterra. ¡Quiero mudarme a España!-

Los padres de Víctor están sorprendidos. Normalmente, Víctor es una persona muy reservada y sensata.

Madre -Pero, ¿por qué España?-

Víctor -¡Porque me encanta!-

Cada año Víctor pasa sus vacaciones en España y le gusta mucho el país.

Padre -Y ¿cuándo te vas, Víctor?-

Víctor -En seis meses, porque primero quiero aprender un poco más de español. -

Víctor ya habla español un poco, pero sabe que para vivir y trabajar en España, necesita hablar bien.

Madre -Pero ¿cómo vas a vivir?-

Víctor -Voy a trabajar ¡claro!-

Durante los próximos días, Víctor busca en Internet para decidir dónde vivir en España. No quiere vivir en una zona muy turística. Prefiere estar en el interior del país. Después de mucho tiempo y muchas investigaciones, decide ir a Toledo.

Toledo es una ciudad muy antigua, romana con mucha historia. Es muy parecida a York. También, Víctor busca una clase de español. Encuentra una clase intermedia en su instituto local.

Victor and his adventures in Spain

Chapter 1

Victor Carlisle is a twenty-five year old youth. He lives in York, in the north of England. He works in an office. His job is boring and Victor isn't happy. He wants to have an adventure!

One day he arrives at his parents' home with unexpected news.

Victor "Dad, Mum, I want to talk with you. I'm not happy in my job. It's not interesting and I'm tired of being in England. I want to move to Spain!"

Victor's parents are surprised. Normally, Victor is a reserved and sensible person.

Mother "But why Spain?"

Victor "Because I love it!"

Each year Victor spends his holidays in Spain and he likes the country a lot.

Father "And when are you going, Victor?"

Victor "In six months because, firstly, I want to learn a little more Spanish."

Victor already speaks a little Spanish, but he knows that in order to live and work in Spain, he needs to speak it well.

Mother "But, how are you going to live?"

Victor "I'm going to work, of course!"

During the following days, Victor looks on the Internet to decide where to live in Spain. He doesn't want to live in a really touristic area. He prefers to be inland. After lots of time and investigation he decides to go to Toledo.

Toledo is an ancient Roman city with a lot of history. It's very similar to York. Victor also looks for a Spanish class. He finds an intermediate class in his local college.

La primera clase empieza el miércoles a las siete de la tarde y Víctor tiene mucha ilusión de empezar.

El miércoles, a las siete, entra en la clase. El profesor ya está allí.

Profesor -¡Hola! Buenas tardes. Soy Manuel González. ¿Cómo te llamas?-

Víctor -Buenas tardes, soy Víctor. Mucho gusto.-

Profesor -Igualmente. Entra, Víctor. La clase empieza en cinco minutos.-

Víctor se sienta y saca su cuaderno y bolígrafo. Tiene mucha ilusión. Quiere mejorar su español rápidamente y sólo tiene seis meses para tener un nivel más o menos aceptable.

El profesor empieza.

Profesor -Buenas tardes a todos. Soy Manuel González y hoy vamos a empezar con lo básico, los saludos. En España, normalmente saludamos así:-

¡Hola! Buenos días.

Buenas tardes.

Buenas noches.

Profesor -Luego decimos:-

¿Cómo estás?

Profesor -O aún más común:-

¿Qué tal?

Profesor -Típicamente, la gente contesta así:-

-Estoy muy bien, gracias. ¿Y tú?-

Profesor -Luego, contestas:-

-Estoy muy bien, también.-

The first class starts on Wednesday at seven in the evening and Victor is very excited to start.

On Wednesday at seven, he enters the class. The teacher is already there.

Teacher "Hi! Good afternoon. I'm Manuel Gonzalez. What's your name?

Victor "Good evening, I'm Victor. Pleased to meet you."

Teacher "The same here. Come in, Victor, the class starts in five minutes."

Victor sits down and takes out his notebook and pen. He's really excited. He wants to improve his Spanish quickly and he only has six months to get it to a more or less acceptable level.
The teacher starts.
Teacher "Good evening everyone. I'm Manuel Gonzalez and today we're going to start with the basics, the greetings. In Spain we greet like this:

Hi! Good morning.

Good afternoon/evening.

Good night.

Teacher "Then we say:"

How are you?

Teacher "Or even more commonly:"

How are things?

Teacher "Typically, people answer like this":

"I'm very well, thanks. And you?"

Teacher "Then you answer:"

"I'm very well, too."

La clase sigue y Víctor toma apuntes de todo lo que dice el profesor. Después de la clase, Víctor habla con él.

Víctor -Gracias por la información esta tarde. El español es muy interesante. Tengo planes de ir a España en seis meses y quiero saber si hay una manera de mejorar mi español rápidamente.-

Profesor -Claro que sí. Hay muchas maneras si tienes tiempo. Sin embargo, en mi opinión, Internet es la mejor opción. Hay millones de páginas para estudiantes como tú. ¿Por qué no empiezas en la sala de chat que se llama Espanglishchat? Su dirección es www.espanglishchat.com y es un sitio lleno de estudiantes hispanohablantes y angloparlantes que se ayudan el uno al otro a aprender. Es un buen sitio y estoy seguro de que vas a echarte unos amigos españoles.-

Víctor -Muchísimas gracias, Manuel. Voy a buscar ese sitio esta misma noche. Hasta luego.-

Profesor -Hasta luego, Víctor.-

The class continues and Victor takes notes on everything that the teacher says. After the class Victor talks with him.

Victor "Thanks for the information this evening. Spanish is really interesting. I've plans to go to Spain in six months and I want to know if there's a way of improving my Spanish quickly."

Teacher "Yes, of course. There are many ways if you have time. However, in my opinion, the Internet is the best option. There are millions of pages for students like you. Why don't you start in the chat room that's called Espanglishchat? The address is www.espanglishchat.com and it's a site filled with Spanish and English speaking students that help each other to learn. It's a good site and I'm sure that you're going to make some Spanish friends."

Victor "Thanks a lot, Manuel. I'm going to look for that site this very night. See you later."

Teacher "See you later, Victor."

Lesson 2. Singular and Plural. / Singular y Plural.

In the Spanish language, words that are singular are very clearly different to those that are plural.

Here's a singular word: EL CIELO (the sky)

And here's a plural word: LOS CIELOS (The skies)

Can you notice what has happened to make it plural?

These are the basic rules.

If a noun (naming word) or an adjective (describing word) ends in an O or an A then you simply ADD the letter S.

Remember that for the nouns, the THE word must also become plural as we explained in Grammar lesson 1.

e.g.

> el VINO (the wine) = los VINOS (the wines)

> la MESA (the table) = las MESAS (the tables)

You may have noticed that some words don't end with O or A.

What do you do to make them plural?

On the words (both nouns and adjectives) that end with any of the other vowels (E,I,U) you ADD the letter S.

e.g.   el HOMBRE (the man) = los HOMBRE**S** (the men)

> VERDE (green) = VERDE**S** (green)

There are some words, however, that end with a consonant (non-vowel letter)

To make these words plural you ADD the letters ES.

e.g.   la MUJER (the woman) = las MUJER**ES** (the women)

> el MANTEL (the tablecloth) = los MANTEL**ES** (the tablecloths)

Ahora te toca a ti / Now it's your turn.

Make the following words plural:

Singular	Plural
1, El chico (the boy)	*los chicos*
2, La mesa (the table)	*las mesas*
3, La silla (the chair)	*las sillas*
4, La oficina (the office)	*las oficinas*
5, El mantel (the tablecloth)	*los manteles*
6, El móvil (the mobile)	*los móviles*
7, El plato (the plate)	*los platos*
8, El tren (the train)	*los trenes*
9, La copa (the wine glass)	*las copas*
10, El portátil (the laptop)	*los portátiles*

Capítulo 2

En casa, Víctor va directamente a su dormitorio y enciende el ordenador. Mientras se carga, piensa en su aventura y en vivir en España. Sin duda va a ser muy interesante. Luego, escribe la dirección para abrir la página principal de Espanglishchat. Víctor, pone su apodo, Vic25 y pica en –enter-. Unos pocos segundos después aparece la sala de chat. Hay ciento veinte usuarios en el chat y va muy rápido. Víctor tiene miedo de empezar. Respira fuerte y empieza a escribir.

Víctor   -Hola. Muy buenas tardes. Me llamo Víctor y soy de Inglaterra.-

De repente aparecen unos mensajes.

Eliana22   -Hola Víctor. ¿De qué parte de Inglaterra eres?-

Madman   -Buenas tardes, Víctor. ¿Qué tal estás?-

Víctor no sabe a quién contestar primero.

Víctor   -@Eliana22...Soy de York, una ciudad en el norte de Inglaterra. @Madman...Estoy muy bien gracias, ¿y tú?-

Eliana22   - ¡Conozco York! Mi hermano estudia en la universidad. Normalmente yo paso dos semanas con él durante el verano. Me gusta mucho la cuidad. ☺ ¿Vives en el centro?-

Madman   -Estoy fenomenal, Víctor. ¿Es ésta la primera vez que entras en el chat?-

Víctor   -No, vivo en las afueras, Eliana, pero mi casa no está lejos del centro. Está a unos diez minutos. Y sí, Madman, es la primera vez que vengo aquí. Me gusta mucho. ☺-

Eliana22   -Y ¿por qué entras en el chat, Víctor?-

Víctor   -Porque voy a mudarme a España en seis meses y necesito mejorar mi español.-

Chapter 2

At home, Victor goes directly to his bedroom and switches on the computer. Whilst it starts up, he thinks about his adventure and about living in Spain. Without doubt it's going to be really interesting. Then, he writes the address to open the main page of Espanglishchat. Victor enters his nickname, Vic25 and presses "enter". A few seconds later the chatroom appears. There are one hundred and twenty users in the chat and it's going really quickly. Victor is frightened to start. He takes a deep breath and starts to write.

Victor   "Hi. Very good evening. I'm called Victor and I'm from England."

Suddenly some messages appear.

Eliana22   "Hi Victor. What part of England are you from?"

Madman   "Good afternoon, Victor. How are you?"

Victor doesn't know who to answer first.

Victor   "@Eliana22...I'm from York, a city in the north of England.
@Madman...I'm very well, thanks. And you?"

Eliana22   "I've been to York. My brother studies in York University. I normally spend two weeks with him during the summer. I really like the city. ☺ Do you live in the centre?"

Madman   "I'm fantastic, Victor. Is this the first time that you've come to the chat?"

Victor   "No, I live on the outskirts, Eliana, but my house isn't far from the centre. It's ten minutes away. And yes, Madman, this is the first time that I've come here. I like it a lot. ☺"

Eliana22   "And why have you come to the chat, Victor?"

Victor   "Because I'm going to move to Spain in six months and I need to improve my Spanish."

Madman   -¿Qué pasa, Víctor, no puedes aguantar más la comida inglesa? Jejeje.-

Eliana22   -¿En qué parte vas a vivir, Víctor?-

Víctor   -Jaja, Madman. No, no es eso. Me encanta España… Eliana, voy a mudarme a Toledo.-

Eliana22   -¡No me digas, Víctor! Yo soy de Toledo. ¡Qué coincidencia! ¿Tienes alojamiento ya?-

Víctor   -No, todavía no. Busco un piso pequeño o un apartamento. -

Eliana22   -Mi padre es arrendador. Le pregunto si tiene algo disponible. ¿Puedes volver al chat mañana, Víctor?-

Víctor -Claro, Eliana. Muchas gracias por la ayuda. Por cierto ¡encantado!-

Eliana22   -Igualmente, Víctor. Mira, tengo que cenar. Te veo en el chat mañana después de las diez, hora española. Hasta luego.-

Víctor -Hasta luego, Eliana.-

Víctor no puede creerlo. Ha tenido mucha suerte de conocer a Eliana. Esa noche chatea durante horas y se acuesta muy tarde. Antes de dormirse piensa en Eliana. Parece muy amable y tiene ganas de hablar con ella de nuevo. Víctor tiene mucha ilusión de ir a España y sabe que su estancia allí va a ser la aventura más grande de su vida.

Madman   "What's wrong, Victor, can't you stand the English food anymore? Hehehe."

Eliana22   "Which part are you going to live in, Victor?"

Victor   "Haha, Madman. No, it's not that. I love Spain…Eliana, I'm going to move to Toledo."

Eliana22   "You don't say, Victor! I'm from Toledo. What a coincidence! Do you have accommodation already?"

Victor   "No, not yet. I'm looking for a small flat or an apartment."

Eliana22   "My father is a landlord. I'll ask him if he has anything free. Can you come to the chat tomorrow, Victor?"

Victor   "Sure, Eliana. Thanks a lot for the help. By the way, nice to meet you!

Eliana22   "You too, Victor. Look, I have to have dinner. I'll see you in the chat tomorrow after ten, Spanish time. See you later."

Victor   "See you later, Eliana."

Victor can't believe it. He's been really lucky to meet Eliana. That night he chats for hours and he goes to bed really late. Before falling asleep he thinks about Eliana. She seems really nice and he's looking forward to talking with her again. Victor's very excited to go to Spain and he knows that his stay there is going to be the biggest adventure of his life.

Lesson 3. Very Important Verbs. (Doing words) / Verbos Muy Importantes.

The first few chapters have introduced us to what is probably the most important verb in the Spanish language which is:

The Verb to BE

And what's even more interesting is that there are two of them!

SER (to be)	ESTAR (to be)	To Be
yo **soy**	yo **estoy**	I am
tú **eres**	tú **estás**	you are (singular)
él/ella/usted **es**	él/ella/usted **está**	he/she is / you (formal)
nosotros/as **somos**	nosotros/as **estamos**	we are
vosotros/as **sois**	vosotros/as **estáis**	you are (plural)
ellos/as/ustedes **son**	ellos/as /ustedes **están**	they are / you all (formal)

"But why have two?" we hear you ask. (or not, as the case may be ;))

Well, the answer in its simplest form is that Spanish speakers choose to describe things in two ways:

Descriptions (**Ser**)	and	States (**Estar**)
e.g. English, female		e.g. angry, happy

Another way of thinking about this is:

Permanent Traits (Ser)   **Temporary States** (Estar)

Task: *Listen to the two songs on the bonus audio that will help you quickly learn the verbs, or, if you prefer, watch the videos on verb conjugation at LightSpeed Spanish.*

Beginners Spanish Podcast 5- Conjugating Spanish Verbs

Let's take a look at some of the describing words that appear in chapter 1 and notice with which verb they have been placed:

"Su trabajo **es** aburrido ..."   "His job is boring..."

Notice that we have used the verb **Ser** (permanent trait or description) to say that his job is boring. It's a boring job, and to him, it always will be.

However, we then go on to say:

"Víctor no **está** contento..."   "Victor is not happy..."

Here, we have used the verb **Estar**, to show that Victor is in a **state of unhappiness**. This is changeable...temporary.

One of the easiest ways to remember which verb to use is to recall that es**t**ar contains the letter, **T**, which in our book stands for **Temporary.**

Now, look through Chapter 1 and 2 and identify all the describing words that are used with Ser and the ones used with Estar. Can you see why we have done that?

¡Te toca a ti! It's your turn!

Which adjectives can be used with Ser and which with Estar? Tick the correct option.

Adjective	Ser	Estar
Feliz (happy)	( )	(✓)
Confundido (confused)	( )	(✓)
Rubio (blond)	(✓)	( )
Duro (hard)	(✓)	( )
Cansado (tired)	( )	(✓)
Inglés (English)	(✓)	( )

Answers in the index on page 212.

Note: The **weird thing** about the verb Estar is that it is also used to describe the location of something, even if that thing has been in the same place for centuries.

e.g. La iglesia **está** en la plaza mayor. The church is in the main square.

Extra note: The website, www.espanglishchat.com mentioned is not a one we just made up, but rather it is real and was fundamental in helping us improve our language. Give it a go, you may just love it!

Capítulo 3

A la noche siguiente, a las nueve y media, Víctor se mete en el chat y espera a Eliana. Ya tiene unos cuantos amigos en el chat y habla con ellos mientras espera. A las diez en punto, entra Eliana. Enseguida ella le manda un mensaje privado.

Eliana22 -Buenas noches, Víctor. ¿Qué tal estás?-

Víctor -Estoy de maravilla, Eliana. ¿Y tú?-

Eliana22 -Me alegro. Yo también. Tengo buenas noticias. He hablado con mi padre y él dice que tiene un apartamento que va a estar disponible en cinco meses. No es gran cosa, pero está amueblado y sólo cuesta trescientos Euros al mes. ¿Qué te parece?-

Víctor -¡Me parece fantástico! ¿Qué tengo que hacer para reservarlo?-

Eliana22 -Mi padre dice que necesitas pagar un mes de depósito y un mes por adelantado. Es lo normal aquí.-

Víctor -Aquí también. Todo me parece bien. Dime lo que tengo que hacer en cuanto a pagar el dinero y lo hago. –

Eliana22 -No lo sé. Mi padre hace todo eso. Mira, le pongo al ordenador. Se llama Alfredo.-

Víctor -Vale, Eliana. Gracias.-

De repente Víctor tiene nervios. No sabe hablar de negocios en español.

Alfredo -Hola, Víctor. ¿Qué tal? Mi hija dice que quieres alquilar el apartamento. -

Chapter 3

The following night, at nine-thirty, Victor logs onto the chat and waits for Eliana. He already has a good few friends in the chat and he talks with them whilst he waits. At ten o'clock on the dot Eliana enters. She sends him a private message straight away.

Eliana22 "Good evening, Victor. How are you?"

Victor "I'm wonderful, Eliana. And you?"

Eliana22 "I'm pleased for you. Me too. I've got good news. I've spoken with my father and he says that he has an apartment that is going to be available in five months. It's nothing fancy, but it's furnished and it only costs three hundred Euros per month. How does that seem?"

Victor "That's seems fantastic! What have I got to do to reserve it?

Eliana22 "My father says that you have to pay a month's deposit and a month in advance. It's the usual thing here."

Victor "Here too. Everything seems fine to me. Tell me what I have to do with regards to paying the money and I'll do it."

Eliana22 "I don't know. My father does all of that. Look, I'll put him on the computer. He's called Alfredo."

Victor "Okay, Eliana. Thanks."

Suddenly Victor is nervous. He doesn't know how to talk about business in Spanish.

Alfredo "Hi, Victor. How are you? My daughter says you want to rent the apartment."

Víctor -Estoy muy bien, Alfredo. Sí, me parece muy bien tu oferta. ¿Qué tengo que hacer?-

Alfredo -Sólo tienes que hacer una transferencia del dinero a mi cuenta y ya, al llegar el dinero, el apartamento es tuyo.-

Víctor -¡Perfecto! ¿Me puedes enviar por correo los detalles? Mañana voy al banco a organizar la transferencia.-

Alfredo -Lo haré en media hora, Víctor. Hasta pronto. Te paso con mi hija, Eliana.-

Víctor - Muchísimas gracias, Alfredo. -

Eliana22 -Hola, estoy de vuelta. ¿Ya lo has arreglado con mi padre, Víctor?-

Víctor -Sí, ya todo está arreglado. Gracias por la ayuda, Eliana. Eres muy amable.-

Eliana22 - De nada, Víctor.-

Víctor y Eliana hablan mucho rato. Eliana parece una persona muy amable y Víctor no puede creer la suerte que tiene. Ya parece que no sólo tiene alojamiento sino también una amiga nueva. Está seguro de que va a pasarlo muy bien en España.

Víctor "I'm very well, Alfredo. Yes, the offer seems great to me. What do I have to do?"

Alfredo "You just have to make a money transfer to my account and that's it, when the money arrives, the apartment is yours."

Víctor "Perfect! Can you send me your details by email? Tomorrow I'll go to the bank to organise the transfer."

Alfredo "I'll do it in half an hour, Victor. See you soon. I'll pass you on to my daughter, Eliana."
Víctor "Thanks a lot, Alfredo."

Eliana22 "Hi, I'm back. Have you fixed it with my father now, Victor?

Victor "Yes, everything is sorted now. Thanks for your help, Eliana. You're very kind."

Eliana22 "You're welcome, Victor."

Victor and Eliana talk for a good while. Eliana seems like a kind person and Victor can't believe his luck. Now it seems that not only does he have accommodation but a new friend too. He's sure he's going to have a good time in Spain.

Lesson 4. Making Basic Sentences. / Hacer Frases Básicas.

By now you have read a number of Spanish sentences. Have you already noticed that the structure isn't quite the same as in English sentences?

Let's look at one of the most important rules of a Spanish sentence.

Where to put the describing word.

In an English sentence, the describing word mostly comes first.

e.g.

> The **red** house.
>
> The **black** and **white** cat.
>
> The **happy** child.

In Spanish, most of the time, it's the opposite.

e.g.

> The house **red**.
>
> The cat **black** and **white**.
>
> The child **happy**.

As well as maintaining this order, when making a sentence in Spanish, there is one rule that must be adhered to at all times.

Everything in the sentence **MUST AGREE** with the **SUBJECT**.

Now, before you go rushing to Wikipedia to find out what the subject is, let us show you. It's easy! **The subject is the thing you are talking about.**

Examples of the subject:

> The **HAT** is big and brown.
>
> The **PEOPLE** are very happy.
>
> A **DICTIONARY** has many words.

So, the subject is the main thing that is mentioned in the sentence. It's a noun or naming word.

In the Spanish language, once you have mentioned the subject, all the describing words must agree with it in GENDER and PLURALITY.

*Let's use the word **SUELO** (floor) in a sentence. Suelo is masculine and singular. Therefore, all the describing words must be the same.*

e.g.

> *The floor is red and black.*

> ***El** suel**o** es ROJ**O** y NEGR**O**.*

However, if you use the same example with the word, house or CASA, we'll see what happens when the word is feminine singular.

e.g.

> ***La** casa es ROJ**A** y NEGR**A**.*

Let's change those two sentences to plural, now. SUELOS and CASAS.

Notice how the describing words change.

e.g.

> ***Los** suel**os** son ROJ**OS** y NEGR**OS**.*

> ***Las** cas**as** son ROJ**AS** y NEGR**AS**.*

When creating a sentence with numerous describing words (adjectives), you only have to separate each one with a comma and put "and" before the last one.

e.g.

> *La col grande, redonda **y** verde.*

> *The big, green, round cabbage.*

Ahora te toca a ti / Now it's your turn.

Translate these sentences and pay special attention to the agreements.

1, The girl is tall and thin. (chica, alto, delgado.)

....

2, The small, shy boy. (chico, pequeño, tímido.)

....

3, The big, black and blue cars. (grande, negro, azul, coche.)

....

4, The tall, pretty women. (alto, guapo, mujer.)

....

5, A wide, brown and comfortable chair. (ancho, marrón, cómodo, silla.)

....

Capítulo 4

Los días pasan rápido y después de poco tiempo Víctor está a punto de salir de casa para Toledo. Ha estudiado mucho español y ya tiene un nivel bastante bueno. Sus padres están muy tristes porque no quieren perder a su único hijo.

Madre -¿Cuánto tiempo piensas estar allí, Víctor?-

Víctor -No sé, Mamá. Depende de muchas cosas. Necesito encontrar trabajo. Tengo dinero suficiente para vivir allí seis meses sin trabajar. Sin embargo, espero encontrar trabajo directamente. Así que, si puedo trabajar en algo permanente, me quedaré más tiempo.-

Padre -Vas a llamarnos cada semana, ¿verdad?-

Víctor -Claro, papá. También voy a tener Internet, así que podemos hablar por Skype.-

Madre -Vamos a echarte de menos, Víctor.-

Víctor -Y yo a vosotros. También podéis visitarme en verano.-

Padre -Eso seguro. Tengo muchas ganas de ver Toledo.-

Chapter 4

The days pass quickly and very soon Victor is on the point of leaving home for Toledo. He has studied a lot of Spanish and has quite a good level now. His parents are very sad because they don't want to lose their only son.

Mother "How long are you thinking of staying there, Victor?"

Victor "I don't know, mum. It depends on a lot of things. I need to find work. I've got enough money to live there for six months without working. However, I hope to find work straight away. So, if I can work in something permanent, I'll stay longer."

Father "You're going to call us each week, aren't you?"

Victor "Of course, dad. I'm also going to get Internet, so we can talk through Skype."

Mother "We are going to miss you, Victor."

Victor "And I'll miss you both. You can come and visit me in summer, too."

Father "That's certain. I'm really looking forward to seeing Toledo."

Lesson 5. Reflexive verbs. / Verbos Reflexivos.

Firstly, let's start by explaining just what a reflexive verb is. They exist in the English language, but we do not use them to the extent that they do in the Spanish language.

We use reflexive verbs when we say things like:

"Have **yourself** a nice cup of tea."

"I'm going to buy **myself** a new coat."

"He's getting **himself** washed."

"Sit **yourself** down."

Can you see what is different about how these verbs are used?

Reflexive verbs include words like: Myself, Yourself, Himself, Herself, Ourselves, Themselves etc.

The most important thing to keep in mind is that **the reflexive action only happens to the people or things mentioned in the sentence**.

Let's take a closer look at the above sentences:

"Have **yourself** a nice cup of tea." The only person having your tea is you.

"I'm going to buy **myself** a new coat." Only you are going to receive the coat.

"He's getting **himself** washed." He's not washing anyone else, just himself.

"Sit **yourself** down." Just yourself, you won't be sitting other people down.

So, these verbs are "reflexive" because they **reflect back** on the person(s) doing them.

In the Spanish language, reflexive verbs are easy to spot. As a student of mine says, many of the reflexive verbs have an **ARSE** on the end.

That's true, at least for the **AR** verbs. The **ER** verbs have an **ERSE** and the **IR** have an **IRSE**.

Here are some Spanish reflexive verbs:

Levantarse = *To get oneself up*   **Sorprenderse** = *To be surprised (oneself)*

Ducharse = *To shower oneself*   **Mantenerse** = *To maintain oneself*

Sentirse = *To feel (emotions)*   **Irse** = *To take oneself off. (To go away)*

*You've probably already noticed that the **SE** part of the verb means **ONESELF**.*

*However, when we break down the reflexive verbs, each person has their own special reflexive word (pronoun). Take a look at how we break down **ducharse** which means **to shower**.*

Yo	**ME** duch**O**	Nosotros/as	**NOS** ducha**MOS**
Tú	**TE** ducha**S**	Vosotros/as	**OS** duchá**IS**
Él		Ellos	
Ella	**SE** duch**a**	Ellas	**SE** ducha**N**
Usted		Ustedes	

*Note: When working with reflexive verbs this order will never change. **ME** is always used with **YO**. **TE** is always used with **TÚ**, **SE** with **ÉL** etc.*

Each one of the pronouns means something slightly different.

ME = *Myself*

TE = *Yourself (singular, informal)*

SE = *Himself/Herself/yourself singular, formal*

NOS = *Ourselves*

OS = *Yourselves*

SE = *Themselves*

We said that a reflexive verb is something that is done only to the group or persons mentioned and so it kind of reflects back on them. Look at the following:

Me lavo = I wash **myself**.   Lavo a los niños. = I wash the children.

The first one is something you do only to yourself, therefore it's reflexive.

The second is something you are doing to others, therefore it is not reflexive.

NOS levantamos a las siete. = We get (**ourselves**) up at seven.

Levantamos la silla. = We lift the chair.

The first is something we do to ourselves. Thus it is reflexive.

The second is something we do to a chair. Thus it's just a normal verb.

It's worth noting that Spanish speakers use reflexive verbs frequently and that, to have a good command of the language, you must understand how these special verbs work.

Your task.

As you read through Victor's Adventures, see how many reflexive verbs you can identify.

Ahora te toca a ti / Now it's your turn

Translate these reflexive sentences.

1, He gets himself up. (Levantarse)

....

2, We shower ourselves. (Ducharse)

....

3, They prepare themselves a coffee. (Prepararse un café)

....

4, We comb our hair. (Peinarse el pelo)

....

5, I brush my teeth. (Lavarse/cepillarse los dientes)

....

Note: In sentences like: "I brush my hair." Spanish speakers say: "I brush myself **the** hair." rather than, "my hair". This is because they've already said "myself", so adding another "my" is unnecessary.

Capítulo 5

Víctor les da un beso a sus padres y sale de casa con sus maletas para ir al aeropuerto de Stansted. Antes de salir, su madre llora y su padre parece muy triste. También Víctor se siente un poco triste. Sin embargo, tiene mucha ilusión de ver Toledo y de conocer a Eliana. Ella va a recoger a Víctor de la estación de trenes en Toledo.

En la estación de York, Víctor espera en el andén número seis. Tiene su billete que ha comprado por Internet. El tren llega a tiempo y Víctor sube, coloca sus maletas en el compartimiento de equipajes y se sienta en un asiento al lado de la ventanilla. A Víctor le gusta viajar en tren y en este viaje tiene planes de estudiar sus libros de español. Desafortunadamente, justo antes de empezar a estudiar, una mujer se sienta a su lado y empieza a hablar.

Mujer -Hola, buenos días. Me llamo Suzy. Soy de Los Estados Unidos y estoy de vacaciones aquí en Inglaterra. ¿Eres inglés, tú?-

Víctor -Sí, soy inglés. Me llamo Víctor. Mucho gusto.-

Mujer -Igualmente. Llevo tres semanas aquí. He visto la ciudad de York y de Newcastle y he pasado una semana en la región de los lagos en Cumbria. Ahora voy a Londres. Me encanta Inglaterra, es muy bonita. Y tú, ¿adónde vas?-

Víctor sólo quiere estar tranquilo y estudiar pero parece que la mujer quiere hablar.

Víctor -Voy a España. Me mudo a Toledo.-

Mujer -¡Qué bien! Me encanta España. ¿Por qué te mudas a España? ¿Tienes familia allí?

-**Víctor** -No, pero tengo una amiga que vive en Toledo. Ella me ha ayudado a encontrar un piso. Todavía no tengo trabajo pero seguro que lo encuentro.-

Chapter 5

Victor gives his parents a kiss and leaves home with his cases to go to Stansted airport. Before leaving, his mum cries and his father looks very sad. Victor feels a little sad too. However, he is really excited to see Toledo and to meet Eliana. She's going to pick Victor up from the train station in Toledo.

In York train station, Victor waits on platform six. He has his ticket that he has bought on the Internet. The train arrives on time and Victor get's on, puts his cases in the luggage compartment and sits in a seat next to the window. Victor likes to travel by train and on this journey he plans to study his Spanish books. Unfortunately, just before he starts to study, a woman sits next to him and starts to talk.

Woman "Hi, good morning. My name's Suzy. I'm from the United States and I'm on holiday here in England. Are you English?

Victor "Yes, I'm English. My name's Victor. Nice to meet you."

Woman "Nice to meet you too. I've been here for three weeks. I've visited York city and Newcastle and I've spent a week in the Lake District in Cumbria. Now I'm going to London. I love England, it's very pretty. And where are you going to?

Victor just wants to be quiet and study but it seems that the woman wants to talk.

Victor "I'm going to Spain. I'm moving to Toledo."

Woman "How nice! I love Spain. Why are you moving to Spain? Do you have family there?"

Victor "No, but I have a friend who lives in Toledo. She's helped me find a flat. I still don't have a job but I'm sure I'll find one."

Mujer -Y ¿hablas español?-

Víctor -Sí, un poco. Entiendo más que hablo. Y tú, ¿hablas español?-

Mujer -¿Quién, yo? ¡En absoluto! Me cuesta hablar inglés bien. Me gustaría aprender pero no soy buena con los idiomas.-

Víctor -A mí me encanta. Estudio todos los días. -

Mujer -¡Qué bien! Admiro a la gente como tú. Mi marido dice que yo no tengo persistencia pero yo creo que sí. Simplemente no se me dan bien los idiomas.-

La mujer sigue hablando sin parar durante mucho tiempo. Víctor no está muy contento. Quiere utilizar el viaje para estudiar, pero la mujer habla por los codos.

Finalmente llega el momento en el que la mujer necesita respirar.

Víctor -Bueno, perdón. Creo que voy al restaurante a comprarme un sándwich. –

Mujer -Vale. Hasta pronto.-

Cogiendo sus cosas Víctor se levanta y baja por el pasillo pero, en vez de ir a por un sándwich, va a otro vagón. Allí, encuentra unos asientos tranquilos y se sienta para estudiar. Ahora puede concentrarse en sus libros.

Al llegar a la estación de King´s Cross, Víctor baja del tren con su maleta y en el andén ve a la mujer americana. Se siente un poco avergonzado pero ella le mira y sonríe.

Mujer -Que lo pases muy bien en España. Siento mucho hablarte tanto. Es que, de verdad, soy muy habladora.-

Víctor -No pasa nada. Disfruta de tus vacaciones. Adiós.-

Woman "And do you speak Spanish?"

Victor "Yes, a little. I understand more than I speak. And you, do you speak Spanish?

Woman "Who me? Absolutely not! It's hard for me to speak English. I would love to learn but I'm not good with languages."

Victor "I love it. I study every day."

Woman "How nice! I admire people like you. My husband says that I don't have persistence but I think I do. It's just that I'm not good with languages."

The woman continues talking without pause for a long time. Victor isn't very happy. He wants to use the journey to study, but the woman is talking non-stop.

Finally the moment arrives in which the woman has to take a breath.

Victor "Well, excuse me. I think I'm going to the restaurant to buy myself a sandwich."

Woman "Okay. See you soon."

Grabbing his things Victor gets up and goes down the aisle but, instead of going for a sandwich, he goes to another carriage. He finds some quiet seats there and sits down to study. Now he can concentrate on his books.

Upon arriving at King's Cross Station, Victor gets off the train with his suitcase and on the platform he sees the American woman. He feels a bit embarrassed but she looks at him and smiles.

Woman "Have a great time in Spain. I'm really sorry about talking so much. It's just that I'm a real chatterbox."

Victor "Don't worry. Enjoy your holidays. Goodbye."

Lesson 6. Possessive Adjectives. Adjetivos Posesivos (my, your, his, her, etc.)

Who is the owner of what?

Just as in English, Spanish speakers have a range of words known as the "possessive adjectives".

These do exactly what they say on the tin and they are used to describe who the owner of a particular item is.

example: **My** car, **your** hat, **their** home, **our** bicycle etc.

Please, note that because these are adjectives (describing words), they must be accompanied by a noun (naming word).

They can't be used on their own.

(Nuestro/as and Vuestro/as can be used alone, but they mean something else as you'll see later.)

Here is the list:

Person/Owner	One item	More than 1 item
Yo	mi = my	mis = my
Tú	tu = your	tus = your
Él/Ella	su = his/her	sus = his/her
Usted	su = your	sus = your
Nosotros/as	nuestro/a = our	nuestros/as = our
Vosotros/as	vuestro/a = your	vuestros/as = your
Ellos/as	su = their	sus = their
Ustedes	su = your	sus = your

Task. As you read through the story, notice how many of these possessive adjectives you can find.

How do I know which one to use?

*When deciding which adjective to choose, all you need do is ask **yourself these questions**:*

Who is the owner?

Is the owned item single or is it plural?

e.g.1 **Her houses**.

Who is the owner? = Ella   (su or sus)

Single or plural? = Plural (houses)   (Thus = sus)

Correct sentence = **Sus casas**.

e.g.2 **Their car**. (My parents' car.)

Who is the owner? = Ellos   (su or sus)

Single or plural? = Single (car)   (Thus = su)

Correct sentence = **Su coche**.

Please, note that Nuestro and Vuestro can be masculine and feminine, singular or plural.

To know which one to use, all you need do is add one extra question to the above:

Is the item owned masculine or feminine?

e.g.1

Our job.

Who is the owner? = Nosotros   (Nuestros/as)

Is job masculine or feminine? = Masculine (el trabajo)   (Nuestros)

Single or plural? = Single (job)   (Nuestro)

Correct sentence = **Nuestro trabajo**.

e.g. 2

Your houses. *(Both of you, my friends.)*   *(Vuestros/as)*

Who is the owner? = Vosotros

Are houses masculine or feminine = Feminine (las casas)   *(Vuestras)*

Single or plural? = Plural (houses)   *(Vuestras)*

*Correct sentence = **Vuestras casas**.*

Ahora te toca a ti.

Here are some sentences. Fill in the gaps with the appropriate adjective.

1. Es _____ coche. (my)

It's my car.

2. Son _____ amigos. (your/vostros)

They are your friends.

3. _____ casa es grande. (their)

Their house is large.

4. Son _____ manzanas. (our)

They are our apples.

5. ¿ Este es _____ perro? (your/usted)

Is this your dog?

6. ¿Cuándo es _____ cumpleaños? (your/tú)

When is your birthday?

7. _____ plátanos están verdes. (their)

Their bananas are green.

8. Te presento a _____ hijos. (my)

These are my children (Literally "I present you to my children)

9. Tú tienes _____ entradas. (our)

You have our tickets.

10. Este es _____ cuaderno (your/tu) y estos son _____ libros. (my)

This is your notebook and these are my books.

Capítulo 6

Ahora, Víctor tiene que hacer transbordo. Va a la estación del Stansted Express y veinte minutos después está en el aeropuerto de Stansted. Entra y busca el mostrador de RapidAir. Lo encuentra, pero nota que tiene una cola muy larga. Tiene tiempo de sobra, así que no se preocupa. Mientras espera, escucha música española en su MP3 y el tiempo pasa rápidamente. Por fin llega al mostrador.

Azafata -Hola, buenas tardes. ¿Adónde vuela?-

Víctor -A Madrid-

Azafata -Muy bien. Su pasaporte y billete por favor.-

Víctor le entrega sus documentos a la azafata y los mira.

Azafata -Todo bien. ¿Tiene una maleta que facturar?-

Víctor -Sí. Aquí está.-

Víctor pone su maleta grande en la cinta al lado del mostrador y la azafata mira el peso.

Azafata -Lo siento, pero lleva sobrepeso. Tiene que quitar tres kilos o pagar sesenta Euros de exceso.-

Víctor -¡Dios mío! No quiero pagar eso pero, ¿dónde puedo meter tres kilos?

Azafata -¿Tal vez en su maleta de mano?-

Víctor -Lo intento.-

Víctor abre su maleta y empieza a sacar cosas. Su maleta de mano no es muy grande y ya está más o menos llena. Después de sacar las cosas más pesadas, pone su maleta otra vez en la cinta.

Azafata -Ya, está bien. Aquí tiene su billete y pasaporte. El avión sale de la puerta de embarque B17 en una hora.-

Víctor -Gracias.-

Chapter 6

Now, Victor has to change trains. He goes to the Stansted Express station and twenty minutes later he's in Stansted airport. He goes in and looks for RapidAir's desk. He finds it, but he notices that it has a long queue. He's got spare time, so he doesn't worry. Whilst he waits, he listens to Spanish music on his MP3 player and the time goes by quickly. Finally he arrives at the desk.

Air Stewardess "Hi, good afternoon. Where are you flying to?"

Victor "To Madrid."

Air Stewardess "Very good. Your passport and ticket, please."

Victor hands over his documents to the stewardess and she looks at them.

Stewardess "Everything's fine. Do you have a case to check in?"

Victor "Yes, here it is."
Victor puts his case on the belt at the side of the desk and the stewardess looks at the weight.

Stewardess "Sorry, but you have excess weight. You have to take out three kilos or pay sixty Euros excess baggage."

Victor "My God! I don't want to pay that but, where can I put three kilos?"

Stewardess "Maybe in your hand luggage?"

Victor "I'll try."

Victor opens his case and starts to take things out. His hand luggage isn't very big and it's already more or less full. After taking out the heaviest things, he puts his case on the belt again.

Stewardess "That's fine now. Here you have your ticket and passport. The plane leaves from gate number B17 in an hour."

Victor "Thank you."

Lesson 7. Talking about the future. Hablar del futuro.

Like English, the Spanish language has a way of talking about the future using the expression, "going to".

This is made up of the verb **IR** which means **"to go"** and the word/letter **A** which means **"to"**.

Unlike the verbs you've been looking at earlier, **IR** is very irregular. Here's how it breaks down:

Yo **VOY** = I'm going/I go   Nosotros **VAMOS** = We are going/we go

Tú **VAS** = You are going/you go   Vosotros **VAIS** = You all are going/you all go

Él/ella **VA**= He/she is going/goes   Ellos/ellas **VAN** = They are going/they go

Usted **VA** = You go (Formal)   Ustedes **VAN** = You all go (Formal)

Typically, this verb is followed by the word/letter A which means "to".

e.g.

> Voy a la playa = I'm going to the beach

> Vamos a comer = We're going to eat

Perhaps you've noticed in the examples that when you use the verb in this way, you can either talk about **where** someone is going (The place) or **what** they are going to do (The action) See also page 191 for "Going to go."

This means that you can either add a verb in infinitive (The whole verb):

e.g.   Ellos van a **nadar** = They are going to swim

Or you can add a place.

e.g.   Tú vas a la **carnicería** = You are going to the butchers.

The only thing you must be aware of, however, is that when you are adding the letter **A** to the masculine article **EL**, you need to join them together.

e.g.   Voy **A EL** cine becomes voy **AL** cine.

With LA, LOS, LAS this exception doesn't apply.

e.g.   Van **a la** frutería. = They go to the fruit shop.

You will also see IR used with the word DE.

e.g.   *Ir de vacaciones = To go on holiday*

                          Ir de compras = To go shopping

                          Ir de fiesta = To go partying

For the moment, however, you should stick to becoming familiar with the main use of IR with A.

Ahora te toca a ti. Translate these sentences. (You may need a dictionary.)

1, I'm going to Spain...

2, We are going to eat a sandwich...

3, They are going to arrive soon..

4, You all are going to the bank..

5, You are going to be a teacher...

6, I'm going to eat chips...

7, He is going to have a coffee.(Tomar)..

8, They are going to talk...

9, She is going to her friend's house. (The house of her friend.)

...

10, We are going to go to the beach. ....

Capítulo 7

Después de facturar la maleta grande, Víctor va directamente al control de seguridad. Otra vez hay una cola muy larga. Ahora la maleta de mano de Víctor pesa mucho y no cierra bien. Quince minutos más tarde llega al control. En una bandeja pone su maleta, su abrigo, su cinturón, el contenido de sus bolsillos, su reloj y, por último, sus zapatos.

Pasa por el escan y, desafortunadamente, pita. El hombre de seguridad saca su detector de metales y empieza a escanear a Víctor. No encuentra nada de metal, así que le registra. Víctor no puede creerlo. Parece que su viaje ha empezado mal. Sólo quiere estar en el avión, tranquilo.

El hombre termina el registro y le dice que ya puede pasar a recoger sus cosas. En cuanto llega a la bandeja, otro hombre le detiene.

Hombre -Perdone, señor pero ¿tiene aerosoles en su maleta de mano?-

Víctor -¡Claro que no! Están en mi maleta.-

Hombre -Entonces, ¿podemos mirar en su maleta de mano, por favor?-

En ese momento Víctor se da cuenta de que había sacado unos artículos de su maleta grande y que había escogido las cosas más pesadas. Víctor abre su maleta y justo encima de todo hay un aerosol de desodorante y uno de espuma de afeitar.

Víctor -Lo siento. Son de mi maleta grande. He tenido que sacar unas cosas por el sobrepeso.-

Hombre -No se preocupe. No pasa nada. Pero claro, no puede pasar con estas cosas. Tiene que dejarlas con nosotros.-

Víctor -Vale. Lo siento.-

Víctor sale del control y empieza a ponerse los zapatos y el cinturón. ¡Qué mala suerte!

Chapter 7

After checking in his suitcase, Victor goes directly to security. Once again there is a long queue. Victor's hand luggage now weighs a lot and it won't close properly. Fifteen minutes later he arrives at security control. He puts his case, his coat, his belt, the contents of his pockets, his watch and lastly, his shoes in the tray.

He passes through the scanner and, unfortunately, it beeps. The security officer takes out his metal detector and starts to scan Victor. He doesn't find any metal, so he frisks him. Victor can't believe it. It seems like his journey has begun badly. He just wants to be on the plane, in peace.

The man finishes the check and tells him that he can go and collect his things. When the tray arrives another man stops him.

Man "Excuse me, Sir, but do you have aerosols in your hand luggage?"

Victor "Of course not! They're in my suitcase."

Man "Then, can we look in your hand luggage, please?"

In that moment Victor realises that he had taken some things out of his suitcase and that he had chosen the heaviest things. Victor opens his case and right on top of everything there's a can of deodorant and a can of shaving foam.

Victor "I'm sorry. They're from my suitcase. I've had to take out some things because of the weight."

Man "Don't worry. There's no problem. But, of course, you can't go through with these things. You have to leave them here with us."

Victor "Okay. I'm sorry."

Victor leaves security and starts to put on his shoes and belt. What bad luck!

Después de recoger sus cosas, va a la sala de espera y mira las pantallas. Según la información, su avión sale a tiempo. Queda una hora hasta el despegue y Víctor decide tomar un café. Va directamente a una cafetería.

Dependiente   -Hola. ¿Qué le pongo?-

Víctor   -Un café cortado, por favor.-

Dependiente   -Un café cortado. ¿Eso es todo?-

Víctor   - Sí. Es todo.-

Dependiente   -Son tres libras con cincuenta peniques.-

Víctor   -Aquí tiene. Gracias.-

Víctor coge su café y se sienta en una mesa para esperar. Le gusta pasar tiempo en los aeropuertos porque, en su opinión, hay un ambiente de ilusión. Cada persona tiene un destino distinto. El café sabe muy bien y, por fin, Víctor empieza a relajarse un poco. Saca un libro de su maleta de mano y lee.

Media hora después, Víctor decide mirar la pantalla de información para ver el estado de su vuelo. ¡No lo puede creer! Pone que su avión viene con una hora de retraso. ¡Ya es el colmo! Primero la mujer habladora, luego su maleta, luego sus aerosoles y ahora el avión. ¿Qué más puede pasar?

No hay nada más que hacer que sentarse y esperar. Pide otro café, encuentra un asiento más o menos cómodo y lee.

After getting his things, he goes to the waiting area and looks at the screens. According to the information, his plane leaves on time. There's an hour until takeoff and Victor decides to have a coffee. He goes straight to a café.

Assistant   "Hi, what can I get you?"

Victor   "An espresso with a dash of milk, please."

Assistant   "An espresso with a dash of milk. Is that all?"

Victor   "Yes, that's all."

Assistant   "That's three pounds fifty."

Victor   "Here you are. Thanks."

Victor takes his coffee and sits at a table to wait. He likes spending time in airports because, in his opinion, there's an atmosphere of excitement. Each person has a different destination. The coffee tastes really nice and, finally, Victor starts to relax a little. He takes a book out his hand luggage and reads.

Half an hour later, Victor decides to look at the information screens to see the status of his flight. He can't believe it! It says that his plane is delayed by an hour. That's the limit! First the chatterbox women, then his suitcase, then the aerosols and now the plane. What more can happen?

There's nothing else to do than to sit and wait. He orders another coffee, finds a seat that's more or less comfortable and reads.

Lesson 8. Saying what you've done. Decir lo que has hecho.

Just as in English, the Spanish language has a way of forming sentences like:

I have eaten my evening meal.

We have taken the children to the park.

They have lived in France.

This is officially known as the **Present Perfect** tense and is made up of two parts.

Part 1.

The doing word, **HABER** which means **TO HAVE** (done)

So how does HABER break down? Well, it's quite irregular.

Yo **HE** = I have	Nosotros **HEMOS** = We have
Tú **HAS** = You have	Vosotros **HABÉIS** = You all have
Él/Ella **HA** = He/She has	Ellos/Ellas **HAN** = They have
Usted **HA** = You have (Formal)	Ustedes **HAN** = You all have (Formal)

Remember: When it's not joined to the letter C, H is the only silent letter in the Spanish language so you mustn't pronounce it.

e.g.   **HE** = A (Similar to the sound of the English letter A)

                 HAS = ASS

                 etc.

Part 2.

The second part of this tense is made up of what we call the **Past Participle** and what you know as words like:

eaten-spoken-written-walked-talked-driven

In English, there are many variables, not only of the spelling but also in pronunciation.

In Spanish, however, apart from a definitive list of irregular forms, making the past participle is really easy.

This is how you do it:

ER and IR verbs.

*Take **off** the **ER** or **IR***

e.g.   *COMER=COM   VIVIR=VIV*

*Then **add IDO***

e.g.   **COMIDO** = Eaten   **VIVIDO** = Lived

AR verbs.

*Take off the **AR***

e.g.   *HABLAR = HABLA*

*Then **add ADO***

e.g.   **HABLADO** = Talked

The next step is to put them together.

I have talked = HE HABLADO

We have lived = HEMOS VIVIDO

They have eaten = HAN COMIDO

Irregular verbs.

As mentioned earlier, there are some verbs that don't follow the usual rules. These simply have to be memorised. The job is easy, however, given that they are some of the most frequently used. Here are some of the most important ones.

abrir (to open)	*abierto*	*morir (to die)*	*muerto*
cubrir (to cover)	*cubierto*	*poner (to put)*	*puesto*
decir (to say)	*dicho*	*resolver (to resolve)*	*resuelto*
escribir (to write)	*escrito*	*romper (to break)*	*roto*
freír (to fry)	*frito*	*ver (to see)*	*visto*
hacer (to do)	*hecho*	*volver (to return)*	*vuelto*

Note:

The verb HABER which means TO HAVE (done) is often confused with TENER which means TO HAVE (got).

In English, we don't differentiate between the two words:

> *"I have a tennis bat."*

and

> *"I have played tennis."*

In Spanish, however, there is a big difference.

*To **check** which verb "To Have" you need to use, all you do is **add** the word "**got**".*

If it doesn't make sense, then Haber will normally be the verb you should use.

e.g.

*I have a car. **Test**. I have GOT a car. This makes sense so the verb will be TENER.*

*I have eaten. **Test**. I have GOT eaten. This doesn't make sense so the verb must be HABER.*

Ahora te toca a ti. / Now it's your turn.

Translate the following sentences:

1, I have spoken with the man. ....

2, I have a fast car. ....

3, Have you eaten? (Tú) ....

4, Do you have a moment? (Vosotros, momento).. ....

5, They have written a book. ....

6, Have you fried the chips? (Usted) ....

7, Have you seen my car? (Tú) ....

8, I have put the coffee on the table. (café, mesa).. ....

9, We have watched the television. (la televisión).. ....

10, Have you drunk a tea? (Ustedes, té) ....

Capítulo 8

Una larga hora después, su avión está listo para el embarque y Víctor va a su puerta. Ya hay una cola muy larga y todos los pasajeros parecen frustrados.

Mientras espera, Víctor nota que una azafata trae un cajón de metal que se usa para medir las maletas de mano. Empieza a obligar a los pasajeros a que pongan sus maletas en el cajón para medir sus dimensiones. La mayoría entra bien, pero de vez en cuando, una maleta cabe con mucha dificultad. Víctor mira su maleta. No cierra bien y parece abarrotada. Empieza a preocuparse. Unos minutos más tarde llega la azafata.

Azafata -Por favor, ¿puede meter la maleta en el cajón?-

Víctor -Claro. Sin problema.-

Víctor mete la maleta en el cajón pero, desgraciadamente, no entra bien. Es demasiado ancha.

Azafata - Parece que no va a entrar. Eso significa que tiene que facturar la maleta. Tenemos que pesarla para saber el coste.-

Víctor -Espere, por favor. Creo que ya entra.-

Desesperado, Víctor empuja muy fuerte y con alivio nota que la maleta entra. La azafata parece un poco mosqueada y tiene cara de pocos amigos.

Azafata -Bueno. Supongo que está bien. Por favor, sáquela del cajón.-

Víctor coge la maleta e intenta sacarla. No se mueve. Intenta otra vez pero no puede sacarla del cajón. Todos los otros pasajeros lo miran y se siente bastante incómodo. De repente, oye la voz de un hombre detrás de él.

Chapter 8

One long hour later, his plane is ready to board and Victor goes to his gate. There is already a long queue and all the passengers look frustrated.

Whilst he waits, he notices that a Stewardess is bringing a metal frame used for measuring the hand luggage. She starts to oblige the passengers to put their luggage in the frame to measure their dimensions. The majority goes in fine but, once in a while, a case fits with great difficulty. Victor looks at his case. It doesn't close properly and it looks fit to burst. He starts to worry. A few minutes later the stewardess arrives.

Stewardess "Please, can you put the case in the frame?"

Victor "Of course, no problem."

Victor puts his case in the frame but, unfortunately, it won't go in properly. It's too wide.

Stewardess "It doesn't seem to fit. That means that you have to check the case in. We have to weigh it to know the cost."

Victor "Wait, please. I think that it fits now."

Desperate, Victor pushes really hard and with relief he notes that the case goes in. The stewardess looks a little ticked off and she's got a face like a smacked bottom.

Stewardess "Well. I suppose that's okay. Take the case out, please."

Victor grabs his case and tries to take it out. It won't move. He tries again but can't free the case from the frame. All the other passengers are looking at him and he feels quite uncomfortable. Suddenly, he hears the voice of a man behind him.

Hombre -¿Te ayudo con eso?-

Víctor -Sí, por favor. Es que no quiere salir.-

Hombre -Apártate, tengo mucha experiencia en esto.-

El hombre es muy grande. Parece un jugador de rugby o algo semejante. Coge la maleta y tira con todas sus fuerzas. Con un chirrido la maleta sale y el hombre se la entrega a Víctor.

Víctor -Muchísimas gracias-

Hombre -De nada. Me ha pasado muchas veces. Ten cuidado porque te cobran mucho por facturar una maleta de mano.-

Man "Can I help you with that?"

Victor "Yes, please. It doesn't want to come out."

Man "Step aside, I have a lot of experience in this."

The man is really large. He looks like a rugby player or something similar. He grabs the case and pulls with all of his might. With a scraping noise the case comes out and the man hands it back to Victor.

Victor "Thanks ever so much."

Man "You're welcome. It's happened to me many times. Be careful because they charge you a lot to check in hand luggage."

Lesson 9. Ser and Estar. Revisited.

Because these verbs are so important, we are going to take another look at them in more detail. By now you will have seen them in action many times in the book and you also should have **listened to the songs on the audio** to help you remember how they break down.

Remember:

<u>Why do they have two verbs?</u>

This is because the Spanish language differentiates between something that has:

Permanent Traits..............SER

and something that has:

Temporary States ....ESTAR

Remember that **ESTAR** *has a* **"T"** *in it, which will help to remind you that it's* **Temporary.**

What do we mean by permanent and temporary?

Although this rule doesn't apply to every case, it's a handy way to know when you should use Ser or Estar.

Example.

In your opinion, which sentence is permanent and which is temporary?

I'm very angry right now!

I'm French.

Have you decided?

Answer.

*Well, once you've calmed down, you won't be angry. So that's **temporary**.*

*However, if you are born French, then you'll be French for your entire life, so that's **permanent**.*

Those two examples are very clear cut. Sometimes it's not so obvious. However, if you use the temporary/permanent guideline, you'll be right 90% of the time.

And that isn't bad for starters.

Here's how the verbs break down again.

SER

Yo **soy**	Nosotros **somos**
Tú **eres**	Vosotros **sois**
Él/Ella **es**	Ellos/Ellas **son**
Usted	Ustedes

ESTAR

Yo **estoy**	Nosotros **estamos**
Tú **estás**	Vosotros **estáis**
Él/Ella **está**	Ellos/Ellas **están**
Usted	Ustedes

*Apart from using the idea of permanent and temporary, it may help to think of **SER** as a verb of **description** and **ESTAR** a verb of **state.***

Let's show you some examples:

SER

Permanent/Description

He is a good boy	**Él es un chico bueno**
She is a teacher	**Ella es profesora**
They are Russian	**Ellos son rusos**
We are tall	**Nosotros somos altos**
You are a happy person	**Tú eres una persona feliz**

Notice that the last example is talking about the person's personality and not a temporary state.

ESTAR

Temporary/State

She is in Canada	**Ella está en Canadá**
He is ill	**Él está enfermo**
They are bored	**Ellos están aburridos**
We are in the square	**Nosotros estamos en la plaza**
You are happy today	**Tú estás contento hoy**

Here are a few examples of some of the ways that **Ser** and **Estar** are used.

SER		ESTAR	
Alto/a (s)	Tall	Bien	Good
Bajo/a (s)	Short	Mal	Bad
Guapo/a (s)	Good looking	Feliz (felices)	Happy
Feo /a (s)	Ugly	Triste	Sad
Inteligente (s)	Intelligent	de buen humor	In a good mood
Estúpido /a (s)	Stupid	de mal humor	In a bad mood
Hombre (s)	Man	Cerca	Near
Mujer (es)	Woman	Lejos	Far
Joven (es)	Young	Sentado /a (s)	Seated
Mayor (es)	Old	de pie	Stood up
de Inglaterra	from England	Vivo /a (s)	Alive!
inglés /inglesa	English	Muerto/a (s)	Dead!
de España	from Spain	Cansado/a (s)	Tired
español/a	Spanish	Listo/a (s)	Ready
Delgado/a (s)	Slim	En la mesa	On the table
Gordo/a (s)	Fat	Borracho/a (s)	Drunk
Simpatico/a (s)	Kind	Antipático /a (s)	Unkind

Now it´s your turn. / Te toca a ti.

Decide whether these sentences should be **Ser** or **Estar** and add the appropriate conjugation.

Here are the verbs again.

SER (to be)	ESTAR (to be)
Yo **soy**	Yo **estoy**
Tú **eres**	Tú **estás**
Él /ella **es**	Él/ella **está**
Nosotros **somos**	Nosotros **estamos**
Vosotros **sois**	Vosotros **estáis**
Ellos/as **son**	Ellos/as **están**

1. Los chicos ………… en la clase.

2. Yo …… profesor de matemáticas.

3. Vivo en Inglaterra pero ……….. en Francia.

4. Mi padre…….... español y mi madre ……. inglesa.

5. Ellos ………… hombres y hoy……….. muy felices.

6. Yo ……….... Marco y ……… en el centro de la ciudad.

7. Nosotros ………… de vacaciones en Australia. (on holiday)

8. Ellos ………… vivos, pero ellas ………… muertas.

9. Mi amigo ……. borracho.

10 Mi hermana ……. muy inteligente.

Capítulo 9

Muy aliviado, Víctor coge su maleta y entra en el avión. Ya está harto del aeropuerto de Stansted y sólo quiere estar en España de una vez. Por supuesto, su viaje no ha terminado todavía y al llegar a Madrid tiene que coger el metro y el tren para ir a Toledo. Con todo su corazón él espera que todo le vaya bien en España.

Después de colocar su maleta arriba en el compartimento, se sienta y espera el despegue. A su lado hay un chaval que parece español. Víctor le saluda.

Víctor -Hola. ¿Qué tal?-

Chaval -Hola. No hablo inglés. Soy español.-

Víctor -No pasa nada. Yo hablo un poco de español.-

Chaval -¡Bien! ¿Vives en España?-

Víctor -Todavía no. ¡Me mudo allí hoy!-

Chaval -Vaya. ¡Qué bien! ¿A qué parte vas?-

Víctor -Tengo un piso en las afueras de Toledo.-

Chaval -¡Qué guay! Toledo es una ciudad muy bonita, de verdad.-

Víctor -Y tú, ¿de qué parte eres?-

Chaval -Soy de Madrid. Me llamo Jorge. Mucho gusto.-

Víctor -Me llamo Víctor. Encantado.-

Jorge -Entonces ¿por qué vienes a España?

Víctor -La verdad es que mi trabajo en Inglaterra no era muy interesante. Llevo siete años trabajando allí y estoy muy aburrido. He decidido hacer un cambio radical y empezar una vida nueva en vuestro país.-

Chapter 9

Very relieved, Victor takes his case and boards the plane. Now he's tired of Stansted airport and just wants to get to Spain, once and for all. Of course, his journey hasn't finished yet and once in Madrid he has to catch the train to Toledo. With all of his heart he hopes that everything goes well in Spain.

After putting his case up in the compartment, he sits down and waits for the take off. At his side there is a youth that seems Spanish. Victor greets him.

Victor "Hi, how are you?"

Youth "I don't speak English. I'm Spanish."

Victor "No problem. I speak a little Spanish."

Youth "Great! Do you live in Spain?"

Victor "Not yet. I've moving there today!"

Youth "Wow. How nice! Which part are you going to?"

Victor "I have a flat in the outskirts of Toledo."

Youth "How cool! Toledo is a really pretty city, for sure."

Victor "And you. What part are you from?"

Youth "I'm from Madrid. I'm called Jorge. Nice to meet you."

Victor "I'm called Victor. A pleasure."

Jorge "So, why are you coming to Spain?"

Victor "The truth is that my job in England wasn't very interesting. I've been working there for seven years and I'm really bored. I've decided to make a radical change and start a new life in your country."

Jorge -Pues, espero que tengas mucha suerte. Seguro que te va a gustar.-

Víctor -Espero que sí.-

Jorge -Ahora, si no te importa, voy a intentar dormir un poco. No me gusta el despegue.-

Jorge cierra los ojos y en dos minutos, ronca ligeramente. Víctor saca su libro de la maleta y estudia español de nuevo.

El vuelo pasa sin problemas y después de dos horas y cuarto la tripulación se prepara para el aterrizaje. Víctor nota que tiene nervios en el estomago. Ya está en España y su aventura empieza de verdad.

Tiene miedo de todo pero, a la vez, se siente muy ilusionado. También tiene muchas ganas de conocer a Eliana. Ha estado hablando mucho con ella durante los últimos meses. Parece una chica muy simpática y, según su foto en Facebook, es bastante guapa.

Jorge "Well, I hope you have lots of luck. It's sure you'll like it."

Victor "I hope so."

Jorge "Now, if you don't mind, I'm going to try and sleep a little. I don't like the takeoff."

Jorge shuts his eyes and in two minutes, is snoring lightly. Victor takes his book from the case and studies Spanish again.

The flight goes by without problems and after two and a quarter hours the crew prepare for the landing. Victor notices that he's got butterflies in his stomach. Now he's in Spain and his adventure is starting for real.

He's frightened of everything but, at the same time, he feels really excited. He's also really looking forward to meeting Eliana. He's been talking to her a lot in the last few months. She seems like a really nice girl and, according to her photo in Facebook, she's quite pretty.

Lesson 10. Making adverbs or the LY words in English. Crear adverbios.

Throughout the story you may have noticed that some of the describing words have **MENTE** tagged on the end.

This is the Spanish version of the English **ADVERB** which we know as words with **LY** tagged on the end.

Example:

> **Happily, Sadly, Quickly, Slowly, Strongly, Normally** etc.

The same words in Spanish are:

> **Felizmente, Tristemente, Rápidamente, Lentamente,**
>
> **Fuertemente, Normalmente.**

How to remember what an ADVERB is, is simple.

It's the LY, or in the Spanish case, the MENTE, and it's an ADjective that enhances the meaning of a VERB.

example: Quick = QuickLY   Rápido = RápidaMENTE

Simple = SimpLY   Simple = SimpleMENTE

The Basic Rules:

If the describing word ends with O normally, when it becomes an Adverb, the O becomes A.

Lent**O** = Lent**A**mente

Segur**O** = Segur**A**mente

If the describing word ends with any vowel other than O, then it remains the same.

Trist**E** = Trist**E**mente

And if the describing word doesn't have a vowel on the end, then there is no vowel added:

Feli**Z** = Feli**Z**mente

Norma**L** = Norma**L**mente

Finally, if you want to use **two or more adverbs in a row** then if they need to, the ones before the last will be feminine without the MENTE and only the last one will have the MENTE added.

Example:

*El chico trabaja feli**z**, rápid**a** y perfecta**mente**. = The boy works happily, quickly and perfectly.*

That's all on ADVERBS for the moment. Watch out for them as you read on. They play an important part in making your Spanish "perfectamente bien".

Ahora te toca a ti.

Convert the following describing words into adverbs.

1, Frecuente. (Frequent) ....

2, Ligero (Light) ....

3, Reciente (Recent) ....

4, Suave (Smooth) ....

5, Afortunado (Fortunate)..........................

Capítulo 10

El aterrizaje pasa sin problemas y Víctor baja del avión y va directamente a la sala de recogida de equipaje. Al llegar allí la cinta ya está en marcha y él espera la llegada de su maleta grande. Hay un montón de maletas de todos los tamaños circulando y la gente recoge su equipaje y se va.

Víctor espera, espera y espera, pero no aparece su maleta. Quince minutos después no queda nadie de su vuelo y la cinta se para. Víctor entra en pánico. ¿Dónde puede estar su maleta grande? Él no lo sabe, pero está seguro de que no está en España.

Enfadado, va a la oficina de reclamaciones. Hay una mujer detrás del mostrador.

Víctor -Buenas tardes. He perdido mi maleta.-

Mujer -Buenas tardes. ¿Dónde la ha perdido?-

Víctor -No sé. He venido de Londres. He facturado mi maleta en Stansted pero no ha llegado.-

Mujer -¿Cuál es el número de su vuelo?-

Víctor -Es el numero 5994.-

Mujer -¿Es un vuelo con escala?-

Víctor -No. Es un vuelo directo.-

Mujer -No se preocupe. Sólo tiene que rellenar esta reclamación y dentro de dos o tres días tiene la maleta de nuevo.-

Víctor -¡¿En dos o tres días?! ¡Dios mío! No puedo esperar tanto tiempo. Tengo que estar en Toledo hoy. Alguien viene a recogerme.-

Mujer -No pasa nada. Deme su dirección aquí en España. Así, podemos enviar la maleta directamente allí.-

Víctor no lo puede creer. Ha sido un viaje del infierno. Ya llega una hora y media tarde.

Chapter 10

The landing goes by without problem and Victor gets off the plane and goes directly to the luggage collection area. When he arrives the conveyor is already in motion and he waits for his suitcase to arrive. There's a pile of suitcases of all sizes going round and the people are collecting their cases and going.

Victor waits, waits, and waits, but his suitcase doesn't appear. Fifteen minutes later, no one from his flight is left and the conveyor stops. Victor begins to panic. Where can his suitcase be? He doesn't know but he's sure that it's not in Spain.

Angry, he goes to the lost property office. There's a woman behind the desk.

Victor "Good afternoon. I've lost my case."

Woman "Good afternoon. Where have you lost it?"

Victor "I don't know. I've come from London. I've checked in my case in Stansted but it hasn't arrived."

Woman "What's the number of your flight?"

Victor "It's number 5994."

Woman "Is it a flight with connection?"

Victor "No, it's a direct flight."

Woman "Don't worry. You just have to fill in this claim form and within two or three days you'll have your case again."

Victor "In two or three days! My God! I can't wait that long. I have to be in Toledo today. Someone is coming to pick me up."

Woman "No problem. Give me your address here in Spain. That way we can send the suitcase directly there."

Victor can't believe it. It's been a journey from hell. Now he's an hour and a half late.

Al salir de la oficina de reclamaciones coge su móvil y marca el número de Eliana. Después de unos segundos ella contesta.

Eliana -Víctor ¿eres tú?

Víctor -Sí, Eliana. He tenido muchos problemas y todavía estoy en el aeropuerto de Barajas. Mi vuelo ha llegado con una hora de retraso y ahora ¡han perdido mi maleta!-

Eliana -Pobrecito. Y ¿qué va a pasar? ¿Tienes que esperar allí?-

Víctor -No. Ellos van a enviarla a mi casa en dos o tres días, dicen.-

Eliana -¡Qué mala suerte, Víctor! Pero no te preocupes. Estoy segura de que mi padre te puede prestar algo de ropa mientras tanto.-

Víctor -Vale, gracias. Voy a coger el metro ahora. He perdido mi tren pero no pasa nada porque compré un billete abierto y puedo coger el siguiente. Salen cada hora.-

Eliana -Vale, Víctor. Espero tu llamada. Llámame en cuanto sepas a qué hora va a llegar el tren. Voy a estar esperándote en la estación. A no ser que te pase algo más antes. Je je-

Víctor -Espero que no, Eliana. Ja ja. Ya he tenido suficiente por un día.-

As he leaves the lost property office he gets his mobile and rings Eliana's number. After a few seconds she answers.

Eliana "Victor, is that you?"

Victor "Yes, Eliana. I've had lots of problems and I'm still in Barajas airport. My flight has arrived an hour late and now they've lost my suitcase!"

Eliana "Poor thing. And what's going to happen? Do you have to wait there?"

Victor "No. They are going to send it to my house in two or three days."

Eliana "What bad luck, Victor! But don't worry. I'm sure my father can loan you some clothing in the meanwhile."

Victor "Okay, thanks. I'm going to catch the Metro now. I've missed my train but there's no problem because I bought an open ticket and I can catch the next one. They leave every hour."

Eliana "Okay, Victor. I'll wait for your call. Call me as soon as you know what time the train is going to arrive. I'm going to be waiting for you at the station. Unless something else happens to you beforehand. He he."

Victor "I hope not, Eliana. Ha ha. I've already had sufficient for one day."

Lesson 11. There is and It is / Hay and Está/n.

You're probably already familiar with these two words. At this stage they are very much two of the most valuable words you could have in your vocabulary.

Because of their similarity, however, they often get confused. Nevertheless, as you will see, there is an easy way not to mix them up. "Está/n" comes from the verb ESTAR (to be) and "hay" comes from the verb HABER(to have done).

HAY means THERE IS/THERE ARE

ESTÁ/N means IT IS/THEY ARE

Although they seem similar, there is a big difference between them.

Look at these two sentences.

> The car is in the street.- There is a car in the street.

> El coche ESTÁ en la calle. – HAY un coche en la calle.

Can you see that when you use a sentence with "There is" or "There are" that you use HAY?

And that, when you use a sentence with "It is" or "They are" then you use Está/n?

Room for error.

Quite often the confusion comes when we use the apostrophe S when we say: THERE'S a car instead of THERE IS a car.

The other confusion comes because of the way that we often incorrectly say:

"THERE'S three cars", when it really should be: "THERE ARE three cars."

In both of these cases many students mistakenly use ES instead of HAY.

The real clue is watching for the word THERE.

That should trigger off the alarm bells to tell you that you need to use HAY.

Last but not least.

Make a special mental note that you CANNOT mix HAY with EL/LA/LOS/LAS:

"Hay EL tren." or "Hay LOS trenes." is not allowed.

In English we can say: "In an emergency there's always THE train."

In Spanish you would have to say: "There is always A train."

A handy word.

The nice thing about HAY is its flexibility. It's a great word to use as a question:

Perdone, ¿hay más pan? = Excuse me, is there more bread?

Disculpe, ¿hay un banco por aquí?= Excuse me, is there a bank around here?

Ahora te toca a ti.

Let's see how you get on translating these sentences.

1, Is there a church around here? (Iglesia)...

2, Is the church around here? ....

3, There's a man in the street. ....

4, The man is in the street. ....

5, Are the people here? ....

6, Are there people here? ....

7, The dogs are here. ....

8, There are dogs here. ....

9, The bank is here. ....

10, There's a bank here. ....

Capítulo 11

Víctor baja las escaleras hasta el Metro y coge un billete de la maquina. Aunque tiene que hacer transbordo, todo parece muy fácil. El metro está limpio y nuevo y no hace tanto ruido como el metro de Londres.

Víctor se siente más relajado. Está casi allí. Quince minutos más tarde, está en la estación de Atocha. Es enorme y él tiene que preguntar en la taquilla por su andén.

Víctor -Perdone. ¿Me puede decir de qué andén sale el tren para Toledo?-

Dependienta -Sí, sale del andén número seis en quince minutos.-

Víctor -y ¿dónde se encuentra?

Dependienta -Siga este pasillo a la derecha y luego baje las escaleras automáticas donde pone "Andén Número Seis".-

Víctor -Muchas gracias.-

Dependienta -De nada. Buen viaje.-

Víctor va directamente al andén y espera la llegada del tren. Mientras espera, llama a Eliana y le da la hora de la llegada. El tren llega a tiempo y Víctor sube y se sienta al lado de la ventanilla. Ya lleva muchas horas viajando y está cansado. Todo ha sido bastante estresante para él.

Esta vez, no estudia en el tren. En vez de eso, mira el paisaje y duerme un poco. Después de una hora el conductor anuncia que la próxima estación es Toledo. Víctor coge su maleta y espera cerca de la puerta.

Tiene mucha ilusión de conocer a Eliana. Baja del tren y mira a su alrededor. Al otro lado del andén ve a una chica. Parece Eliana. Víctor la saluda con la mano y ella empieza a andar hacia él.

Chapter 11

Victor goes down the stairs to the Metro and takes a ticket from the machine. Although he has to change trains, everything looks easy. The Metro is clean and new and it doesn't make as much noise as the London underground.

Victor feels more relaxed. He's nearly there. Fifteen minutes later, he's in Atocha station. It's enormous and he has to ask in the ticket counter for his platform.

Victor "Excuse me. Can you tell me which platform the train for Toldeo leaves from?"

Assistant "Yes, it leaves from platform six in fifteen minutes."

Victor "And where is it?"

Assistant "Follow this aisle on the right and then go down the escalator where it says, "Platform Six".

Victor "Thanks a lot."

Assistant "You're welcome. Have a good journey."

Victor goes straight to the platform and waits for the arrival of the train. Whilst he waits, he calls Eliana and gives her the arrival time. The train arrives on time and Victor gets on and sits next to the window. He's been travelling for many hours and he's tired. Everything has been quite stressful for him.

This time he doesn't study in the train. Instead of that, he looks at the countryside and sleeps a little. After an hour the driver announces that the next station is Toledo. Victor grabs his case and waits near the door.

He's really excited to meet Eliana. He gets off the train and looks around. At the other end of the platform he sees a girl. It looks like Eliana. Victor waves at her with his hand and starts to walk toward her.

Eliana -Bueno, ¡por fin llegas! ¿Qué tal estás?-

Eliana coge a Víctor por los brazos y le da dos besos.

Víctor -Ahora mejor, gracias. Vaya viaje ¡Qué estrés!-

Eliana -No te preocupes. Ahora estás aquí. ¿Tienes hambre?-

Víctor -La verdad es que sí. No he comido desde esta mañana.-

Eliana -Mi madre ha preparado algo de comer en casa. Mis padres quieren conocerte.-

Víctor -Muchas gracias, Eliana. No tienen por qué hacer eso. Yo puedo comprarme un sándwich.-

Eliana -¡Qué va! De todas las maneras quieren verte. Mi padre quiere saber qué tipo de persona va a alquilar su piso. Míralo como una combinación de comida y entrevista. Ja ja.-

Víctor -¡Dios mío! Mi español no es suficientemente bueno para hablar con ellos. Van a pensar que soy un paquete.-

Eliana -Para nada, Víctor. Sólo estoy de broma. De verdad, quieren conocerte. Ya le caes muy bien a mi padre.-

Eliana "Well. You've arrived, finally! How are you?"

Eliana takes Victor by the arms and gives him two kisses.

Victor "Better now, thanks. What a journey. What stress!"

Eliana "Don't worry. You're here now. Are you hungry?"

Victor "I really am. I haven't eaten since this morning."

Eliana "My mother has prepared something to eat at home. My parents want to meet you."

Victor "Thanks a lot, Eliana. They don't have to do that. I can buy myself a sandwich."

Eliana "No way! Regardless, they want to see you. My father wants to know what type of person is going to rent his flat. Look at it as a combination of lunch and interview. Ha ha."

Victor "My God! My Spanish isn't good enough to talk with them. They are going to think that I'm useless."

Eliana "Not at all. I'm just joking. They really want to meet you. My father already really likes you."

Lesson 12. Stress and emphasis on words. / El golpe de voz.

You may or may not have noticed, as you listen to some of the words in the audio, that the emphasis falls on different places within words.

Is there a pattern to this?

Of course!

Let's get familiar with the Nose Rule.

The 'nose rule' helps you understand perfectly how to pronounce any word with the correct emphasis.

THE NOSE RULE.

Any word that ends with an N, S or any vowel (the O and the E in NOSE stand for all vowels) has the emphasis on the second last....or if you're a bookworm...the penultimate vowel.

For example:

As you can see, where the peaks appear is where the emphasis must go. In Spanish this is called "el golpe de voz" or "the hit of the voice." All words have it, English ones included.

Say some English words out loud and try to work out where the emphasis goes. Then, put the emphasis on another vowel and notice how weird and "wrong" it makes the word sound.

THE BROKEN NOSE RULE

The second rule is the 'broken nose rule' and this is when a word finishes with any consonant other than the N or S of the previous rule. When this happens, then the emphasis or 'golpe de voz' falls on the LAST VOWEL.

For example:

Mantel

Hablar

Ciudad

Madrid

As you can see, where the peaks appear is where the emphasis is placed.

NOTE: In both rules, the words do not require an accent because the emphasis falls naturally in the word.

NOTE: If two vowels are side by side, they generally count as ONE.

EVERYTHING ELSE

You may be wondering, then, why is it that many words have accents? The answer is easy. The words that have accents don't follow any rules. At some point, some-one decided that the word should be pronounced in a different way, and they added an accent.

So, an accent on a word shows that IT IS NOT following any rule. It simply IS like that.

Once you become skilled at hearing the emphasis, you'll know if a word needs an accent as soon as you hear it. You'll know because you'll be able to hear that the emphasis isn't in the correct place. Here are some examples. Try to work out where the emphasis would be if the words followed the normal rules:

Estación = Station   Árbol = Tree   Ratón = Mouse

Sillón = Armchair   Sartén = Frying pan   Bolígrafo = Pen

Televisión = Television   Fotografía = Photograph   Cajón = Draw

Capítulo 12

Aun así, Víctor tiene nervios. La casa de Eliana está a sólo cinco minutos de la estación. Mientras andan y hablan Víctor mira a Eliana. Es una chica muy guapa. Tiene el pelo negro, largo y rizado y los ojos muy oscuros. No es muy alta y es delgada. Tiene una sonrisa muy bonita.

Pronto llegan al chalet de Eliana. Es bastante grande, de tres plantas con un jardín impresionante. Entran por la puerta y van directamente a la cocina donde los padres de Eliana están preparando la comida.

Eliana -Mamá, papá, éste es Víctor. Víctor, éste es mi padre, Alfredo, y mi madre, Mercedes.-

Mercedes le da un beso a Víctor y Alfredo le estrecha la mano.

Víctor -Mucho gusto.-

Mercedes -Igualmente, Víctor. ¡Por fin llegas! ¿Qué tal el viaje?-

Alfredo -Un poco problemático ¿verdad?-

Víctor -Un poco mucho. Fue un desastre. No tengo ropa ni nada. Sólo tengo lo que llevo en mi maleta de mano.-

Mercedes -No es para tanto. Seguro que Alfredo tiene algo de ropa que puedes usar durante unos días. Si no te molesta llevar ropa de un viejo. Je je.-

Alfredo -¿Qué dices de "viejo"? Mi ropa siempre está de moda.-

Mercedes -Sí, claro, de moda de anciano.-

Los padres de Eliana parecen muy simpáticos. A Víctor le caen muy bien y se siente cómodo.

Chapter 12

Even so, Victor is nervous. Eliana's house is only five minutes away from the station. Whilst they walk and talk, Victor looks at Eliana. She's a very good looking girl. She has long, dark, curly hair and very dark eyes. She's not very tall and she's slim. She has a really pretty smile.

They soon arrive at Eliana's villa. It's quite big, with three storeys and an impressive garden. They go in through the door and go straight to the kitchen where Eliana's parents are preparing the lunch.

Eliana "Mum, Dad, this is Victor. Victor, this is my father, Alfredo, and my mother, Mercedes.

Mercedes gives him a kiss and Alfredo shakes his hand.

Victor "Nice to meet you."

Mercedes "The same here. You've finally arrived! How was the journey?"

Alfredo "A little bit problematical, no?"

Victor "A bit too much. It was a disaster. I don't have any clothes or anyting. I only have what I've brought in my hand luggage."

Mercedes "It's no big deal. I'm sure that Alfredo has some clothing that you can use for a few days. If you don't mind wearing old mens clothes. He he."

Alfredo "What are you saying, "old man"? My clothes are always in the fashion."

Mercedes "Yes, right. The fashion of an old codger."

Eliana's parents seem really nice. Victor likes them a lot and he feels very comfortable.

Eliana -No les hagas caso, Víctor. Mis padres son muy cachondos. Oye, ¿vamos a tomar algo antes de comer?

Mercedes -Claro. ¿Qué quieres tomar, Víctor?-

Víctor -Me gustaría una cerveza, por favor.-

Mercedes -Tenemos Mahou. ¿Te gusta?-

Víctor - ¡Me encanta! Y además, tengo mucha sed.-

Eliana "Don't take any notice of them, Victor. My parents are real jokers. Listen, are we going to drink something before lunch?"

Mercedes "Sure. What do you want to drink, Victor?"

Victor "I'd like a beer, please."

Mercedes "We have Mahou. Do you like it?"

Victor "I love it! And what's more, I'm really thirsty."

Lesson 13. The personal A.

Perhaps you've noticed, as you've been reading and translating the story that sometimes an A appears in the Spanish that does not have any translation in English.

This is the "Personal A". Its job is one of respect and it's used to show that an interaction is happening between people, or pets with human names.

In English this "A" mostly doesn't exist, although to give you an idea of how it works we can consider the sentence:

I often say that TO my mum. = A menudo le digo eso A mi madre.

Most times, however, this A appears in sentences where, in English, it doesn't exist.

Ejemplo:

Visito A mi padre. = I visit (to) my father.

Paseo A mi perro. = I walk (to) my dog.

Vemos A Juan. = We see (to) Juan.

There are times when even though people are mentioned in a sentence, the personal A is not necessary. Here are the main exceptions.

A Non-Specific person.

If you are talking about a certain type of person, rather than an actual person, then it isn't necessary for you to use the personal A.

I'm looking for a good plumber. = Busco un fontanero bueno.

He needs a hard working secretary. = Necesita una secretaria trabajadora.

We want a Boxer dog. = Queremos un perro boxer.

With HAY *(there is/are)* and ESTAR *(to be)*

It isn't necessary to use the personal A when you are describing what there is/are.

There's a man in the garden. = Hay un hombre en el jardín.

The man is in the garden. = El hombre está en el jardín.

There are three people here. = Hay tres personas aquí.

Three people are here. = Tres personas están aquí.

There's an old woman in that house. = Hay una mujer mayor en esa casa.

The old woman is in the house. = La mujer mayor está en la casa.

With TENER *(to have)*

When you are describing the family that you have, you don't need to use the personal A.

I have three brothers. = Tengo tres hermanos.

I have a sister that lives in Spain. = Tengo una hermana que vive en España.

NOTE*: Although the personal A isn't used with TENER in the examples above, most text books do not mention that it IS used with the verb TENER in the following situation:*

I have my parents with me at home this week.= Tengo A mis padres en casa conmigo esta semana.

I have my brother with me now. = Tengo A mi hermano conmigo ahora.

Although this may seem a little confusing, you will soon begin to get the idea of how the personal A is used. As you read on through the story, see if you can notice when it appears.

Ahora te toca a ti / Now it's your turn.

Decide whether these sentences need the personal A or not.

1, Veo (?) mi amigo.

2, Veo (?) mi casa.

3, Tengo (?) mi amigo aquí conmigo.

4, Tengo (?) muchos amigos.

5, Busco (?) Jorge.

6, Busco (?) mi perro.

7, Busco (?) un fontanero.

8, Hay (?) cuatro personas en el salón.

9, Están (?) las cuatro personas en el salón.

10, Busco (?) tu hermano.

Capítulo 13

Todos salen fuera y se sientan en el patio. Hace calor y sol y mientras Víctor escucha la conversación animada de la familia de Eliana nota que se siente bastante contento y relajado.

Alfredo -Víctor, Eliana dice que necesitas encontrar trabajo. ¿Qué piensas hacer?-

Víctor -Realmente, no me importa. Estoy dispuesto a hacer cualquier cosa.-

Alfredo -Es que tengo un amigo que busca camareros para su restaurante nuevo que abre la semana que viene. ¿Alguna vez has trabajado de camarero?-

Víctor -Cuando tenía dieciséis años trabajaba en McDonald's. No sé si vale eso.-

Alfredo -Bueno, tampoco lo sé yo, pero si quieres, puedo organizar una entrevista con él para ti. ¿Te parece bien?-

Víctor -Eso sería fantástico, Alfredo. Muchísimas gracias. Seguro que podría hacerlo. Aprendo rápidamente y tampoco me importa trabajar duro.-

Alfredo -Pues, vale. Hablo con él mañana. Ahora, a comer, ¿no?-

Todos entran en casa y se sientan a la mesa en el comedor. La comida huele muy bien y Víctor se da cuenta del hambre que tiene. De primer plato Mercedes trae tortilla española, lonchas de chorizo, una ensalada y pan. Él come con gusto. Le gustan mucho el chorizo y la tortilla. Después de horas sin comer, todo sabe a gloria.

De segundo plato, Mercedes trae una paella. Encima de la paella hay cuatro gambas enormes.

Víctor -¡Qué bien parece! ¿Qué lleva exactamente la paella?

Alfredo -Bueno, depende. Ésta es una paella de marisco, así que lleva calamares,

Chapter 13

Everyone goes outside and they sit in the patio. It's hot and sunny and whilst Victor listens to the lively conversation of Eliana's family, he notices that he feels quite happy and relaxed.

Alfredo "Victor, Eliana says that you need to find work. What are you thinking about doing?"

Victor "I really don't mind. I'm willing to do anything."

Alfredo "It's just that I have a friend who's looking for waiters for his new restaurant that opens next week. Have you ever worked as a waiter?"

Victor "When I was sixteen I worked in McDonald's. I don't know it that's any good."

Alfredo "Well, I don't know either, but if you like, I can organize an interview with him for you. Is that okay for you?

Victor "That would be great, Alfredo. Thanks ever so much. I'm sure that I could do it. I learn quickly and I don't mind working hard either."

Alfredo "Okay then. I'll speak with him tomorrow. Now, let's eat, shall we?"

Everyone goes indoors and they sit at the table in the dining room. The food smells really good and Victor realises how hungry he is. For first course Mercedes brings Spanish omelette, sliced chorizo, a salad and bread. He eats heartily. He likes the chorizo and the omelette a lot. After hours without eating, everything tastes delicious.

For second course, Mercedes brings a paella. On top of the paella there are four enormous prawns.

Victor "It looks great! What does the paella have in it, exactly?"

Alfredo "Well, it depends. This is a seafood paella, so it has squid,

mejillones y gambas. Pero, de verdad, puede llevar muchas cosas.-

Eliana -¿Sabes, Víctor? Mi padre no sabe cocinar en absoluto, pero, como la mayoría de los hombres españoles, puede describir perfectamente cómo se prepara todo, je je.-

Alfredo -¿Qué dices? ¡Yo preparo un buen plato de jamón y chorizo!-

Eliana - Ah sí, es verdad. Papá sabe muy bien cortar.-

Mercedes - Es que, aquí en España, los hombres no suelen cocinar. Y tú, Víctor, ¿sabes cocinar?

Víctor -Claro. Cocino bastante bien. A mí me encanta preparar platos variados. En particular me gusta la comida italiana. Si tengo tiempo, preparo pasta, o pizza yo mismo. Es bastante fácil. Sólo hacen falta unos ingredientes básicos.-

Mercedes -¡Qué impresionante, Víctor! Tal vez puedas darle a mi marido unas clases de cocina.-

Alfredo -No te preocupes, Víctor. Con lo deliciosa que es la comida que me prepara mi esposa no hace falta que cocine yo.-

Mercedes -¿Ves, Víctor? Alfredo no es un hombre moderno como tú. Pero, de todas formas, lo quiero.-

mussels and prawns. But, in truth, it can have lots of different things in it."

Eliana "You know, Victor, my father doesn't know how to cook at all, but, like the majority of Spanish men, he can describe perfectly how everything is prepared. He he."

Alfredo "What do you mean? I make a great plate of ham and chorizo."

Eliana "Ah yes, that's true. Dad knows how to cut really well."

Mercedes "It's just that, here in Spain, the men don't usually cook. And you, Victor, do you know how to cook?"

Victor "Of course. I cook quite well. I love to cook different dishes. In particular I like Italian food. If I have time, I prepare pasta, or pizza myself. It's quite easy. You only need some basic ingredients."

Mercedes "How impressive, Victor! maybe you can give my husband some cookery classes."

Alfredo "Don't worry, Victor. Given the delicious food that my wife prepares I don't need to cook."

Mercedes "You see, Victor? Alfredo isn't a modern man like you. But I love him anyway."

Lesson 14. The verb Tener = To have

The verb TENER is an interesting and very important Spanish verb. Let's firstly see how it conjugates. (It's quite irregular.)

Yo **tengo** = I have   Nosotros **tenemos** = We have

Tú **tienes** = You have   Vosotros **tenéis** = You all have

Él/Ella **tiene** = He/She has   Ellos **tienen** = They have

Usted **tiene** = You have(Formal)   Ustedes **tienen** = You all have (formal)

Notice how, no matter how irregular the verb, in the nosotros and vosotros form, it is never irregular!

As a verb, Tener is very versatile and has a much bigger job than it does in the English language. It is used in many of the sentences in which English speakers might say: "I AM." I contrast, Spanish speakers say: I HAVE. One example that you may be familiar with is age:

Tener años. Spanish speakers don't say "I am twenty years old." They say, "I have twenty years."

Tengo veinte años.

Here is a list of some the verb TENER's main jobs.

Tener hambre. = To be hungry.

Tener sed. = To be thirsty.

Tener miedo. = To be frightened.

Tener prisa. = To be in a hurry.

Tener vergüenza = To be embarrassed or ashamed.

Tener sueño = To be tired.

Tener frío = To be cold.

Tener calor = To be hot.

Tener suerte = To be lucky.

Apart from the above jobs, TENER is also used to make "HAVE TO" sentences.

To do this, you just need to add **QUE** to your conjugation. Notice that after the QUE you add a verb in its infinitive form (that means the full version like COMER, HABLAR etc.)

e.g.

*Tengo **que** comer lentamente.* = I have to eat slowly.

*Tenemos **que** estar allí mañana.* = We have to be there tomorrow.

*Tienen **que** devolver el regalo.* = They have to return the present.

Ahora te toca a ti.

Translate the following sentences.

1, We are frightened. ....*Tenemos miedo*......

2, They are hungry. ......*Tienen hambre*.......

3, Pedro is ashamed. ......*Pedro tienes vergüenza*

4, I'm thirsty. ......*Tengo sed*......

5, You are normally in a hurry. ....*Normalmente tienes prisa*

6, Are you tired? (Formal) ....*¿Tiene sueño? usted*....

7, I have to work tomorrow. ......*Tengo que trabajar mañana*

8, They have to eat now. (Ahora) ....*Ahora tienen que comer*

9, We have to be there, soon. (pronto) ....*Pronto tenemos que estar allí*

10, I have to sleep. I'm tired. ......*Tengo que dormir Estoy cansada*

Capítulo 14

Pasan la próxima hora comiendo y hablando. Víctor se siente como en casa con la familia. Después de la comida, Alfredo va a buscar algo de ropa para Víctor. Luego Eliana y él llevan a Víctor a su piso nuevo que está en un bloque no muy lejos de la casa de Eliana. No es muy grande pero está muy limpio y bien amueblado. En el salón hay un sofá y una mesa pequeña con dos sillas. En la esquina hay una televisión y al lado de la televisión hay una puerta que da al balcón. La cocina también es pequeña y tiene un horno, una nevera con congelador, un microondas y una lavadora.

Hay solamente un dormitorio pero es bastante grande y bien iluminado. En una esquina hay un armario y a su lado una cómoda. La cama parece nueva y, de repente, Víctor tiene ganas de meterse en ella y dormir durante tres días.

Alfredo -Bueno, Víctor. ¿Cómo te parece?-

Víctor -Me parece muy bien, Alfredo. Me encanta. Es justo lo que quería.-

Alfredo -Pues, ahora te dejamos. Que pases una buena noche. Mañana hablo con mi amigo sobre el trabajo ése y te avisaré, ¿vale?

Víctor -Muchísimas gracias, Alfredo. Eres muy amable.-

Eliana -¿Qué vas a hacer esta tarde, Víctor?-

Víctor -No sé. Creo que voy a dormir un poco y luego voy a dar un paseo por la ciudad.-

Eliana -Si quieres, te acompaño.-

Víctor -¡Perfecto!-

Chapter 14

They spend the next hour eating and talking. Victor feels at home with Eliana's family. After eating, Alfredo goes to look for some clothing for Victor. Then he and Eliana take Victor to his new flat that is in a block not very far from Eliana's house. It's not very big but it's very clean and well furnished. In the living room there is a sofa and a small table with two seats. In the corner there's a television and to the side of the television there's a door that leads to the balcony. The kitchen is also small and it has a cooker, a fridge with a freezer, a microwave and a washing machine.

There's only one bedroom but it's quite big and well lit. In one corner there's a wardrobe and at its side a chest of drawers. The bed looks new and, suddenly, Victor has the desire to get in it and sleep for three days.

Alfredo "So, Victor, how does it look?"

Victor "It seems really good, Alfredo. I love it. It's just what I wanted."

Alfredo "Well, we'll leave you now. Have a good night. Tomorrow I'll talk with my friend about that work and I'll let you know, okay?"

Victor "Thanks a lot, Alfredo. You're very kind."

Eliana "What are you going to do this evening, Victor?"

Victor "I don't know. I think I'm going to sleep a little and then I'm going to have a walk around the city."

Eliana "If you want I'll come with you."

Victor "Perfect!"

Los dos quedan para las nueve y media de esa tarde y luego Eliana sale con su padre. Víctor se sienta en el sofá. Ha sido un día muy concurrido y tiene mucho sueño. Piensa en todo lo que ha ocurrido y sabe que sus aventuras ya han empezado de verdad. Cinco minutos después, Víctor se queda profundamente dormido y ronca suavemente

They both agree to meet at nine-thirty that evening and then Eliana leaves with her father. Victor sits on the sofa. It has been a very busy day and he is very tired. He thinks about everything that has happened and he knows that his adventures have now started for real. Five minutes later he's deeply asleep and he snores gently.

Lesson 15. The Weather. El Tiempo.

In many cases, Spanish speakers talk about the weather in a different way to English speakers. Often, when they describe the weather, they use the verb:

HACER = To make/do.

As an example, instead of saying, "It's hot." They say, "It makes heat."

To ask how the weather is you can say:

¿Qué tiempo hace hoy? = What's the weather like today?

¿Cómo está el tiempo hoy? = How's the weather today?

Here are the types of weather that are typically used with the verb **HACER**.

Hace calor = It's hot.

Hace frío = It's cold.

Hace sol = It's sunny.

Hace viento = It's windy.

Hace buen tiempo = The weather's nice.

Hace mal tiempo = The weather's bad.

Hace fresco = It's fresh/cool

Hace bochorno = It's stifling

Notice that when we use HACER, it's always conjugated in the third person singular, (the "it" form).

The same applies when using the weather verbs. They will always be in third person, singular. (That's the él/ella person.)

Here are the principal verbs used:

LLOVER = to Rain   LLUEVE = It's raining (Note that this verb is irregular.)

NEVAR = to Snow   NIEVA = It's snowing (Irregular, too.)

GRANIZAR = To hail   GRANIZA = It's hailing.

CHISPEAR = To drizzle CHISPEA = It's drizzling

*You may also see these verbs used with ESTAR, making up what is called 'The present continuous' which **can only be used when that particular kind of weather is happening right now**.*

Está lloviendo. = It is raining (right now)

Está nevando = It is snowing (right now)

Está granizando = It is hailing (right now)

Está chispeando = It's drizzling (right now)

Here are another few expressions that use ESTAR:

Está nublado = It's cloudy

Está despejado = The skies are clear.

Está fresco = It's cool/fresh.

Note: Sometimes HAY (there is/are) is used to describe what kind of weather there is:

Hoy, hay mucha niebla. = There's a lot of fog today.

Hay escarcha = There's a frost.

Ahora te toca a ti.

Translate the following sentences:

1, It's sunny and hot today. ....*Hace sol y calor hoy*....

2, It rains a lot in England. ....*Hace Llueve mucho en Inglaterra*

3, It's raining in England. ....*Está lloviendo* — " —

4, It's stifling because it's not windy. ....*Hace bochorno prque no hace viento*

5, There's frost on the cars. ....*Hay escarcha en los coches*

Capítulo 15

A las nueve y media en punto, Eliana llega al portal del edificio de Víctor y llama. Espera un rato y cuando Víctor no contesta, llama de nuevo. Finalmente, Víctor contesta, todavía medio dormido.

Víctor -¿Eliana?

Eliana -Sí, Víctor, soy yo. ¿Qué pasa?-

Víctor -Me quedé dormido en el sofá. Acabo de despertarme. ¿Qué hora es?-

Eliana -Son las nueve y media. Mira, no pasa nada. Si quieres, lo podemos dejar para mañana. No me importa.-

Víctor -No, no. Está bien. Sólo necesito un ratito para arreglarme. ¡Sube!

Víctor aprieta el botón del portero para abrir la puerta del portal. Luego abre la puerta del piso. Un minuto después entra Eliana sonriendo.

Eliana -¡Qué dormilón! Te has quedado dormido ¿eh?-

Víctor -¡Qué vergüenza! Lo siento mucho. Es que no me di cuenta de la hora. Sólo me hacen falta cinco minutos para vestirme.-

Eliana -Tranquilo. Te espero aquí. No tenemos prisa.-

Mientras Eliana espera en el salón, Víctor va al cuarto de baño; se ducha y se afeita rápidamente. Luego, se echa desodorante y un poco de colonia. Después, se viste. Lleva la ropa del padre de Eliana. Realmente no es su estilo, pero está limpia y hasta que venga su maleta, no tiene alternativa.

Víctor -Ya, estoy listo. Gracias por esperarme.-

Eliana - De nada. Bueno, ¿te apetece tomar algo?

Chapter 15

At nine-thirty exactly, Eliana arrives at the entrance of the Victor's building and buzzes. She waits a while and when Victor doesn't answer, she calls again. Finally, Victor answers, still half asleep.

Victor "Eliana?"

Eliana "Yes, Victor, it's me. What's happening?"

Victor "I fell asleep on the sofá. I've just woken up. What time is it?"

Eliana "It's nine-thirty. Look, don't worry. If you want, we can leave it until tomorrow. I don't mind."

Victor "No, no. It's fine. I just need a momento to get myself ready. Come up!"

Victor pushes the button to open the main entrance door of the block of flats. Then he opens the door of the apartment. A minute later, Eliana comes in smiling.

Eliana "What a sleepy head! You've fallen asleep eh?"

Victor "How embarressing! I'm really sorry. It's just I didn't realise the time. I only need five minutes to get dressed."

Eliana "Take it easy. I'll wait for you here. We aren't in a hurry."

Whilst Eliana waits in the living room, Victor goes to the bathroom; he has a shower and shaves quickly. Then, he puts on some deodorant and a little bit of aftershave. Then, he gets dressed. He's wearing Eliana's father's clothing. It's not really his style, but it's clean and until his suitcase arrives, he doesn't have an alternative.

Victor "I'm ready, now. Thanks for waiting for me."

Eliana "You're welcome. So, do you fancy eating something?"

Víctor -Sí. De verdad tengo algo de hambre. ¿Ya has cenado?

Eliana -Yo, sí, pero no pasa nada, podemos pedir unas raciones. De todas maneras, nos van a poner tapas con la bebida. Conozco un buen bar muy cerca de aquí.-

Víctor -¡Perfecto!-

Víctor "Yes. In fact I'm a bit hungry. Have you had dinner already?"

Eliana "I have, but there's no problem, we can order some food to share. Anyway, they're going to give us tapas with the drinks. I know a good bar really close to here."

Victor "Perfect!"

Lesson 16. The present continuous. El presente continuo.

Although we are giving you the names of many grammar tenses, you don't need to get too concerned about recalling their names. The most important thing is to understand the rules that go with this particular tense when you use it.

The present continuous is the same in Spanish as it is in English. Here are some examples:

I am looking in the mirror.

I am eating fish.

We are walking home.

They are thinking about the party.

The structure.

Just as in English, the present progressive tense is made up of **two parts**.

The first part is the verb "to be", which is ESTAR.

This is how it breaks down:

Yo estoy	Nosotros estamos
Tú estás	Vosotros estáis
Él, ella está	Ellos, ellas están
Usted está	Ustedes están

The second part is what is called the "gerund", in Spanish, "el gerundio".

This is the second verb that in English ends with "ING".

e.g.

walking, talking, eating, looking, reading, etc.

In Spanish it's very easy to make the gerund.

AR verbs lose the AR and gain ANDO.

ER and IR verbs lose ER/IR and gain IENDO.

e.g.

> *Hablar = To talk   Hablando = Talking*
>
> *Correr = To run   Corriendo = Running*
>
> *Abrir = To open   Abriendo = Opening*

Once you've got the two parts, then all we do is add them together.

Note: The Present Progressive is always used with ESTAR.

Can you work out why?

Well, firstly we know that ESTAR is a verb that describes temporary situations or states. It typically describes something that won't last forever.

Thus, the Present Progressive is doing exactly that. If you are running, walking, reading, listening, or whatever, the action will always come to an end.

This brings us to another point.

In English you can ask someone at a party:

"Where are you working now?" = "¿Dónde estás trabajando ahora?"

In Spanish this is PROHIBITED.

The reason for this is that, to a Spanish speaker, the present progressive describes things that are happening right now!

When to use it.

You only use this tense when you are talking about an action that is happening at the moment, in real time.

On the phone to a friend...

> *¿Qué estás haciendo? = What are you doing (right now)?*

Having been interrupted...

> *Perdona, ¡estoy hablando yo! = Excuse me. I'm talking!*

Of course, you don't need to use this tense in these circumstances.

You can simply use the present (indicative) tense.

This is because, to a Spanish speaker, when you say something like:

Yo hablo

They understand it as both..."I speak"...and..."I am speaking".

So, the examples above could just as easily be like this:

> *¿Qué haces? = What are you doing?*

> *Perdona, ¡hablo yo! = Excuse me, I'm speaking!*

So, if you don't need to use it, why does it exist?

Basically, the Present Progressive is used very much as a way of emphasising speech.

Using it in conversation makes what you say, very "real-time" and very alive.

However, like anything used for emphasis, it should be used sparingly, and certainly not at the level that it's used in the English language.

Overuse it and it will make your Spanish sound weird and foreign.

Ahora te toca a ti.

Convert the following sentences into Spanish. Be careful. There are some sentences that cannot be translated into the present continuous.

1, I'm eating fish. (Comer) .... *Estoy comiendo*

2, On Monday, I'm eating with friends. ...... *El lunes, Como con amigos*

3, Pablo is running. (Correr) ..... *Pablo está corriendo*

4, I'm working in the office tomorrow. ..... *Mañana trabajo en la oficina*

5, She's working in the office today. (Trabajar) *Hoy está trabaja en la oficina*

6, I'm thinking about going to Spain. (Pensar en) *Yo pienso en España* *Estoy pensando en ir a España*

7, We are listening to the music. (Escuchar) *Estamos escuchando la música*

8, They are fighting in the street. (Luchar) *Están luchando en la calle*

9, We are going out on Friday. (Salir) *Salimos el viernes*

10, He's writing a book. (in general)(Escribir) *Escribe un libro*

Capítulo 16

Los dos salen de la casa y andan hasta el bar Paco. Allí hay mucha gente sentada en la terraza y el ambiente parece bueno. Eliana escoge una mesa con dos sillas y se sientan. Unos minutos más tarde llega el camarero.

Camarero -Hola, buenas noches. ¿Qué les traigo?-

Eliana -Por favor, ¿me trae un Bitter Kas? Y tú, Víctor ¿Qué tomas?-

Víctor -Creo que voy a tomar una cerveza.-

Camarero -¿Quiere caña, botellín, jarra?-

Víctor -¿Me trae una jarra, por favor?-

Eliana -¿Y no querías pedir una ración, Víctor?-

Víctor -Sí. ¿También me trae una ración de alitas de pollo?-

Camarero -Sí, enseguida se lo traigo todo.-

Eliana -Entonces, ¿qué tal tu primer día aquí en Toledo?-

Víctor -Muy bien. Tu familia es encantadora y me cae fenomenalmente bien. Al pensarlo mi día ha empezado mal, pero ha terminado muy bien.-

Eliana -Que no hables tan rápido, ¡todavía no ha terminado! jaja-

Justo en ese momento, alguien se acerca a ellos. Los dos piensan que es el camarero con las bebidas pero están equivocados. Es un chico muy grande y musculoso de un metro noventa que, sin decir ni una palabra, se sienta a su mesa. De repente, Eliana parece muy incómoda.

Eliana -Hola, Hugo. ¿Qué haces aquí?-

Hugo -Más importante, ¿qué haces tú?-

Chapter 16

They both leave the house and walk to Paco's bar. There are many people seated on the terrace and the atmosphere seems nice. Eliana chooses a table with two seats and they sit. A few minutes later the waiter arrives.

Waiter "Hello. Good evening. What can I bring you?"

Eliana "Could you bring me a Bitter Kas, please? And you, Victor. What are you having?"

Victor "I think I'm going to have a beer."

Waiter "Do you want a glass, a bottle, a pint?"

Victor "Can you bring me a pint, please?"

Eliana "And didn't you want to order a plate of chicken wings?"

Victor "Yes. Can you bring me a plate of chicken wings, as well?"

Waiter "Yes, I'll bring everything right away."

Eliana "So, how has your first day in Toledo been?"

Victor "Really good. Your family is lovely and I like them a lot. Thinking about it, my day has started badly but has finished very well."

Eliana "Don't speak too soon. It isn't over yet! Haha."

Just at that moment, someone comes up to them. They both think that it's the waiter with the drinks but they are wrong. It's a very large, muscular youth more than six feet tall. Without saying a single word he sits at their table. Suddenly, Eliana seems very uncomfortable.

Eliana "Hello, Hugo. What are you doing here?"

Hugo "More importantly, what are you doing?"

Eliana -Nada. Tomando algo con el inquilino de mi padre. Se llama Víctor y acaba de llegar hoy.-

Hugo no saluda a Víctor, y él no sabe qué decir ni hacer. Opta por no hacer nada. Hugo tiene pinta de estar muy cabreado.

Hugo -Creo que no es normal salir a tomar algo con un desconocido; así que ¿me vas a decir dónde has conocido a este guiri?-

Eliana -Hugo, no seas maleducado y, para empezar, no es asunto tuyo. Tú ya no figuras en mi vida y no tengo por qué darte explicaciones.-

Hugo se gira hacia Víctor y le mira a los ojos.

Hugo -¿Qué haces tú con Eliana? ¿Quieres que sea tu novia o qué? ¿Qué pasa, que no hay bastantes chicas inglesas?-

Víctor no sabe qué decirle. Hugo parece muy enfadado y a punto de explotar.

Víctor -Eliana es amiga mía y me ha ayudado mucho con la mudanza. Sólo eso, Hugo.-

Hugo -Sólo eso- dices. Bueno, para ser sólo amigos parecéis muy cómodos aquí, tomando algo y charlando.-

Eliana -Hugo, por favor. Déjame en paz. Ya hace seis meses que lo hemos dejado. No queda nada. Ya no me interesas. ¿Me entiendes? Entonces, ¿te vas o tengo que llamar a alguien?-

Hugo - Ya os dejo, pero este asunto no ha terminado todavía y tú lo vas a pagar. Hablaremos de esto otro día cuando tu guiri no esté para protegerte.-

Luego, sin decir más, Hugo se va, dejando a los dos bastante asustados.

Víctor -¡Dios mío!, ¿quién era ese hombre?-

,

Eliana "Nothing. Having a drink with my father's tenant. He's called Victor and he's just arrived today."

Hugo doesn't say hello to Victor, and he doesn't know what to say or do. He opts for doing nothing. Hugo looks very angry.

Hugo "I don't think it's normal to go out for a drink with a stranger; so, are you going to tell me where you've met this foreigner?"

Eliana "Don't be rude, Hugo, and, to start with, it's none of your business. You aren't part of my life anymore and I don't have to explain things to you."

Hugo turns toward Victor and looks at him in the eyes.

Hugo "What are you doing with Eliana? Do you want her to be your girlfriend, or what? What's wrong, aren't there enough English girls?"

Victor doesn't know what to say. Hugo looks really angry and about ready to explode.

Victor "Eliana is my friend and she's helped me a lot with the move. That's all, Hugo."

Hugo "That's all,' you say. Well, for being only friends you both look very comfortable here, having something to drink and chatting."

Eliana "Hugo, please. Leave me in peace. We finished six months ago. There's nothing left. You don't interest me anymore. Do you understand? So, are you going or do I have to call someone?"

Hugo "I'm leaving now, but this isn't over yet and you're going to pay. We'll discuss this another day when your Brit isn't here to protect you."

Then, without saying more, Hugo goes, leaving them both fairly shocked.

Victor "My God! Who was that man?"

Eliana -Lo siento, Víctor. Fue mi novio durante un año. Hace seis meses que lo dejamos o mejor dicho, lo dejé yo. No podía aguantar más sus celos.

Al principio todo iba bien, luego, poco a poco, se volvió cada vez más celoso. No me permitía salir con mis amigos, me seguía por todas partes y decía que tenía aventuras. Todavía me sigue. Me da mucho miedo. No sé lo que es capaz de hacer.-

Víctor -Bueno, ya se ha ido. No te preocupes. No va a hacer nada en plena calle.-

Eliana -Menos mal que estás conmigo.-

Víctor -¿En serio? Creo que lo he enfadado aún más.-

Eliana -Tal vez. Es que no sé qué le pasa, Víctor. Mis padres me dicen que debería denunciarle pero prefiero no hacer nada. No quiero causar más problemas ni para mí ni para mi familia.-

Víctor -Te entiendo, Eliana.-

El camarero llega con las bebidas y la ración de alitas de pollo. Después de todo eso Víctor no tiene mucho apetito. Terminan rápidamente y Víctor pide la cuenta. Eliana intenta pagar todo pero Víctor la para.

Víctor -Quiero pagar yo.-

Eliana -No, Víctor. Te he invitado yo. Aquí en España, la persona que invita, paga.-

Víctor -En Inglaterra pagamos a medias. Parece más justo.-

Eliana -No importa, Víctor. La próxima vez, pagas tú.-

Eliana "I'm sorry, Victor. He was my boyfriend for a year. Six months ago we finished, or better said, I finished it. I couldn't stand his jealousy any more.
At the start everything was going well, then, little by little, he became more and more jealous. He wouldn't let me go out with my friends, he followed me everywhere and said I was having affairs. He still follows me. He makes me really frightened. I don't know what he's capable of doing."

Victor "Well, he's gone now. Don't worry. He's not going to do anything in the middle of the street."

Eliana "It's a good job that you're with me."

Victor "Really? I think I annoyed him even more."

Eliana "Maybe. It's just that I don't know what's wrong with him. My parents say that I should report him but I prefer not to do anything. I don't want to cause more problems for me or my family."

Victor "I understand you, Eliana."

The waiter arrives with the drinks and the plate of chicken wings. After all that Victor doesn't have much of an appetite. They finish quickly and Victor asks for the bill. Eliana tries to pay for it all but Victor stops her.

Victor "I want to pay."

Eliana "No, Victor. I've invited you. Here in Spain, the person who invites, pays."

Victor "In England, we pay half each. It seems fairer."

Eliana "Don't worry, Victor. The next time, you pay."

Al oír eso, Víctor se alegra. Significa que Eliana quiere salir de nuevo con él. Es una chica muy simpática y la encuentra muy atractiva. Dicho esto, le preocupa mucho su ex. Espera que ese Hugo no sea un problema en el futuro.

Los dos van a sus casas y quedan para el día siguiente por la tarde. Víctor se acuesta directamente. Antes de dormirse, piensa en todo lo que ha pasado ese día. Ha sido un día largo y lleno de experiencias nuevas. La mujer habladora, el retraso del vuelo, la maleta perdida, la familia de Eliana, y luego, el impresionante Hugo. ¡Vaya día más interesante!

Enseguida se duerme y sueña con maletas voladoras que le persiguen por la calle.

As he hears that, Victor feels happy. That means that Eliana wants to go out with him again. She's a really nice girl and he finds her very attractive. That said, he's very worried about her ex. He hopes that Hugo won't be a problem in the future.

They both go home and agree to meet the next day in the evening. Victor goes to bed right away. Before going to sleep he thinks about everything that has happened that day. It's been a long day filled with new experiences. The chatty women, the flight delay, the lost case, Eliana's family and then, the impressive Hugo. What a very interesting day!

He falls asleep straight away and dreams of flying suitcases that chase him along the street.

Lesson 17. The Time / La Hora

The time in Spanish isn't quite the same as in English, so let us show you the different ways you can tell the time.

Firstly, this is how you ask for the time:

¿Qué hora es?

(What hour is it?)

or

¿Tienes la hora?

(Do you have the hour?)

To answer this question, you use the verb SER. (to be)

You'll either use:

ES = It is.

or

SON = They are.

ES is only used when talking about one o'clock or any variation around that time.

e.g. One o'clock, a quarter to one, half past one, etc.

SON is used for all the other hourly numbers from 2 to 12.

This is how you use them:

It's one o'clock. = **Es** la una.

It's two o'clock. = **Son** las dos.

It's three o'clock. = **Son** las tres. etc.

Note: One of the most common mistakes is saying: "Son las tres HORAS."

However, there is no need to mention the word, "horas" because the word "LAS" refers to "LAS HORAS".

Thus, the sentence:

Son las cuatro. 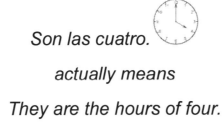

actually means

They are the hours of four.

(Son)   (las)   (cuatro)

Although this may sound quite strange to us, you can trust that to a Spanish speaker, it sounds like the best thing since sliced bread! lol

The Nuts and Bolts.

There are two main parts to telling the time beyond the "o'clocks".

1. Everything up to "half past the hour".

2. Everything from "29 minutes to the hour" onwards.

Let's deal with the first part.

Past the hour.

*To say whatever minutes past the hour it is, then you use "**Y**" = "AND".*

*e.g.   Son las tres **Y** cinco. = It's five past three.*

*   Son las nueve **Y** veintcinco. = It's twenty-five past nine.*

Quarter/Half past.

Like ours, the Spanish clock divides itself into quarters.

Quarter past = Y cuarto

Half past = Y media

The second part.

As soon as we pass half past, we move to the next hour and start saying:
MENOS = LESS.

e.g.

Twenty to six

is:

Son las seis menos veinte.
(Literally, "It's the hours of six less twenty".)

Ten minutes to nine

is:

Son las nueve menos diez.
(Literally, "It's the hours of nine less ten".)

At the "quarter to" point, you say: "Menos cuarto."
e.g.

Son las siete menos cuarto.= It's a quarter to seven.

How to say, "At nine o'clock" etcétera.

When you want to tell someone at which time something will happen, then all you do is use the letter:

A = at

e.g.

El tren llega **A** las tres. = The train arrives AT three o'clock.

Voy a estar allí **A** las dos y media. = I'm going to be there AT two thirty.

Just remember. In your mind, you only need to replace **AT** with **A.**

So when you want to ask something like

"What time are you going?"

you simply put the A at the beginning of the sentence.

e.g.

¿A qué hora te vas?

which literally means:

At what time are you going?

Ahora te toca a ti.

Convert these times to Spanish.

1, It's a quarter to three. ..... Son las Tres menos cuarto

2, It's ten past two. ..... Son las dos y diez

3, It's one fifteen. ..... Es la una y cuarto

4, It's twenty-five to eleven. ..... Son las once menos veinte cinco

5, It's ten to seven. ..... Son las siete menos diez

6, It's twenty-three minutes past five. ..... Son las cinco y veintitrés

7, It's three minutes to twelve. ..... Son las doce menos tres

8, It's one-thirty. ..... Es la una y media

9, It's six forty-five. ..... Son las siete menos quince

10, It's nine o'clock. ..... Son las nueve

11, I'm going to arrive (llegar) at three o'clock. ..... Voy a llegar a las tres

12, What time are they coming? (venir) ..... ¿A qué hora vienen?

13, We are going to be (estar) there at a quarter past nine. ..... Vamos a estar allí a las nueve y cuarto

14, What time do you eat? ..... ¿A qué hora comes?

15, He's going to call (llamar) at midnight. ..... Él llamar a las media noche
El va a

Capítulo 17

Al día siguiente una llamada telefónica despierta a Víctor. Coge su móvil que está al lado de la cama y contesta.

Víctor -¿Sí? Dígame.-

Mujer -Hola, buenos días. ¿Hablo con el señor Víctor Carlisle?-

Víctor -Sí, soy yo.-

Mujer -Llamo desde el aeropuerto. Tenemos buenas noticias. Su maleta está con nosotros y se la enviaremos por taxi esta mañana. Debería estar con usted antes de las doce. ¿Usted va a estar en casa toda la mañana?-

Víctor -Sí, no hay problema. Puedo esperar aquí.-

Mujer -Perfecto. Si tiene problemas no dude en llamarme. Que tenga un buen día. Adiós.-

Víctor -Gracias, adiós.-

Víctor se siente muy alegre. Son muy buenas noticias. Va a la cocina a preparar un café. Los padres de Eliana han comprado unas cositas como leche, café, pan y un poco de queso y chorizo para él. Prepara un bocadillo de queso y chorizo y un café fuerte y se sienta a la mesa. De repente suena su móvil otra vez.

Víctor - ¿Hola?-

Alfredo - ¿Víctor? Soy Alfredo. ¿Qué tal estás?

Víctor -Muy bien, gracias. Han encontrado mi maleta. Me la van a entregar esta mañana.-

Alfredo -Me alegro mucho, Víctor. Pues también tengo buenas noticias. Mi amigo del restaurante quiere verte hoy. Dice que tiene

Chapter 17

The next day a telephone call wakes Victor up. He grabs his mobile that's at the side of the bed and answers.

Victor "Yes. Who's speaking?"

Woman "Hello, good morning. Am I speaking with Mr Victor Carlisle?"

Victor "Yes, that's me."

Woman "I'm calling from the airport. We have good news. Your suitcase is with us and we will send it to you by taxi this morning. It should be with you before twelve. Will you be at home all morning?"

Victor "Yes, there's no problem. I can wait here."

Woman "Perfect. If you have problems feel free to call me. Have a good day. Goodbye."

Victor "Thank you, goodbye."

Victor feels very happy. It's really good news. He goes to the kitchen to prepare a coffee. Eliana's parents have bought some things like milk, coffee, bread and a little bit of cheese and chorizo for him. He prepares a cheese and chorizo baguette and a strong coffee and he sits at the table. Suddenly, his mobile rings again.

Victor "Hello?"

Alfredo "Victor? It's Alfredo. How are you?"

Victor "Very well, thank you. They've found my suitcase. They are going to deliver it to me this morning."

Alfredo "I'm really pleased, Victor. Well, I've also got good news. My friend from the restaurant wants to see you today. He says that he has

un puesto disponible y que sí, quiere hablar contigo sobre la posibilidad de trabajar allí.-

Víctor -¡Qué bien, Alfredo! Muchas gracias. ¿A qué hora tengo que estar allí?-

Alfredo - Dice que tienes que estar allí para las cuatro de la tarde. ¿Sabes dónde está el restaurante?

Víctor -No tengo ni idea, Alfredo, pero puedo preguntar fácilmente. ¿Cuál es la dirección?-

Alfredo -Está en la calle Descalzos, número 10A y se llama el Mesón de Cervantes. Está a unos diez minutos a pie. Sigue los carteles hacia el centro y luego pregúntale a alguien.-

Víctor -Sin problema, Alfredo. Voy a estar allí a las cuatro en punto.-

Alfredo -Bien. Llámame después para contarme todo. Por cierto, el hombre se llama Guillermo. Buena suerte, Víctor. Hasta luego-

Víctor -Gracias. Hasta luego, Alfredo.-

Víctor está encantado. Ya no sólo tiene su maleta sino una entrevista para tener un trabajo. Parece que todo sale muy bien.

A las once y media un taxista llama al timbre y Víctor baja a recoger su maleta.

Taxista -Hola, buenos días. Tengo su maleta aquí. Sólo tiene que firmar este papel para decir que ha recibido la maleta en un buen estado.-

Víctor -Vale. Parece que todo está en orden. Muchas gracias. Aquí tiene algo para usted.-

Víctor le da cinco euros de propina al taxista.

Taxista -Muchísimas gracias. Que pase un buen día. Adiós.-

Víctor -Y usted. Adiós.-

a position available and that he does want to talk with you about the possibility of working there."

Victor "That's great, Alfredo! Thanks a lot. What time have I to be there?"

Alfredo "He says that you have to be there by four this afternoon. Do you know where the restaurant is?"

Victor "I don't have a clue, Alfredo, but I can easily ask. What's the address?"

Alfredo "It's in Descalzos street, number 10A and it's called Cervantes Tavern. It's ten minutes on foot. Follow the signs for the town centre and then ask someone."

Victor "No problem, Alfredo. I'm going to be there at four on the dot."

Alfredo "Good. Call me afterwards to tell me everything. By the way, the man is called Guillermo. Good luck, Victor. See you later."

Victor "Thanks. See you later, Alfredo."

Victor is over the moon. Now he doesn't only have his suitcase but has an interview for a job. It seems that everything is turning out well.

At eleven thirty a taxi driver rings the bell and Victor goes down to pick up his suitcase.

Taxi driver "Hello, good morning. I have your case here. You just have to sign this paper to say that you have received the case in a good state."

Victor "Okay. Everything seems in order. Thanks a lot. Here is something for you."

Victor gives a five Euro tip to the taxi driver.

Taxi driver "Thanks a lot. Have a god day. Goodbye."

Victor "And you. Goodbye."

Víctor sube con su maleta y luego pasa el resto de la mañana ordenando la casa y poniendo su ropa en su sitio.

Victor takes his case up and then he spends the rest of the morning straightening out the house and putting his clothing away.

Lesson 18. Saber and Conocer. The verbs To Know.

In English, we have only one verb "to know", however, the Spanish language has two.

This is because they choose to differentiate between knowing information, things, "stuff" and knowing people and places.

Knowing "Stuff" = **Saber** (Both begin with S)

This is how it breaks down. It´s irregular only in the first person, "Yo" form.

Saber

Yo sé	Nosotros sabemos
Tú sabes	Vosotros sabéis
Él/Ella sabe	Ellos/Ellas saben
Usted sabe	Ustedes saben

A common form of this is heard when people talk about not knowing something.

"*No sé.*" they say. "*I don't know.*"

or

"*No lo sé.*" which means, "*I don't know it.*"

Here are some examples of how this verb is used in the following way:

"I know a lot about English." = "Yo sé mucho sobre el inglés."

"We know a lot about Spanish." = "Sabemos mucho sobre el español."

Saying "How to".

In English we say things like, "I know how to do something…."

*In Spanish, the verb Saber means "**to know how to**".*

Thus, to say:

"I know how to swim..." you merely have to say:

"Yo sé nadar."

"I know how to paint well."

"Yo sé pintar bien."

and, of course, to say that you don't know is easy... just add "no"

"I don't know how to ride a bicycle." = "No sé montar en bicicleta."

"You all don't know how to read maps." = "No sabéis leer mapas."

Conocer = To know/meet people and to know places

Like Saber, Conocer is irregular in the first person. After that, it follows the normal rules.

Yo conozco	Nosotros conocemos
Tú conoces	Vosotros conocéis
Él/Ella conoce	Ellos/Ellas conocen
Usted conoce	Ustedes conocen

Here are some examples of how it´s used to describe knowing people:

Conozco muy bien a Jorge. = I know Jorge really well.

¿Conoces a mi hermano? = Do you know my brother?

Ellos conocen a mis padres.   = They know my parents.

Note: You can know a person, by face, (conocer) but not know anything about them (saber).

e.g.

Conozco a esa mujer pero no sé nada sobre ella. = I know that woman (recognize her) but I know nothing about her.

Notice that when Spanish speakers use "nada" they make a double negative which isn´t allowed in English, yet is perfectly acceptable in Spanish.

No sé nada = I don't know anything/I know nothing

(lit. I don't know nothing.)

In addition to that, you can use it to show which countries or places you´ve visited:

Conozco Francia y Béligica. = I've been to France and Belgium.

¿Conoces mi pueblo? = Have you been to my home town?

No conozco Los Estados Unidos. = I haven't been to the United States.

So, what does this sentence mean?

"No conozco a Brad Pitt personalmente, pero sé mucho de él."

"I haven't met Brad Pitt, but I know a lot about him."

Thus, to be clear, Conocer has a dual meaning. When you say:

"Conozco tu país."

You are saying...

"I'm familiar with your country because I have been there."

When you say:

"Conozco a esa mujer."

You are saying that you have either met her, or you know her face, but it does not mean that you know anything about her.

Intensifiers.

To intensify your knowing, whether it is the knowing of things or people and places, then you use BIEN = well.

e.g.

Conozco bien España. = I am very familiar with Spain.

(Because I've been there.)

Sé hacerlo bien. = I know how to do it well.

Conozco muy bien a tu madre. = I know your mum very well.

Sé nadar muy bien. = I know how to swim very well.

Ahora te toca a ti.

Fill in the blanks, choosing the correct verb and person.

1.-Margarita ......*sabe*.....hablar francés.

2.-¿Tú .*conoces*..a Julio Iglesias?

3.-Disculpe, ¿usted ..*sabe*....donde está la biblioteca?

4.-Nosotros *sabemos*....nadar muy bien.

5.-Ellos .*conocen*.al doctor Ramírez.

6-7.-Nosotros .*sabemos*.quién es el presidente de los Estados Unidos, pero no

lo...*conocemos*.personalmente.

8.-Ella es una estudiante nueva, y no...*conoce*....bien la universidad.

9. ¿*Conoces* (tú) la ciudad de Madrid?

10.-Ella...*sabe*..muy bien todos los verbos nuevos.

11. ¿A qué deportes ..*sabes*....(tú) jugar bien?

12. ¿*Conocen*... tus compañeros a tus abuelos?

Capítulo 18

A las dos decide salir a comer. Busca un bar o restaurante en la zona con un menú del día. En una esquina él ve un restaurante que se llama -Jamón Jamón-. En un cartel pone que sirven un menú del día por diez euros. Incluye el primer plato, el segundo plato, postre, bebida o café. Entra por la puerta y se sienta a la mesa. Un camarero viene directamente a tomar su pedido.

Camarero -Buenos días, ¿qué va a tomar?-

Víctor -El menú del día, por favor.-

Camarero -Por supuesto. ¿De primero?

Víctor -De primero la paella.-

Camarero -¿Y de segundo?-

Víctor -El filete, por favor.-

Camarero -Perfecto. Y ¿cómo lo quiere?-

Víctor -Eh...No entiendo.-

Camarero -Quiero decir que si lo quiere vuelta y vuelta, medio hecho o bien hecho.-

Víctor -Ah, ya entiendo. Bien hecho, por favor.-

Camarero -Y ¿de beber?-

Víctor - Voy a tomar una Fanta naranja.-

Camarero -Enseguida se lo traigo.-

Mientras espera la comida, Víctor piensa en su entrevista de hoy. Tiene nervios al imaginarse hablando con el dueño del restaurante. Todavía no entiende todo y a veces le cuesta expresarse bien en español. Realmente quiere conseguir el trabajo aunque ser camarero no es lo que quiere hacer para siempre. Llega la comida y come con hambre. La comida está riquísima y le gusta todo. Al terminar, él pide la cuenta.

Chapter 18

At two he decides to go out to eat. He looks for a bar or a restaurant in the area with a menu of the day. On a corner he sees a restaurant called "Ham Ham". On a sign it says that they serve a menu of the day for ten Euros. It includes a first course, a second course, a dessert, a drink or coffee. He goes through the door and sits at a table. A waiter comes directly to take his order.

Waiter "Good morning, what are you going to have?"

Victor "The menu of the day, please."

Waiter "Of course. For first course?"

Victor "For first course, the paella."

Waiter "And for second course?"

Victor "The steak, please."

Waiter "Perfect. And how do you want it?"

Victor "Eh...I don't understand."

Waiter "I mean if you want it, rare, medium or well done."

Victor "Ah, now I understand, well done, please."

Waiter "And to drink?"

Victor "I'll have an orange Fanta."

Waiter "I'll bring it right away."

Whilst he waits for the food, Victor thinks about his interview today. He gets nervous imagining talking with the owner of the restaurant. He still doesn't understand everyone and sometimes it's hard for him to express himself in Spanish. He really wants the job although being a waiter isn't what he wants to do forever. The food arrives and he eats hungrily. The food is delicious and he likes everything. When he finishes he asks for the bill.

Víctor -Perdone.-

Camarero -Sí, ¿desea algo más?-

Víctor -No, gracias. ¿Cuánto le debo?-

Camarero -Son diez euros.-

Víctor -Aquí tiene. Muchas gracias.-

Camarero -Y a usted. Que pase un buen día.-

Víctor le da al camarero once euros. Diez por el menú y un euro de propina. A eso de las tres de la tarde, sale del restaurante y anda hacia el centro. Todavía no conoce la ciudad de Toledo y al llegar a la plaza de Zocodóver le pregunta a alguien por la dirección.

Víctor -Perdone. ¿Me puede decir por dónde está la calle Descalzos?-

Persona -Lo siento, no soy de aquí. Sólo estoy de visita.-

Víctor -No pasa nada. Gracias.-

La verdad es que toda la plaza está llena de turistas y Víctor sabe que sería difícil encontrar un ciudadano. Decide preguntar en una tienda. A un lado hay un estanco. Entra y pregunta.

Víctor -Perdone, ¿la calle Descalzos?-

Dependiente -Sí, mire. Al salir de la tienda, doble a la derecha y siga todo recto por la calle del Comercio. Siga hasta el final y allí, doble a la izquierda. Esa calle se llama la calle de la Trinidad. Siga hasta el cruce y coja la calle de Rojas a la izquierda. Baje esa calle unos veinte metros y luego doble a la derecha por la calle del Taller del Moro. De allí, siga todo recto unos doscientos metros y allí está.-

Víctor -Muchas gracias. Es muy amable.-

Dependiente -De nada.-

Victor "Excuse me."

Waiter "Yes, would you like something else?"

Victor "No, thanks. How much do I owe you?

Waiter "That's ten Euros."

Victor "Here you have it. Thanks a lot."

Waiter "To you too. Have a good day."

Victor gives the waiter eleven Euros. Ten for the menu and one Euro tip. At about three in the afternoon, he leaves the restaurant and walks toward the centre. He still doesn't know Toledo city and once he arrives at Zocodóver Square, he asks someone the direction.

Victor "Excuse me. Can you tell me the way to Delcalzos street, please?

Person "Sorry, I'm not from here. I'm just visting."

Victor "No problem. Thanks."

In truth, the whole square is filled with tourists and Victor knows that it would be difficult to find a local. He decides to ask in a shop. To one side there's a tobacconists. He goes in and asks.

Victor "Excuse me. Descalzos Street?"

Assistant "Yes, look. As you go out of the shop, turn to the right and follow straight on along Comercio street. Continue to the end of the street and, there, turn left. That street is called Trinidad street. Continue to the cross road and take a left onto Rojas street. Go down that street some twenty metres and then, turn to the right, along Taller del Moro street. From there, continue straight on some two hundred metres and there it is."

Victor "Thanks a lot. You're very kind."

Assistant "You're welcome."

Víctor tiene una confusión de nombres en su mente, pero por lo menos puede recordar que tiene que doblar a la derecha y seguir la calle del Comercio. La calle es muy interesante y tiene tienda tras tienda de todo tipo de cosas. Casi todas son turísticas y venden recuerdos y suvenires de Toledo. Es un paseo muy agradable y a Víctor le gusta el ambiente de estar de vacaciones que tiene el centro.

Al final de la calle, entra en otra tienda y pregunta de nuevo por la calle Descalzos. Otra vez, el dependiente le da un montón de instrucciones pero Víctor solamente se enfoca en las primeras dos o tres. Finalmente, después de haber preguntado otras dos veces, encuentra la calle. A las cuatro menos veinte se encuentra fuera del restaurante el Mesón de Cervantes. Todavía es temprano, así que entra en una cafetería local y pide un café. Está muy tranquila y no hay nadie.

Víctor -¿Me pone un café cortado, por favor?-

Camarero -Aquí tiene. Y usted, ¿de dónde es?-

Víctor -Soy de Inglaterra, del norte.-

Camarero -¿Ah, sí? Pero ¿cómo es que habla tan bien el español?

Víctor -Gracias, pero todavía mi español no es muy bueno. Estudio todos los días pero aún me falta mucho.-

Camarero -Bueno, muchos ingleses vienen para acá y la mayoría no habla ni una palabra. Piden en inglés y luego se enfadan si no les entendemos.

Víctor -Eso cambia. Muchos ingleses ya aprenden el español. Ya sabemos que no se puede ir a otros países hablando solamente en inglés.-

Victor has a confusion of names in his head, but at least he can remember that he has to turn to the right and go along Comercio street. The road is very interesting and it has shop after shop of all kinds of things. Nearly all of them are touristic and they sell mementos and souvenirs from Toledo. It's a very pleasant walk and Victor likes the holiday atmosphere that the town centre has.

At the end of the street, he goes into another shop and asks for Descalzos street. Once more, the assistant gives him a pile of instructions but Victor only focuses in the first two or three. Finally, after having asked another two times, he finds the street. At twenty to four he finds himself outside the restaurant, Cervantes Tavern. It's still early so he goes into a local café and orders a coffee. It's quiet and there's no one there.

Victor "Can you give me a coffee with a dash of milk, please?"

Waiter "Here you have it. And where are you from?"

Victor "I'm from England, from the north."

Waiter "Ah, yes? But, how is it that you speak Spanish so well?"

Victor "Thanks, but my Spanish still isn't very good. I study every day but I'm still have more to do."

Waiter "Well, many English come over here and the majority don't even speak a word. They order in English and then they get annoyed if you don't understand them."

Victor "That's changing. Many English are now learning Spanish. Now we know that you can't go to other countries speaking only in English."

Camarero -Pues, tal vez cambie por allá pero por aquí no veo mucho cambio. Aun así, no me puedo quejar. Sois muy generosos a la hora de dejar propinas.-

Víctor -¿De verdad? Cuando trabajaba de camarero en Inglaterra, dejaban propinas muy malas.

Camarero -No sé. Aquí en España somos muy malos en cuanto a dejar propinas. Dicen que somos los peores de Europa, mientras los ingleses soléis dejar mucho más, especialmente los grupos.

Víctor -Bueno, ahora me siento obligado a dejarle una buena propina, ja ja. ¿Cuánto le debo?-

Camarero - Un euro y cincuenta céntimos, por favor.-

Víctor -Tome, aquí tiene dos euros. Muchas gracias.-

Camarero -Y a usted. Hasta luego.-

Víctor -Hasta luego.-

Waiter "Well, maybe it's changing over there but around here I don't see much change. Still, I can't complain. You're very generous when you leave a tip."

Victor "Is that so? When I worked as a waiter in England, the used to give really bad tips.

Waiter "I don't know. Here in Spain, we are really bad when leaving tips. They say that we are the worst in Europe, whilst the English normally leave much more, especially the groups.

Victor "Well, now I feel obliged to leave you a good tip. Haha. How much do I owe you?

Waiter "One Euro and fifty cents, please."

Victor. "Here. There you have two Euros. Thanks a lot."

Waiter "And you. See you later."

Victor "See you later."

Lesson 19. Gustar to like / to be pleasing.

One of the most useful verbs you'll ever learn is **Gustar**. It's a great conversation piece and a very handy Spanish tool to aid your chatting skills.

The only issue is that it can be a little confusing!

The Big Mistake

In many grammar books the verb **Gustar** is often translated as "To like", however, that's not really the case.

A better translation is "To please" or "To be pleasing" and we"ll show you why.

Look at this sentence:

I like chocolate → **Me gusta el chocolate**.

In English we say:

"I like chocolate."

But in Spanish, it's **the other way around**.

What they say is:

"To me it's pleasing the chocolate."

So, to make a sentence with **Gustar** we need only ask ourselves:

Three simple questions!

Question 1, Who is the pleasing happening to?

To do this part you need to choose from the list of what are called "Indirect Object Pronouns". Many students freeze when they hear names like that!

To help them stay calm, we like to call it the **"Furniture Movers List."**

Why? *Because when you read them in English they sound like something furniture removers would say. They go like this: "to me, to you, to him...etc.*

To me	=	**ME**
To you	=	**TE**
To him/her =		**LE**
To us	=	**NOS**
To you all =		**OS**
To them	=	**LES**

So, as in the sentence, "I like chocolate", or in Spanish style, "To me, it pleases, the chocolate." the person being pleased is yourself (ME.). Thus you would choose ***"ME".***

*In the sentence, "You like chocolate." the person receiving the pleasing is YOU and so you would choose "**TE**".*

 Question 2, Is the thing that's pleasing singular or is it plural?

If what the person likes is: **Singular** *we choose* **GUSTA.**

If what the person likes is: **Plural** *we choose* **GUSTAN.**

Ejemplo:

If it was **EL FÚTBOL** *that was doing the pleasing then you would use* **GUSTA**

This is because it's singular.

If it was **LAS PELÍCULAS** that was doing the pleasing then you would use **GUSTAN**

This is because they are plural.

Question 3, What is doing the pleasing?

Once you have the person who's being pleased then **gusta** or **gustan** in place, all you need to do is to add the thing that's doing the pleasing.

Note: You just about always need to use the word "the" in front of the noun.

e.g.

Me gusta **EL** fútbol.

Me gustan **LAS** películas.

And that's it!! That's the formula. If you follow it, you´ll always get the sentence right!

Tip. To use Gustar well, you **MUST** take the word "**like**" out of your mind. It only causes confusion and some very dodgy sentences. (Technical term)

Here's a summary of the Formula.

1. Who is being pleased?

2. Is it singular or plural?

3. What is the thing that's pleasing?

Let"s try a couple of sentences: **He likes sports. (los deportes)**

1.Who is being pleased?   *He is!*   *So we put* **LE**

2. Are sports singular or plural?   *Plural!*   *So we put* **GUSTAN**

3. What is pleasing?   **LOS DEPORTES.**

So the sentence would be: **Le gustan los deportes.**

We like beer. (la cerveza)

1. Who is being pleased?   *We are!*   *So we put* **NOS**

2. Is beer singular or plural?   *Singular!*   *So we put* **GUSTA**

3. What is pleasing?   **LA CERVEZA**

So the sentence would be: **Nos gusta la cerveza.**

Getting the idea?

Saying that you don't like.

*To make a **like** into a **don't like**, all you do is add **NO** before the me, te, le, etc.*

I don't like beer → **No me gusta la cerveza.**

They don´t like beer → **No les gusta la cerveza.**

She doesn´t likes animals → **No le gustan los animales**.

To like to do THINGS.

When you want to say that you like to do something, then all you need do is add the entire verb, or infinitive as it's known, after the word **gusta**.

Note: Verbs (even if you put one after another) are **always** singular.

So:

> **Me gusta correr y jugar al tenis.** = I like to runand play tennis.

> **Os gusta comer pescado.** = You all like to eat fish.

> **Les gusta ver la televisión.** = They like to watch the television.

Mentioning People

If we want to mention a person when we use **Gustar**, for example:

> **George likes to eat paella.**

All we need to do is to **begin** the sentence with the **name** of the person (or title) preceded by "**A**".

> **A + name**

e.g.

> **A George, le gusta comer paella.**

Some further examples.

Marta likes cooking. → **A** Marta le gusta cocinar.

John and Julia don"t like fish. → **A** Juan y **A** Julia no les gusta el pescado.

My sister likes pop music. → **A** mi hermana le gusta la música pop.

Does your brother like potatoes? → ¿**A** tu hermano le gustan las patatas?

If you want to mention the person but not the name, for example: Me, You, Him, Her etc. then all you do is add the following at the beginning of the sentence:

A mí *(me)*	**A nosotros** *(nos)*
A ti *(te)*	**A vosotros** *(os)*
A él/ A ella *(le)*	**A ellos** *(les)*
A usted *(le)*	**A ustedes** *(les)*

e.g.

I like chicken. → **A mí me gusta el pollo.**

They *don"t like going shopping.* → **A ellos no les gusta ir de compras.**

Do **you all** *like vegetables?* → **¿A vosotros os gustan las verduras?**

Asking someone, "And you?"

*In normal questions, we have learned to ask "**Y tú**?" when we want to say. "And you?"*

*However, due to the way we make the sentences with **Gustar** (and similar verbs), when you want to ask somebody, "and you?" you need to say, "and **to** you?" which is "**¿Y a ti**?"*

e.g.

I like dogs. And you?

which is:

*Me gustan los perros, **y ¿a ti?***

Ahora te toca a ti. ¡¡Buena suerte!!

1. I like dogs. (los perros) ...... *Me gustan los perros*

2. Do you like animals? (los animales) ...... *¿Te gustan los animales?*

3. We don"t like this house. (esta casa) ... *nos nosgusta esta casa*

4. Samantha likes tea. (el té) .... *A Samantha le gusta el té*

5. Raúl and Elsa like going to the theatre. (IR) .. *A Raúl y Elsa les gusta ir al teatro*

6. I like chocolate ice-cream, and you? (el helado de chocolate)
.... *me gusta* ———— *¿y a ti?*

7. Does Peter like French? (el francés) ... *A Peter le gusta el francés*

8. I like reading and writing. (leer, escribir) ... *me gusta leer y escribir*

9. My sister doesn"t like cake. (la tarta) .. *A mi hermana no le gusta la tarta*

10. I don"t like bugs, and you? (los bichos) *no me gusta los bichos ¿y a ti?*

11. I like them! ... *me gustan mucho*

12. I don"t like it. .... *No me gusta*

And finally, let's look at how to emphasise your preferences.

To say "I like something **a lot**" you add:

Mucho

e.g

Me gusta mucho.

If you really like it, you add:

Muchísimo

e.g.

Me gusta muchísimo.

*And, if you like it even more than that, you can change the verb to **Encantar**. That means to adore it!!*

e.g.

¡Me encanta!

So, there you have your first delve into the impersonal verb, Gustar. We hope you found the information useful.

Remember, this is something you will continue to return to and to add to. And what's more, it's a great verb to have in your Spanish language tool box.

Capítulo 19

Víctor sale de la cafetería y va directamente al restaurante El Mesón de Cervantes. Parece vacío pero la puerta está abierta. Entra y busca a Guillermo. Al fondo del restaurante hay un hombre rubio y alto. Víctor lo saluda.

Víctor -¡Hola! Busco a Guillermo.

Guillermo -Soy yo. Debes de ser Víctor, ¿verdad?-

Víctor -Sí. Mucho gusto.-

Guillermo -Lo mismo digo. Alfredo dice que buscas trabajo. Aquí hace falta gente. Vamos a abrir en dos días y necesitamos camareros y gente para la barra. ¿Tienes experiencia?-

Víctor quiere el trabajo pero tampoco quiere mentir para conseguirlo. Decide decirle la verdad.

Víctor -Bueno, no mucho. Trabajé en McDonald's cuando era estudiante. Sólo eso.-

Guillermo -En verdad busco a gente con experiencia pero, bueno. Alfredo me dice que eres un buen chico. Sin embargo, trabajar de camarero es duro. ¿Tendrías problemas con eso? Si no eres trabajador no vales aquí.

Víctor -No me da miedo trabajar duro, Guillermo. Nunca he tenido problemas con eso.

Guillermo -Pues, mira, lo que te propongo: puedes empezar este viernes, nuestra primera noche, pero estarás de prueba. Si te apañas bien, no habrá problema. Sólo pago el mínimo, como todos los restaurantes. Te puedo ofrecer veinte horas por semana que son cuatro noches. Empiezas a las ocho y terminas a la una, más o menos. ¿Eso te vale? –

Chapter 19

Victor leaves the café and goes straight to the restaurant Cervantes Tavern. It looks empty but the door is open. He goes in and looks for Guillermo. At the back of the restaurant there's a tall blond man. Victor waves at him.

Victor "Hi! I'm looking for Guillermo."

Guillermo "That's me. You must be Victor, right?"

Victor "Yes. Nice to meet you."

Guillermo "The same here. Alfredo says that you're looking for work. We are short of people here. We're going to open in two days and we need waiters and people for the bar. Do you have experience?"

Victor wants the job but he doesn't want to lie to get it. He decides to tell him the truth.

Victor "Well, not a lot. I worked in McDonalds when I was a student. Only that."

Guillermo "In truth, I'm looking for people with experience but, well, Alfredo tells me that you're a good guy. However, working as a waiter is hard. Would you have problems with that? If you're not a worker, you're no good here.

Victor "I'm not afraid of hard work, Guillermo. I've never had problems with that."

Guillermo "Well, look what I propose to you: you can start this Friday, our first night, but you'll be on trial. If you manage well, there won't be a problem. I only pay the minimum, like all the restaurants. I can offer you twenty hours a week, which is four nights. You start at eight and you finish at around one. Is that okay?"

Víctor se asusta un poco por el horario. En Inglaterra los restaurantes abren mucho más temprano y cierran a las once. En este trabajo no va a acostarse hasta las dos de la madrugada. Se da cuenta de que tendrá que acostumbrarse al horario español.

Víctor -Perfecto, Guillermo. Muchísimas gracias. ¿A qué hora vengo el viernes y qué llevo de ropa?-

Guillermo -Estate aquí para las siete. Así podemos darte algo de formación antes de empezar la faena. De ropa, sólo tienes que llevar una camisa blanca y pantalones y zapatos negros.-

Víctor -Vale. Te veo a las siete.-

Guillermo -Hasta el viernes.-

Víctor -Hasta entonces.-

Víctor se siente muy contento de tener el trabajo, pero, a la vez, tiene un nudo en el estomago. No sabe nada de ser camarero. ¿Y si le cuesta entender a la gente? ¿Y si lo hace mal? Por otro lado, Guillermo parece un buen hombre y seguro que le va a ayudar. Para calmarse un poco, Víctor entra en un bar y toma un par de cervezas antes de volver a casa. Nada más entrar por la puerta, suena su móvil. Es Alfredo.

Alfredo -Hola, Víctor. ¿Qué tal te fue con Guillermo? ¿Te ha ofrecido un trabajo?-

Víctor -Sí, Alfredo. Empiezo este viernes.-

Alfredo -Me alegro, Víctor. ¿Y cómo lo ves?

Víctor -¿Perdón?

Alfredo -Quiero decir: ¿qué piensas de eso?

Víctor -Ah. Estoy muy contento, pero también tengo miedo, Alfredo. No sé si voy a hacerlo bien.-

Victor is a bit shocked about the hours. In England the restaurants open much earlier and close at eleven. In this job he's not going to get to bed until two o'clock in the morning. He realises that he'll have to get used to the Spanish timetable.

Victor "Perfect, Guillermo. Thanks a lot. What time do I come on Friday and what do I wear for clothing?"

Guillermo "Be here for seven. That way we can give you some training before the rush starts. For clothing, you just need to wear a white shirt and black trousers and shoes."

Victor "Okay. I'll see you at seven."

Guillermo "Until Friday."

Victor "See you then."

Victor feels really happy to have the job, but, at the same time, he has a knot in his stomach. He doesn't know anything about how to wait tables. What if he can't understand the people? What if he does it badly? On the other hand, Guillermo looks like a good man and he's sure he'll help him. To calm down a bit, Victor goes into a bar and has a couple of beers before returning home. Just as he gets through the door, his mobile rings. It's Alfredo.

Alfredo "Hi Victor. How did the interview go with Guillermo? Has he offered you a job?"

Victor "Yes, Alfredo. I start this Friday."

Alfredo "I'm pleased, Victor. And how does it look to you?"

Victor "Sorry?"

Alfredo "I mean, what do you think about it?"

Victor "Ah. I'm very happy, but I'm frightened, too, Afredo. I don't know if I'm going to do it well."

Alfredo -No te preocupes, Víctor. Lo vas a hacer fantásticamente. Después de dos días allí vas a ser como un profesional.

Víctor -Eso espero. Por cierto, gracias por recomendarme. Sé que sin tu ayuda no tendría ese trabajo.

Alfredo -De nada, Víctor. Por lo menos, así con trabajo, voy a estar seguro de que pagues el alquiler. Ja ja. ¿Y qué haces ahora?

Víctor -Nada. Pienso echarme una siesta.-

Alfredo -Pues nada, te dejo. Por cierto Eliana ha preguntado si quieres quedar esta tarde a las nueve. Ahora está estudiando pero dice que va a estar libre más tarde. Entonces, si quieres salir a tomar algo tienes que enviarla un SMS, ¿vale?-

Víctor -Vale, Alfredo. Lo haré. Hasta luego.-

Alfredo -Hasta luego, Víctor.-

Víctor cuelga y se tumba en el sofá. Piensa en los últimos días. Tantas cosas han pasado que todo parece muy borroso en su mente. Su trabajo nuevo, su nueva amistad con Eliana, su nueva vida aquí en Toledo y claro, el preocupantemente fornido ex novio, Hugo.

Esta tarde va a salir con Eliana otra vez y al pensarlo nota que tiene nervios en el estomago. Le gusta mucho pasar tiempo con ella y encima, su familia le cae muy bien. Antes de quedarse dormido le envía un mensaje a Eliana que dice que va a ir a recogerla a su casa a las nueve y media.

Alfredo "Don't worry, Victor. You're going to do it wonderfully well. After two days there you're going to be like a professional."

Víctor "I hope so. By the way, thanks for recommending me. I know that, without your help, I wouldn't have gotten that job."

Alfredo "You're welcome, Victor. At least, this way, with work I'm going to be sure that you pay the rent. Haha. And what are you doing now?"

Víctor "Nothing. I'm thinking about having a siesta."

Alfredo "Well, anyway, I'll let you go. By the way, Eliana has asked if you want to meet this evening at nine. She's studying now but she says that she's going to be free later. So, if you want to go out with her you have to send her a text message, okay?"

Víctor "Okay, Alfredo. I'll do it. See you later."

Alfredo "See you later, Victor."

Victor hangs up and lies down on the sofa. He thinks about the last few days. So many things have happened that everything seems blurry in his mind. His new job, his new friendship with Eliana, his new life in Toledo and, of course, Eliana's worryingly enormous ex-boyfriend, Hugo.

That evening he's going to go out with Eliana again and when he thinks about it, he notices that he has butterflies in his stomach. He really likes to spend time with her and, what's more, he really likes her family. Before falling asleep, he sends Eliana a message that says that he's going to pick her up from home at nine-thirty.

Lesson 20. Useful Questions / Preguntas Útiles.

In this lesson we'd like give you a range of useful questions that will help you, just like Victor, to instigate and carry on conversations in Spanish.

Of course, we haven't included everything you'll need, but as a start it will launch you into the fascinating world of the Spanish language and conversation.

Here we go:

¿Dónde vives? = **Where do you live?**

Note: The fact that "vives" finishes with an S, shows that you are talking to one person in an informal way.

Vivo en... (Add place) = **I live in...**

Note: **En** can mean In and On. Also the V is typically pronounced like a B. You say. Bibo instead of Vivo.

¿De dónde eres? = **Where are you from?**

Literally: From where are you?

Soy de ... (add place) = **I'm from...**

or

Soy inglés (man) or *inglesa* (woman) = **I'm English**

Soy de los Estados Unidos = **I'm from the United States**

or

Soy español (man) or *española* (woman) = **I'm from Spain**

Soy de España = **I'm from Spain**

Asking about someone's job.

There are three main ways that you can ask someone what they do for work.

Here they are in order of difficulty of pronunciation. We particularly like option two as it's easy to say and doesn't readily cause confusion.

1. *¿Qué haces?* = What do you do?

2. *¿En qué trabajas?* = What do you work in?

3. *¿A qué te dedicas?* = What do you dedicate yourself to?

Note: The word "qué" means "what". The Spanish have the following questioning words which are really worth committing to memory:

¿Qué? = What?

¿Cuándo? = When?

¿Cómo? = How?

¿Cuál? = Which?

¿Quién? = Who?

¿Cuánto? = How much?

¿Dónde? = Where?

To answer the question about your job, all you need to do is this:

Soy .... *(add your profession)* = **I am...**

e.g.

Soy profesor (teacher)

Soy fontanero (plumber)

Soy carpintero (carpinter)

Soy marinero (sailor)

To say you're retired, Spanish speakers normally say:

Estoy (sometimes Soy) jubilado (man) **jubilada** (woman)

Asking about family.

¿Tienes familia? = **Do you have family?**

You answer by saying:

Tengo...(Add family members) = **I have...**

e.g.

Tengo dos hermanos y una hermana.

= I have two brothers and a sister.

Asking about hobbies.

To do this all you say is:

¿Tienes pasatiempos? = **Do you have pastimes/hobbies?**

The easiest way of answering this is to find the verb that describes what you do and break it down to say what it is.

e.g.

Correr = **To run**
Corro = **I run**
Nadar = **To swim**
Nado = **I swim**
Leer = **To read**
Leo = **I read**

If you play a sport you use the verb JUGAR. This verb is irregular and it breaks down like this:

Juego   *Jugamos*
Juegas   *Jugáis*
Juega   *Juegan*

When you use this verb you normally follow it with **A** and link it to the sport.

 e.g.

Football = **el fútbol**

So to say "I play football" you say:

Juego AL fútbol.

Note: When you join **A** with **EL** it becomes **AL**. However **A LA, A LOS** and **A LAS**, stay the same.

A+EL = AL

Most sports are masculine although not all. Thus, most times you´ll say, **Juego al...**

e.g.

Juego al rugby
Juego al cricket
Juego al tenis
Juego al squash
Juego al golf

but

Juego a las cartas (Cards)
Juego a la comba (Skipping)

You can also use the verb **Gustar**, which is mentioned in lesson 19. In its simplest form, all you say to say what you do is this:

Me gusta el fútbol (I like football)
Me gusta el rugby (I like rugby)

or

Me gusta leer. I like to read.
Me gusta andar. I like to walk.
Me gusta conducir. I like to drive.

To ask someone what they like to do, you say:

¿Qué te gusta hacer? = What do you like to do?

Ahora te toca a ti.

Have a go at answering these questions. Firstly, say the answers and then write them down.

1. ¿Dónde vives? ..... *Vivo en Londres*

2. ¿De dónde eres? ..... *Soy de Grays*

3. ¿En qué trabajas? ..... *Soy ingeniero*

4. ¿Tienes familia? ..... *Si tengo familia*

5. ¿Tienes pasatiempos? ..... *Si juego a golf*

6. ¿Qué te gusta hacer? ..... *Me gusta el fútbol*

Now, translate these answers.

7. I live in France. ..... *Vivo en Francia*

8. I'm from Spain. ..... *Soy de España*

9. I'm a carpenter. ..... *Soy un carpintero*

10. I have three sisters. ..... *Tengo tres hermanas*

11. I like to go out with friends. ..... *Me gusta salir con amigos*

12. I like to read novels. ..... *Me gusta leer novelas*

Capítulo 20

Un par de horas más tarde se despierta y se prepara un café fuerte. Luego, se ducha y se viste. Son las ocho y media y decide salir y tomar algo rumbo a casa de Eliana. Todavía no conoce muy bien la zona, y da una vuelta mirando lo que hay en su barrio. Cerca de su casa hay un supermercado. Al lado del supermercado hay un gimnasio y en frente del gimnasio está la comisaría.

Lo que nota Víctor es que en cada calle hay por lo menos un bar, pero frecuentemente hay hasta dos o tres.

No están muy ocupados pero siempre hay algunas personas adentro. Más interesante es que el suelo de cada bar está lleno de deshechos como servilletas y restos de comida. Parece que la gente tira su basura directamente al suelo.

Entra en un bar medio lleno de gente y pide una caña. Un hombre a su lado lo saluda.

Hombre   -Hola, buenas tardes. ¿Qué tal?-

Víctor   -Bien, gracias. ¿Y tú?-

Hombre   -Fenomenal, gracias. No eres de aquí, ¿verdad?-

Víctor   -No. Soy inglés, pero ahora vivo aquí.-

Hombre   -Ah, bien. ¿A qué te dedicas?-

Víctor   -Acabo de llegar; pero el viernes empiezo como camarero en el restaurante, El Mesón de Cervantes.-

Hombre   -¡Qué bien! Trabajé de camarero durante una temporada. Es un buen trabajo aunque no me gustó mucho el horario.-

Chapter 20

A couple of hours later he awakes and prepares himself a strong coffee. Then, he showers and get's dressed. It's eight-thirty and he decides to go out and have something on the way to Eliana's house. He still doesn't know the area well and he walks around looking at what there is in his neighbourhood. Close by his home there's a supermarket. To the side of the supermarket there's a gymnasium and in front of the gymnasium is the police station.

What Victor notices is that in each street there is, at least, one bar, but often there are up to two or three.

They aren't very busy but there's always someone in there. More interesting is that the floor in each bar is full of rubbish like serviettes and leftover food. It looks like the people throw their rubbish straight onto the floor.

He goes in a half-filled bar and orders a beer. A man at his side greets him.

Man   "Hello, good evening. How are you?"

Victor   "Fine, thanks. And you?"

Man   "Phenomenal. You're not from here, right?"

Victor   "No, I'm English, but I live here now."

Man   "Ah, good. What do you do?"

Victor   "I've just arrived but on Friday I start as a waiter in the restaurant, Cervantes Tavern."

Man   "That's good! I worked as a waiter for a while. It's a good job although I didn't like the hours much."

Víctor -A mí tampoco, pero por lo menos tengo algo. Más tarde puedo buscar algo más de mi estilo. Tengo una pregunta. ¿Por qué la gente tira todo al suelo en los bares?-

Hombre -¿Cómo dices?-

Víctor -Es que, en Inglaterra, nunca haríamos eso. La mayoría de los bares tiene moqueta y tirar basura al suelo sería muy mal educado.-

Hombre -Ah, ya veo. Aquí es la costumbre. De verdad, para nosotros, los mejores bares son los de los suelos más sucios. Eso significa que el bar es popular y que las tapas son buenas.-

Víctor -Vale, ya entiendo, gracias. Aun así, me daría cosa hacerlo a mí.-

Hombre -No te preocupes, después de pasar seis meses aquí vas a estar tirando tú servilletas como cualquiera, jaja.-

Víctor -Creo que tienes razón, jeje. ¿Y porque hay tantos bares en cada calle? Es que, en Inglaterra, sí tenemos bares, pero no tantos como aquí.-

Hombre -Bueno. Lo que pasa es que aquí en España, somos muy callejeros. Nos gusta salir a tomar algo. No es que bebamos mucho volumen, sino que bebemos muy frecuentemente. Muchos bloques de pisos tienen su propio bar y tienda que vende cosas como pan y leche y, antes de la hora de comer o cenar, por ejemplo, se ve mucha gente tomando algo en el bar.-

Víctor -Sí, es verdad. Cada vez que he estado en España, no he visto a un español borracho.-

Hombre -No. Ése es el trabajo de los guiris. Para ver eso tienes que ir a la costa, a Benidorm o lugares así. Allí, vas a ver borrachos por un tubo.-

Víctor "Me neither, but at least I have something. I can look for something more my style later on. I've got a question. Why do the people throw everything on the floor in the bars?"

Man "What do you mean?"

Víctor "It's just, in England, we'd never do that. Most of the bars have carpets and throwing rubbish on the floor would be very rude."

Man "Ah, now I see. It's the custom here. In truth, for us, the best bars are the ones with the dirtiest floors. That means that it's a popular bar and the tapas are good."

Victor "Okay, now I understand, thanks. Even so, I'd feel bad doing it."

Man "Don't worry, after spending a couple of months here you're going to be throwing serviettes down like anyone else, haha."

Victor "I think you're right, hehe. And why are there so many bars in each street? It's just that in England, we do have bars, but not as many as here."

Man "Well. What happens is that here in Spain, we are street people. We like to go out and have something to eat or drink. It's not that we drink a lot, but rather we drink frequently. Many blocks of flats have their own bar and shop that sells things like bread and milk and, before lunchtime or the evening meal, for example, you'll see a lot of people having a drink in the bar."

Victor "Yes, it's true. Each time that I've been in Spain, I haven't seen a Spanish person drunk."

Man "No. That's the job of the foreigners. To see them you have to go to the coast, to Benidorm or places like that. You're going to see drunks in their thousands there."

Víctor -Nunca he estado en Benidorm. Prefiero el interior. Así puedo vivir la cultura.-

Hombre -Y, claro, puedes alimentarte con nuestra comida tan buena, ¿eh? ¿A que está riquísima?-

Víctor -Sí, me gusta mucho. Mi favorita es la tortilla española.-

Hombre -¿Alguna vez has probado una loncha de jamón?-

Víctor -Sí, varias veces ya.-

Hombre -¿A qué está bueno?-

Víctor -Sí. Me encanta de verdad.-

Hombre -Para hacer un jamón hay un proceso muy largo. Se producen por todas partes pero uno de los mejores viene de León.-

Víctor -¿De verdad? ¿De león? Siempre he pensado que el jamón venía del cerdo. Jaja.-

Hombre -... Supongo que ése es el famoso sentido del humor inglés.-

Víctor -Lo siento. Es que me gusta bromear un poco.-

Hombre -Dicen que por allí se come mal. ¿Es cierto?-

Víctor -¿Por allí?-

Hombre -Digo, allí en Inglaterra. Dicen que la comida no es muy buena y que coméis mal.-

Víctor -Bueno, no diría eso. Nuestra comida tiene su encanto como cualquiera.-

Hombre -Ah. Pero no está tan buena como la nuestra, ¿verdad?-

Víctor -Pues, a mí me gusta todo tipo de comida, la nuestra, la vuestra, la comida italiana, hindú, tailandesa, bueno de todo.-

Victor "I've never been to Benidorm. I prefer inland. That way I can experience the culture."

Man "And, of course, you can feed yourself on our great food, eh? It's fantastic isn't it?"

Victor "Yes, I like it a lot. My favourite is Spanish omelette."

Man "Have you ever tried a slice of ham?"

Victor "Yes, many times now.

Man "It's lovely, isn't it?"

Victor "Yes. I really love it."

Man "There's a very long process to make a ham. It's made in most places but one of the best comes from Leon." (Leon also means lion.)

Victor "Really? From a lion? I always thought that ham came from pork, haha."

Man "...I suppose that that is the famous English sense of humour."

Victor "Sorry. I just like to joke a little bit."

Man "They say that you don't eat very well, over there. Is it true?"

Victor "Over there?"

Man "I'm saying, there in England. They say that the food isn't very good and that you eat badly."

Victor "Well, I wouldn't say that. Our food has its charm like any other."

Man "Ah. But it isn't as nice as ours, is it?"

Victor "Well, I like all kinds of food, ours, yours, Italian food, Indian, Thai, well everything."

Hombre -Hombre, no sé nada de las demás comidas. Sólo sé que no hay nada mejor en el mundo que una buena paella o un buen filete español.-

Víctor -Tal vez tengas razón. Mira, ahora me tengo que marchar porque he quedado con una amiga y llego tarde. Gracias por la charla. Hasta luego.-

Hombre -Hasta luego, hombre. Y por cierto. Para ser inglés hablas muy bien español. ¡Enhorabuena!-

Víctor -Gracias.-

Man "I don't know anything about other food. I just know that there's nothing better in the world that a good paella and a great Spanish steak."

Victor "Maybe you're right. Look, I've got to run now because I've agreed to meet a friend and I'm late. See you later."

Man "See you later, pal. And by the way. For an English person you speak Spanish very well. Congratulations!

Victor "Thanks."

Lesson 21. Food and drinks. Comida y Bebida.

In this lesson we will give you all the vocabulary you need to safely manage your way round any Spanish speaking restaurant or bar. At this point you will probably have seen Victor in various situations in which he has ordered food and you may have noticed that at no time did he say to the barman:

"Dos cervezas, por favor."

We say that because we have noticed that whenever someone says to us that they can get by in Spain, they invariably say the above sentence. The strange thing is that they always ask for 'two' beers, never one or three!

Sounding like a Native.

Normally, if you want to order a drink, you can either say:

At the bar:

"¿Me pone...?"

which means "Will you put me...?"

or

At the table.

"¿Me trae...?"

which means, "Will you bring me...?"

Then, all you need to do is fill in the gap with what you want.

Attracting the waiter's attention.
When attracting the waiter's attention it is quite acceptable to say:

¡Oiga! (Listen!)

However, for many, this can feel a little uncomfortable. An easier way is just to say:

¡Perdone! (Excuse me!)
Waiters respond very well to this. ☺

The Bill

When you want to pay at the bar then there are various options. You can, of course, use the old favourite:

¡La cuenta por favor! *(The bill please!)*

However, far more common is:

¿Cuánto es? *(How much is it?)*

¿Cuánto le debo? *(How much do I owe you?)*

Try them out. These simple expressions will take you from the level of novice to someone who knows about the Spanish language!

The Restaurant.

Entering a restaurant needn't be a stressful event. When you enter, all you need say is:

Somos....personas. *(We are ......persons) Just add the number.*

or

Una mesa para ..... personas. *(A table for ...... people) Just add the number.*

In the event of all this slipping from your mind... stick the right amount of fingers up at the waiter and say the number.

(A timely "por favor" always helps to sweeten the pill, too!)

If you want to reserve a table, either face to face or even by phone (gulp!) then just follow the steps below.

Quiero reservar una mesa para....

I want to reserve a table for...

(add number) **personas, para** .....

...people, for...

(add day) **a las**… *(add time)*

…at…

A nombre de …*(add name)* **por favor.**

In the name of…please.

e.g.

Hola. Quiero reservar una mesa para cinco personas, para este sábado a las tres, a nombre de Smith-Durán.

In the Restaurant

Once in the restaurant, the waiter will typically come and ask you for drinks, and then for food. We have placed a lot of the vocabulary you'll need below.

However, if there's something on the menu that you don't recognise, then all you need do is ask the waiter:

¿Esto qué lleva? *(What does this have in it?)*

Say that whilst pointing at the item. The waiter will then set about tellingl you whilst you pray that you understand him!!

Giving appreciation.

To say that the food is nice, you can say:

¡Está muy buena!

or

¡Está muy rica!

Warning: *You must only use this expression with food. If you use it when talking about people, you will be saying that they are very sexy!*

Leaving a tip.

Every country has is customs around leaving tips. The Spanish are not Europe´s biggest tippers. In fact, they have been voted Europe's worst tippers!

So, when eating in Spain, the waiters will expect some kind of "**propina**" but you don't have to go mad!

Leaving 50 **céntimos** or 1 **Euro** after having only a coffee is excessive. The Spanish tend to leave twenty or thirty **céntimos**.

(In tourist resorts, this rule doesn't apply as, generally, they will take your eyes out and come back for the sockets! lol)

In Mexico, however, it's expected that you leave 15-20% of the bill as a tip given that the waiters' wages are some of the lowest.

The best way of dealing with this is to check on the Internet before travelling to any country and see what the custom is in that country.

One last point.

The Spanish say:

¡Que aproveche!

which means

Enjoy your meal.

It's very common for people who are walking to their table to say, "**que aproveche**" to the people on the other tables as they pass. It's seen as the polite thing to do.

In Mexico they say: "**Buen provecho**." which is the same thing in a different format.

The Vocabulary.

Here is some vital vocabulary that will help you sound like a real native.

¿Qué va/van a tomar?

What are you going to have?

¿Para beber / de beber?   To drink?

¿Para comer / de comer?   To eat?

Para mí...	For me...
de primero	for first course
de segundo	for second course
de postre	for dessert
Quiero...	I want
Quisiera...	I would like

¿Me trae......, por favor? Could you bring me......, please?

¿Me pone......, por favor? Could you "put" me........, please?

La cuenta, por favor The bill, please

or

¿Me cobra, por favor? Will you charge me, please?

Una propina	A tip.
Otro/a	Another

A spoon= **(Una) cuchara**   A serviette = **(Una) servilleta**

A knife= **(Un) cuchillo**   A plate= **(Un) plato**

A fork = **(Un) tenedor**   The dressing = **(El) aliño**

Drinks / Las bebidas.

Note. All coffees are made from a base of an espresso.

Un café con leche.	Coffee with milk.
Una café cortado.	Espresso with a dash of milk.
Un manchado (de café).	Very milky, weak coffee.
Un café solo.	An expresso. No milk.
Un café bombón.	Coffee with condensed milk.
Un café americano.	American coffee (not so strong)
Un té.	A tea
Un café con hielo.	Ice coffee (Coffee with ice)
Una copa de…	A glass of…(for wine etc.)
Vino blanco/tinto/rosado	White/red/rosé wine
Una botella de…	A bottle of…
Un vaso de…	A glass of… (For soft drinks)
Una taza de...	A cup of...
Un Ginebra	A gin
Un whisky	A whisky
Un vodka	A vodka
Un ron	A rum
Un Coñac (Cognac), Brandy	Brandy
Un cubata	A spirit with mixer
Un cubalibre	A rum with coke
Una tónica	A tonic
Un agua sin/con gas	A still/fizzy water
Un zumo de… naranja/piña…	Fresh orange juice/pineapple…
Una coca cola (light)	A coke (diet)

Una sidra	A cider
Una cerveza	A beer
Una caña	A fifth of a litre of draught beer
Una jarra	A large glass of beer, like a pint.
Una pinta	A pint (not common in traditional bars)
Un botellín	A little bottle of beer

Las tapas típicas.

In some areas of Spain, tapas come free with your drink and are usually served on a small plate.

Tortilla	Potato omelette
Patatas Bravas	Potatoes in spicy tomato sauce
Alitas de pollo	Chicken wings
Jamón Serrano/Ibérico	Cured ham off the bone
Queso Manchego	Goats cheese
Gambas	Prawns
Pincho Moruño	Meat on skewers
Aceitunas	Olives
Boquerones	Anchovies
Empanadas	A thin pie. Usually with tuna.
Chorizo	Sausage with smoked paprika
Salchichón	Sausage like pepperoni
Cacahuetes	Nuts.

Raciones

Las raciones are big tapas. These must be paid for.

Una ración de...

Calamares a la romana	Battered squid

Chopitos	Fried baby octopus
Chorizo al vino	Chorizo cooked in wine
Morcilla de arroz/ de cebolla	Similar to black pudding (with rice or onion)
Caracoles	Snails in sauce
Tortilla española	Spanish omelette (with potato and onion)
Patatas ali-oli	Alli-olli potatoes
Oreja a la plancha	Grilled pig's ears.
Criadillas	Bull's testicles. (Sin comentarios/No comment)
Albóndigas	Meat balls
Ensaladilla rusa	Potatoes with mayonnaise, tuna, onion...
Croquetas	Croquettes.
Boquerones en vinagre	Raw anchovies in vinagre

Remember, in most of the world and none more than in Spain, food is a favourite subject. It's worth learning about it because when you are there, you'll hear them talking about it constantly!

¡Que aproveche!

Translate these exchanges

Excuse me! Could you bring me more bread and a bottle of red wine.

....

Also, can you bring me a coffee with milk and the bill please?

....

Hello, good afternoon. Can I get a beer and a gin and tonic, please?

....

Excuse me, could you give me another beer and a water, please?

....

Capítulo 21

Víctor sale del bar y anda con rapidez a la casa de Eliana. Al llegar Eliana le está esperando en el portal de su casa. Le sonríe y le da un beso.

Eliana -Hola Víctor. ¿Dónde has estado?-

Víctor -He estado en un bar hablando de comida buena y mala.-

Eliana -O sea, de la comida española e inglesa, ¿verdad? Ja ja.

Víctor -Algo así pero, oye, la comida inglesa no es tan terrible, ¿sabes?-

Eliana -Lo sé, Víctor. Sólo te estoy picando un poco. De verdad, cuando he estado en Inglaterra he probado mucha comida divina. Lo que pasa es que los españoles somos muy orgullosos de nuestra cocina. Sabemos que la comida española es la mejor. Ja ja. Y, además, sentimos pena por los pobres ingleses que no tienen nada más que los fish and chips y verduras cocidas.-

Víctor -Ya he hablado suficiente de la comida. Me toca comer algo de esta famosa comida española. ¿Adónde vamos?-

Eliana -Pensaba que podríamos ir a un bar cerca. Allí te ponen una tapa grande con cada bebida y puedes escoger lo que quieras. Y después, ¿te parece ir al cine?-

Víctor -Me parece bien. ¿Qué echan?-

Eliana -Hay una película nueva de terror. Empieza a las diez y media.-

Víctor -Ya son las nueve y diez. No queda mucho tiempo para cenar antes. Si quieres, podemos coger algo en el cine. Venden perritos calientes y eso, ¿no?-

Chapter 21

Victor leaves the bar and walks quickly to Eliana's house. As he arrives, Eliana is waiting for him in the porch of her house. She smiles at him and greets him with a kiss on the cheeks.

Eliana "Hello, Victor. Where have you been?"

Victor "I've been in a bar talking about good and bad food."

Eliana "So, about Spanish and English food, right? Haha."

Victor "Something like that but, listen, English food isn't so terrible, you know."

Eliana "I know, Victor. I'm just winding you up a bit. In truth, when I've been in England I've tried lots of lovely food. What happens is that we Spanish are very proud of our food. We know that Spanish food is the best. Haha. And what's more, we feel sorry for the poor English who don't have anything else but fish and chips and boiled vegetables."

Victor "I've talked enough about food. It's my turn to eat some of this famous Spanish food. Where are we going?"

Eliana "I thought we could go to a bar close by. They give you a large tapa there with each drink and you can choose what you want. And afterwards, do you fancy going to the cinema?"

Victor "That seems great. What are they showing?"

Eliana "There's a new horror film. It starts at ten thirty."

Victor "It's ten past nine already. There's not much time left to eat beforehand. If you want, we can grab something in the cinema. They sell hot dogs and that, don't they?"

Eliana   -Sí, por supuesto. A mí, no me importa. Me conformo con unas palomitas y una coca-cola.-

Víctor   -Muy bien. Pues, ¡vámonos al cine!-

Los dos van andando al cine y hablan animadamente mientras pasan por las calles. Víctor se siente muy cómodo con Eliana. Cada vez más parece una persona buena y muy amistosa. También, según parece, a Eliana le gusta su compañía. Después de veinte minutos andando llegan al centro comercial donde se encuentra el cine. Realmente, a Víctor no le gustan las películas de terror pero no quiere decir nada.

Taquillera   -Hola, buenas noches. ¿Qué película quieren ver esta noche?-

Eliana   -Dos entradas para la peli "El Sótano", por favor.-

Taquillera   -Son quince euros.-

Eliana   -Aquí tiene.

La taquillera le entrega las entradas a Eliana.

Eliana   -Empieza a las diez y media, ¿verdad?-

Taquillera   -Sí, pero se puede entrar a partir de las diez.-

Eliana   -Gracias, hasta luego.-

Eliana le da a Víctor su entrada.

Víctor   -Toma, Eliana. Te debo siete con cincuenta.-

Eliana   -¡Qué va! Te invito yo.-

Víctor   -Gracias. Pues te invito a un perrito caliente.-

Eliana   -Prefiero palomitas, Víctor, si no te importa.-

Víctor   -Claro. ¿Quieres uno grande, mediano o pequeño?-

Eliana   "Yes, of course. I don't mind. I'm happy with some popcorn and a coke."

Victor   "Very good, then, let's go to the cinema!"

The two of them set about walking to the cinema and they talk excitedly whilst they pass through the streets. Victor feels very comfortable with Eliana. She seems more and more like a very friendly, nice person. Also, from what it seems, Eliana likes his company too. After walking for twenty minutes, they arrive at the shopping centre where the cinema is. Actually, Victor doesn't like horror films but he doesn't want to say anything.

Ticket seller   "Hello, good evening. What film do you want to watch this evening?"

Eliana   "Two tickets for the film, The Basement", please."

Ticket Seller   "That's fifteen Euros."

Eliana   "Here you are."

The ticket seller hands over the tickets to Eliana.

Eliana   "It starts at ten thirty, doesn't it?"

Ticket Seller   "Yes, but you can go in from ten."

Eliana   "Thanks, see you later."

Eliana gives Victor his ticket.

Victor   "Here, Eliana. I owe you seven-fifty."

Eliana   "No way! I'm paying."

Victor   "Thanks. Well, I'll pay for a hotdog for you."

Eliana   "I prefer popcorn, Victor, if you don't mind."

Victor   "Sure. Do you want large, medium or small?"

Eliana -Mediano, por favor, con azúcar.-

Víctor -Si compro uno grande, ¿podemos compartirlas?-

Eliana -Claro, Víctor. ¿Y vas a comerte un perrito caliente también?-

Víctor -Sí, Eliana. Es que tengo muchísima hambre.-

Víctor va al kiosco donde venden la comida y bebida. Un asistente lo atiende.

Asistente -Sí, ¿qué desea?

Víctor -Palomitas con azúcar, dos coca-colas y un perrito caliente, por favor.-

Asistente -¿De qué tamaño las palomitas?-

Víctor -Grande, por favor. De hecho, todo grande, ja ja. Es que tengo mucha hambre.-

Asistente -Vale. Aquí tiene todo. Son veintitrés euros.-

Víctor paga y los dos van directamente a la sala. La película dura dos horas y a las doce y media los dos salen del cine y andan para casa. Es una noche calurosa pero con una brisa muy placentera.

Eliana -¿Qué te parece la película, Víctor?-

Víctor -De verdad, no sé. Mantuve mis ojos cerrados durante la mitad de ella. No me gustan mucho las películas de terror.-

Eliana -¿Por qué no me lo has dicho antes? Desde luego, Víctor, qué tontería. Había muchas otras películas. Podríamos haber visto otra.-

Víctor -No pasa nada, Eliana. Sé que tenías muchas ganas de verla. No me importa sufrir por ti. Ja ja.-

Eliana -Ah, ¡qué bonito! Gracias, Víctor. Sin embargo, la próxima vez escoges tú.-

Mientras andan, Eliana le coge del brazo y Víctor se siente muy contento. Parece que

Eliana "Medium, please, with sugar."

Victor "If I buy a large one, can we share them?"

Eliana "Sure, Victor. And are you going to have a hotdog, too?"

Victor "Yes, Eliana. It's just that I'm extremely hungry."

Victor goes to the kiosk where they sell the food and drinks. An assistant serves him.

Assistant "Yes, what would you like?"

Victor "Popcorn with sugar, two cokes and a hotdog, please."

Assistant "What size popcorn?"

Victor "Large, please. In fact, everything large, haha. I'm very hungry."

Assistant "Okay. Here you have everything. That's twenty-three Euros."

Victor pays and they both go straight to the theatre. The film lasts two hours and at twelve-thirty they both leave the cinema and walk home. It's a warm night but with a very pleasant breeze.

Eliana "What do you think of the film, Victor?"

Victor "In truth, I don't know. I kept my eyes closed for half of it. I don't like horror films much."

Eliana "Why haven't you told me before? Goodness, Victor, what a silly thing. There were lots and lots of other films. We could have seen another."

Victor "Not a problem, Eliana. I know that you were really looking forward to seeing it. I don't mind suffering for you. Haha."

Eliana "Ahh, how lovely! Thanks, Victor. however, the next time, you choose."

Whilst they walk, Eliana takes him by the arm and Victor feel really happy. It seems that

la relación con Eliana va cada vez mejor. Ninguno de los dos ha hablado de su amistad pero Eliana pasa mucho tiempo con él y siempre parece feliz cuando están juntos.

Víctor -Mañana empiezo mi nuevo trabajo en el restaurante. Tengo nervios.-

Eliana -Lo sé. ¡Qué ilusión! ¿Ya sabes que la mayoría de los clientes son turistas? Así que vas a tener que hablar en inglés mucha parte del tiempo.-

Víctor -¿De verdad? ¡Qué bien! Ya no tengo tanto miedo. Es que el inglés lo domino yo, ja ja.-

Eliana -Ya, lo he notado, Víctor. Y, por cierto, tú español también ha mejorado muchísimo. Puedes estar muy orgulloso de tu progreso. ¡Eres un crack!-

Víctor -¿Qué significa crack?-

Eliana -Ja ja, es una palabra inglesa. ¿No la conoces? Significa experto.-

Víctor -Ah, ya veo. Gracias, Eliana, pero todavía me queda mucho que aprender. Con algunas personas no tengo problemas, pero si la persona tiene un acento fuerte, no entiendo nada.-

Eliana -Eso pasa en cualquier país con cualquier idioma. Sólo es cuestión de acostumbrarte. Ya verás, en seis meses vas a hablar como un verdadero español.-

Víctor -Eso espero, Eliana. Es que, me encanta estar aquí y aún más, me gusta pasar tiempo contigo. Eres muy amable, Eliana. Gracias por todo lo que has hecho por mí.-

Eliana le mira a los ojos y sonríe. Hay un momento de silencio mientras se miran el uno al otro.

---

the relationship with Eliana is getting better and better. Neither of the two have talked about their friendship but Eliana is spending a lot of time with him and she always seems happy when they are together.

Víctor "Tomorrow I'm starting my new job in the restaurant. I'm nervous."

Eliana "I know. How exciting! You do know that the majority of the customers are tourists? So you'll have to speak in English most of the time."

Víctor "Really? That's good! I'm not so frightened any more. I have a good command of English, haha."

Eliana "I've noticed already, Victor. And, by the way, your Spanish has improved massively too. You can be very proud of your progress. You're a crack!"

Víctor "What does 'crack' mean?"

Eliana "Haha, it's an English word. Don't you know it? It means an expert."

Víctor "Ah, I see. Thanks, Eliana, but I've still got lots left to learn. With some people I don't have problems, but if the person has a strong accent, I don't understand anything."

Eliana "That happens in any country with any language. It's just a question of getting used to it. You'll see, in six months you're going to speak like a true Spaniard."

Víctor "I hope so, Eliana. It's just that I love being here and even more, I like spending time with you. You're very nice, Eliana. Thanks for everything you've done for me."

Eliana looks him in the eyes and smiles. There's a moment of silence whilst they look at each other.

Eliana -Me encanta ayudarte, Víctor. La verdad es que, a mí, me caes genial y a mis padres también. Eres un chico muy simpático.-

Víctor -Eliana, sé que no me conoces al cien por cien y que acabo de llegar, pero te he cogido mucho cariño y... me encantaría que fueras mi novia. ¿Qué te parece? ¿Quieres salir conmigo?-

Tras una pausa muy larga Eliana le contesta.

Eliana -Víctor, no es que no me gustes ni nada así, pero en este momento no puedo. Ya sabes que mi último novio, Hugo, me trataba mal. Bueno, más que mal, me trataba horriblemente. Todavía no lo he superado. Aún no sólo tengo miedo de él sino de las relaciones también. Prefiero que seamos amigos por ahora, si no te importa. Lo siento, Víctor. ¿Me entiendes?-

Víctor -Claro, Eliana. No quiero ponerte bajo presión ninguna. Puedo esperar hasta que estés más segura.-

Eliana -Gracias, Víctor. De todas las maneras, ya salimos juntos, solamente no como novios, ¿verdad?-

Víctor -Así es, Eliana. Me conformo con eso.-

Eliana "I love helping you, Victor. The fact is that I really like you a lot and my parents like you too. You're a really nice guy."

Victor "Eliana, I know that you don't know me a hundred percent and that I've just arrived, but I like you a lot and...I'd love it if you were my girlfriend. What do you think? Do you want to go out with me?"

After a very long pause Eliana answers him.

Eliana "Victor, It's not that I don't like you or anything like that but right now I can't. You already know that my last boyfriend, Hugo, treated me badly. Well, more than badly, he treated me horribly. I still haven't gotten over it. I'm not only still frightened of him, but of relationships too. I prefer that we are friends for now, if you don't mind. Sorry, Victor. Do you understand me?

Victor "Sure, Eliana. I don't want to put you under any pressure. I can wait until you are more sure."

Eliana "Thanks, Victor. Anyway, we are already going out together, just not as boyfriend and girlfriend, right?"

Victor "That's right, Eliana. I can live with that."

Lesson 22. Directions. / Direcciones

As we saw earlier, when Victor was asking for directions, things can get a little complicated. However, if we keep it simple, everything will more straightforward.

Most students of the Spanish language learn to ask for directions by saying:

Perdone, ¿me puede decir dónde está el banco?

Excuse me, could you tell me where the bank is?

You don't have to be in a Spanish speaking country for long for you to realise that this isn't normally the case.

For myself, (Gordon) this realisation came one day in Spain when I saw a car come to a stop and the driver shout at a pedestrian:

¡Perdone! ¿La Plaza Mayor?

Excuse me! The main square?

How simple, I thought. After so many years of struggling to pluck up the courage to say the full blown sentence here was a man breaking all the rules!

And this is the tip that we want to share with you. Sometimes we make Spanish more complicated than it actually is.

Many times there's an easier way to say things. So, when you are in any Spanish speaking country, listen out for what they say. The reality is that the best tips are taken from real life and are more valuable than anything you could ever get from a book. (Even this one! ;))

So here, in their simplest forms are the ways to ask for directions.

*Excuse me = **Perdone / Disculpe** .*

*Can you tell me where..? = **¿Puede decirme dónde está...?***

*Where is (the Square)? = **¿Dónde está (la Plaza)?***

*The Square, please? = **¿La Plaza, por favor?***

However, once you've asked the question, you've then got to understand the answer. And that's where your challenge lies.

The problem is that it's difficult to remember directions even in your own language.

Normally, after having received about three or four instructions in a row it all gets a little blurry. Our advice is to remember the first three directions and then ask again.

"Right" and "Left" are the key words to pick out. An easy way to get them fixed in your mind is the following:

*Left is **IZQUIERDA***

which to us, always sounds like: "THIS KEY HERE DEAR"

*Right is **DERECHA**.*

Which sounds a bit like "THE REACH"

Imagine in your left hand a big key. In the future when you hear the word,

"izquierda"

You'll remember your key in the left hand.

And, imagine that with your right hand you're reaching out, so when you hear the word

"derecha"

You'll remember to reach out your right hand.

*Interestingly, just as in English, the word "**Derechos**" mean "your rights" in law.*

So, now that you have left and right sorted out, here are the principle ways of giving directions. The language used in these instructions is in the formal "usted" or "you" (someone you don't know).

Directions. / Direcciones.

Go straight on	→	*Siga recto*
Until/Up to	→	*Hasta*
Stop.	→	*Pare*
Turn.	→	*Gire*
Turn to the left	→	*Gire a la izquierda*
Turn to the right.	→	*Gire a la derecha*
Take	→	*Tome*
The first (street)	→	*La primera (calle)*
The second (street)	→	*La segunda (calle)*
The third (street)	→	*La tercera (calle)*
Exit	→	*La salida*
Entrance	→	*La entrada*
There it is	→	*Allí está*
Then	→	*Luego*
After	→	*Después*
In front of…	→	*Enfrente de… / Delante de...*
Next to…	→	*Junto a… / Al lado de...*
Behind…	→	*Detrás de…*
At the end of the street	→	*Al final de la calle*
Round the corner	→	*A la vuelta de la esquina*
The street ...	→	*La calle (C/...)*
The avenue	→	*La avenida (Av. / Avda.)*
The road	→	*La carretera*
The roundabout	→	*La rotonda / La glorieta*
The traffic lights	→	*Los semáforos*

Ahora te toca a ti.

How would you say…

1, Go straight on up to the roundabout.

....

2, Then turn left and continue to the traffic lights.

....

3, After (that), take the third street on the right.

....

4, At the end of the street, turn left.

....

5, Go straight until the traffic lights and stop. There it is on the left.

....

Capítulo 22

Pronto están fuera de la casa de Eliana. Víctor se despide de ella y va para casa. Mañana tiene su primera noche en el restaurante. Después de hablar con Eliana sobre eso se siente mejor. De hecho, la idea de trabajar allí le da un poco de ilusión. Mientras piensa en eso escucha la voz de un hombre detrás de él.

Hombre   -¡Oye, guiri!-

Víctor mira hacia atrás y ve el perfil de alguien acercándose con rapidez. Lo reconoce en seguida. Es Hugo.

Víctor   -¿Hugo? ¿Qué haces aquí?-

Hugo   -Nada. Solamente paseando un poco, observando a la gente, a los novios y tal.-

Víctor   -¿Me has estado siguiendo, Hugo?-

Hugo   -Sólo un poco, pero suficiente para saber lo que pretendes con mi novia.-

Víctor -Pero, Hugo, Eliana no es tu novia. Hace mucho que ella cortó la relación entre vosotros. ¿No deberías dejarla en paz, ya?-

Hugo -No la corté yo y eso quiere decir que sigue siendo mi novia. Así que te aviso que dejes de salir con ella. Es mía, ¿sabes? y si sigues intentando robármela, vas a tener muchísimos problemas conmigo.-

Víctor -Mira, Hugo, no quiero problemas contigo pero tienes que ver que Eliana ya no te quiere. De hecho, tiene miedo de ti. Déjala en paz, por favor.-

Hugo   -No, hombre, eso es lo que tienes que hacer, tú. Éste es mi último aviso. La próxima vez, ya verás. No estoy de broma, ¿me entiendes?-

Chapter 22

They are soon outside Eliana's house. Victor says goodbye to her and heads home. Tomorrow he has his first night in the restaurant. After talking to Eliana about that he feels better. In fact, the idea of working there makes him feel a little excited. Whilst he's thinking about that he hears a voice of a man behind him.

Man   "Hey, foreigner!"

Victor looks behind and sees the outline of someone closing in on him quickly. He recognises him straight away. It's Hugo.

Victor   "Hugo? What are you doing here?"

Hugo   "Nothing. Just having a stroll, looking at the people, at the couples and that."

Victor   "Have you been following me, Hugo?"

Hugo   "Just a bit, but enough to know what you are after with my girlfriend."

Victor   "But, Hugo, Eliana isn't your girlfriend. She finished the relationship between you both a long time ago. Shouldn't you leave her in peace now?"

Hugo   "I didn't end it, and that means that she's still my girlfriend. So I'm warning you to stop going out with her. She's mine, you see? And if you keep trying to steal her from me, you're going to have a lot of problems with me."

Victor   "Look, Hugo, I don't want problems with you but you have to see that Eliana doesn't love you anymore. In fact, she's scared of you. Leave her in peace, please."

Hugo   No, man, that's what you have to do. This is my last warning. The next time, you'll see. I'm not joking, do you understand me?"

Víctor   -Hugo, a mí, no me das miedo. Eliana es mi amiga. Encima, no se merece todo esto. La tienes llena de miedo.-

Hugo   -Pues, tú mismo. Te lo he dicho. Mantente lejos de ella o habrá consecuencias.-

Víctor   -Estás loco, Hugo. Ya voy para casa. No quiero hablar contigo más.-

Víctor le da la espalda a Hugo y anda rápidamente hacia su casa. De verdad tiene mucho miedo. Hugo no sólo es un tío enorme sino que también parece estar mal de la cabeza y Víctor no sabe realmente qué podría hacer.

Victor   "Hugo, you don't frighten me. Eliana is my friend. On top of that, she doesn't deserve all this. You've got her scared out of her wits."

Hugo   "Well, it's your funeral. I've told you. Keep away from her or there'll be consequences."

Victor   "You're crazy, Hugo. I'm going home now. I don't want to talk to you anymore."

Victor turns his back on Hugo and walks quickly home. He really is frightened. Hugo isn't just a massive guy but he seems crazy too and Victor doesn't know what he really could do.

Lesson 23. The Numbers / Los Números.

Pronunciation.

As you may have noticed whilst following Victor's story, there aren't many times when he has to use his numbers. Yet, it is important to have a good command of them if only because the times you most need them is when you are dealing with money. (And people want to take it off you.)

We've noticed that one of the biggest issues with Spanish numbers, however, is their pronunciation. To help you with that, we've added a table below which includes the phonetic spelling (phonetic means 'what you see you say') of each number. All you need to do is read the word as it is written and you'll have the sound as it should be. Pay special attention to numbers with an asterix as these are the ones frequently mispronounced.

Number	Real spelling	Phonetic Pronunciation	Number	Real spelling	Phonetic Pronunciation
0	cero	thero	11	once	on-th-ay
1	uno	uno	12	doce	do-th-ay
2	dos	dos	13	trece	tr-eth-ay
3	tres	tres	14	catorce	kat-or-th-ay
4	cuatro	kwatro	15	quince	kin-th-ay
5	cinco	thinko	16	dieciséis	dee-eth-ee-saiys
6	seis *	saiys	17	diecisiete	dee-eth-ee-see-et-ay
7	siete	see-et-ay	18	dieciocho	dee-eth-ee-ot-show
8	ocho	otshow	19	diecinueve	dee-eth-ee-noo-ay-bay
9	nueve	noo-ay-bay	20	veinte *	b-ain-tay
10	diez	dee-eth			

Num-ber	Real spel-ling	Pronunciation	Number	Real spelling	Phonetic Pronunciation
30	treinta	train-ta	100	cien	thee-en
40	cuarenta	kwa-ren-ta	200	doscientos	dos-thee-entos
50	cincuenta	thin-kwen-ta	300	trescientos	tres-thee-entos
60	sesenta	ses-en-ta	400	cuatrocientos	cwatro-thee-entos
70	setenta	se-tent-a	500	quinientos *	kin-ee-entos
80	ochenta	ot-shen-ta	600	seiscientos	saiys-thee-entos
90	noventa	no-ben-ta	700	setecientos *	set-aiy-thee-entos
100	cien	th-ee-en	800	ochocientos	otshow-thee-entos
			900	novecientos *	no-bay-thee-entos
			1000	mil	meel

When and when not to use AND ...Y.

As you may have noticed, the word "AND" or "Y" in Spanish is used to join numbers, but not every time!

Firstly, let's look at when not to...

From 16 to 19.

Once you get to the number 16, you'll notice that the number actually says "ten and six". e.g.

"**dieciséis**" which is really: "diez-y-seis".

However, as you can see, instead of putting a "Y" in between the two numbers, the letter "I" is used, allowing it to be one word.

From 21 to 29.

The same applies for the number twenty. Notice how the "E" in "**veinte**" becomes an "I" and so, for example, makes the number twenty-one: "Twenty-and-one"...

e.g.

"**veintiuno**" which is effectively: "veinte-y-uno".

From 101 upwards.

As soon as you arrive at **101**, you drop the "**Y**" and just place the numbers directly after each other. (Notice that "**CIEN**" becomes "**CIENTO**".)

e.g.

ciento uno, ciento dos, ciento tres.

The same applies all throughout the hundreds to the thousands. There is no "**Y**" needed. (Notice that from **200**, **CIENTO** becomes **CIENTOS**, but **MIL** doesn't change)

e.g.

mil doscientos treinta (1230), tres mil quinientos tres (3503)

So when do we use the "Y"?

The Spanish numbers have the "**Y**" only b**etween 31 and 99.**

. e.g.

*treinta **y** tres (33), cuarenta **y** cinco (45),*

*setenta **y** nueve (79), noventa **y** dos (92)*

Other tips.........

To remember the numbers from 30 upwards you just need to notice how similar they are to the numbers from 1 to ten. It's as if they have just stuck an "enta" on the end. So, you only really need to remember the numbers from 11-15. After that they are easy as they are just "ten and six", "ten and seven" etc. e.g. **dieciséis, diecisiete.**

Don't sweat the BIG numbers.

It's actually fairly easy to construct the big numbers. Here's a list up to one million: (Important: you don't say "un mil", but rather "mil".)

(Even more important: Where we use a comma, the Spanish use a point and our point is their comma!)

Number	Real spelling	Pronunciation
1.000	Mil	Meel
2.000	Dos mil	Dos meel
3.000	Tres mil	Tres meel
4.000	Cuatro mil	Cwatro meel
5.000	Cinco mil	Thinko meel
6.000	Seis mil	Saiys meel
7.000	Siete mil	See et aiy meel
8.000	Ocho mil	Otsho meel
9.000	Nueve mil	Noo eb aiy meel
10.000	Diez mil	Dee eth meel
100.000	Cien mil	Thee en meel
1.000.000	Un millón	Oon mee john
2.000.000	Dos millones	Dos mee john es

Now it's you turn! ¡Te toca a ti!

How would you write the following numbers?

1. *1.234* ....

2. *367* ....

3. *465* ....

4. *579* ....

5. *5.743*...

6. *24.999*...

7. *362.756*...

8. *82* ....

9 *3.496.821*

....

10. *7.326* ....

Note: Numbers aren't for everyone. In nearly every class that we've given there have been a good few students who get very confused with the numbers. We often find that these same people aren't big fans of numbers in their own language either.

Just keep working at them and little by little they will become clearer and easier to manage.

Capítulo 23

Al día siguiente, llama a Eliana y le cuenta todo lo que ha pasado con Hugo. La chica parece muy consternada y habla de llamar a la policía y denunciarlo. Ella tiene que ir a la universidad así que quedan para tomar un café después de comer.

Víctor empieza su trabajo esta tarde y quiere comprarse unas camisas y pantalones negros. También necesita hacer la compra. No tiene nada de comida en casa. Ha comido fuera casi todos los días pero no puede continuar así. Es demasiado costoso vivir de esta manera y él sabe que tiene que empezar a cocinar en casa.

En las afueras de la ciudad hay una gran superficie que vende de todo. Víctor camina por las calles. Hace mucho calor y sol y el cielo está despejado. A pesar de los problemas con Hugo, se siente muy alegre de estar allí en España y de haber conocido a Eliana. Ella no quiere ser su novia pero, aun así, sale con él y pasan mucho tiempo juntos. ¡Todavía tiene esperanzas!

Por fin, llega a la gran superficie. Coge un carro y entra por la puerta principal. Va directamente a la sección de ropa. Busca camisas blancas. Una dependienta se le acerca y pregunta:

Dependienta -¿Le puedo ayudar en algo?-

Víctor -Sí. Busco unas camisas blancas. Son para el trabajo. No tienen que estar muy de moda.-

Dependienta -Ya entiendo. ¿Qué talla tiene?-

Víctor -Soy de talla mediana. También busco unos pantalones negros.-

Dependienta -Tenemos estas camisas. Vienen en pares y sólo cuestan diez euros.-

Víctor -¡Perfecto! ¿Y pantalones?-

Chapter 23

The next day, he calls Eliana and tells her everything that has happened with Hugo. The girl seems very worried and talks of calling the police and reporting him. She has to go to the university so they agree to meet for a coffee after lunch.

Victor is starting his job this evening and he wants to buy himself some shirts and black trousers. He also needs to do the shopping. He doesn't have any food at home. He's eaten out nearly every day, but can't continue like that. It's too expensive to live that way and he knows that he has to start cooking at home.

In the outskirts of the city there's a great shopping centre that sells everything. Victor walks along the streets. It's hot and sunny and the sky is clear. Despite the problems with Hugo, he feels very pleased to be in Spain and to have met Eliana. She doesn't want to be his girlfriend but, even so, she's going out with him and they are spending a lot of time together. He still has hope!

Finally, he arrives at the shopping centre. He takes a trolley and goes in through the main door. He goes straight to the clothing section. He's looking for white shirts. A sales assistant comes up to him and asks:

Assistant "Can I help you with anything?"

Victor "Yes. I'm looking for some white shirts. They are for work. They don't have to be very fashionable."

Assistant "I understand. What's your size?"

Victor "I'm a medium. I'm looking for some black trousers, as well."

Assistant "We have these shirts. They come as a pair and only cost ten Euros."

Victor "Perfect! And trousers?"

Dependienta -Sí, tenemos estos. No son de marca pero son de buena calidad. Cuestan quince euros.-

Víctor -Está bien. Creo que las camisas me valdrán pero prefiero probarme los pantalones. ¿Dónde están los probadores?-

Dependienta -Están allí, al fondo de este pasillo a la derecha.-

Víctor -Gracias por la ayuda.-

Dependienta -De nada.-

Víctor va a los probadores y se prueba los pantalones. Son buenos pero le quedan un poco pequeños. Vuelve a la sección de ropa.

Dependienta -Hola de nuevo. ¿No le valen los pantalones?-

Víctor -No. Me están pequeños. ¿Tiene una talla más grande?-

Dependienta -Sí, aquí tiene.-

La dependienta le entrega a Víctor los pantalones y él va directamente a probárselos. Le quedan perfectamente bien. Los mete en su carro con las camisas y luego busca la sección de comida.

Necesita muchas cosas para la casa y va por cada pasillo cogiendo lo que hace falta. En su carro pone pan, leche entera y varios embutidos como jamón, chorizo y salchichón. A él le gusta la fruta y en la sección de verduras y fruta coge unas naranjas, un kilo de manzanas, una sandía grande, una cajita de cerezas, una lechuga, dos pepinos y tres kilos de patatas.

Luego va al puesto de pescado y mariscos. Allí trabaja un hombre.

Víctor -Buenos días. ¿Me da dos filetes de bacalao, por favor?

Assistant "Yes, we have these. They aren't branded but they are good quality. They cost fifteen Euros."

Victor "That's fine. I think the shirt will be fine, but I prefer to try the trousers on. Where are the changing rooms?"

Assistant "There they are, at the bottom of this aisle to the right."

Victor "Thanks for your help."

Assistant "You're welcome."

Victor goes to the changing rooms and tries on the trousers. They are nice but they're a bit small for him. He returns to the clothing section.

Assistant "Hi again. Don't the trousers fit you?

Victor "No. They're too small. Do you have a larger size?"

Assistant "Yes, here you are."

The assistant gives Victor the trousers and he goes straight to try them on. They fit him perfectly. He puts them in his trolley with the shirts and then he looks for the food section.

He needs a lot of things for the house and he goes down every aisle getting what he's short of. In his trolley he puts bread, whole milk and various cured meats like ham, chorizo and salchichon. He likes fruit and in the fruit and vegetable section he gets some oranges, a kilo of apples, a large watermelon, a little carton of cherries, a lettuce, two cucumbers and three kilos of potatoes.

Then, he goes to the fish and seafood stall. A man is working there.

Victor "Good morning. Can you give me two cod steaks, please?"

Victor -También quería medio kilo de gambas.-

Hombre -Los dos filetes cuestan siete euros. ¿Está bien?-

Víctor -Es un poco caro. ¿Me puede quitar un poco, por favor?-

Hombre -Claro. Éste cuesta cinco.-

Víctor -Perfecto.-

Hombre -Y aquí tiene las gambas. ¿Algo más?-

Víctor -Nada más gracias.-

Luego Víctor va a la caja para pagar la compra.

Cajera -Hola, buenos días. ¿Tiene la tarjeta de cliente?-

Víctor -¿Perdón? ¿Qué es eso?-

Cajera -La tarjeta de la tienda. Le damos puntos por cada compra, y luego usted puede tener descuentos y gastar los puntos aquí.-

Víctor -¡Ah! Ya entiendo. No, no tengo una. Lo siento.-

Cajera -No pasa nada. ¿Usted necesita bolsas? Son tres céntimos cada bolsa.-

Víctor -¿Me da tres, por favor?-

La cajera escanea la comida y la mete en las bolsas.

Cajera -Son treinta y ocho euros con veinte céntimos.-

Víctor -Aquí tiene. Muchas gracias. Hasta luego-

Cajera -De nada. Hasta luego.-

Victor "I also wanted half a kilo of prawns."

Man "The two fillets cost seven Euros. Is that okay?"

Victor "It's a bit expensive. Can you take a little bit off, please?"

Man "Sure. This costs five."

Victor "Perfect."

Man "And here are you prawns. Anything else?"

Victor "Nothing more, thanks."

Victor then goes to the till to pay for the shopping.

Assistant "Hello, good morning. Do you have your customer card?"

Victor "Sorry? What's that?"

Assistant "The shop card. We give you points for each purchase, and then you can have discounts and spend the points here."

Victor "Ah! I understand now. No, I don't have one. Sorry."

Assistant "Don't worry. Do you need bags? They are three cents per bag."

Victor "Can you give me three, please?"

The assistant scans the food and puts it in the bags.

Assistant "That's thirty-eight Euros and twenty cents."

Victor "Here you are. Thanks a lot. See you later."

Assistant "You're welcome. See you later."

Lesson 24. The Preterite past. / El Pretérito

You may notice (with some trepidation) that as our story of Victor's Adventures reaches chapter 24 it begins to be told in the past.

Don't Panic!

Let us explain to you a little about one of these past tenses called the Preterite or as we like to call it, the "I ate" tense.

In English, the Preterite is this:

I **ate** a sandwich.

I **called** my mother.

We **bought** a car.

This tense is used when describing "one off" actions that are measurable. It is used a lot when talking about sequential events:

"Firstly, I did this, then, I did that."

"He said this to me, then, he said that."

How it's made.

To make the Preterite with AR verbs you do the following:

Take off the AR and then add...

yo	é	nosotros	amos
tú	aste	vosotros	asteis
él		ellos	
ella	ó	ellas	aron
usted		ustedes	

Note: The past tense conjugation of WE is AMOS and is the same as present tense. Surprisingly, this never gets confusing as it's always understood through the context of what you are saying.

To make the Preterite with ER and IR verbs you do this:

Take the ER or IR off and then add…

yo	í	nosotros	imos
tú	iste	vosotros	isteis
él		ellos	
ella	} ió	ellas	} ieron
usted		ustedes	

Let's try some examples together.

If you want to say: **I spoke with my friend yesterday.**

We would use the verb Hablar.

You simply take off the AR:

Habl

And then you add **é**.

Hablé

So the sentence would be:

Ayer, **hablé** *con mi amigo.*

On Saturday I ate chips.

You would use Comer.

You take off the ER

Com

And then you add **í**

Comí.

So the sentence would be:

El sábado **comí** *patatas fritas.*

I lived in Spain.

You would use Vivir.

You take of IR.

Viv

and add í

Viví

So the sentence would be:

Yo **viví** en España.

Ahora te toca a ti.

Have a go at writing these basic past tense sentences.

1, We walked through the park. (caminar por el parque)

....

2, I ordered a hamburger. (pedir una hamburguesa)

....

3, They went into the house. (entrar en la casa)

....

4, You all played in the snow. (jugar en la nieve)

....

5, You (one person) listened to the music.(escuchar la música)

....

Capítulo 24

Una vez fuera de la tienda, Víctor va para casa. Otra vez hace buen día y el sol brilla en un cielo azul, despejado. Tiene ilusión de empezar su trabajo esta tarde y claro, le vendría también bien un sueldo.

Llega a casa y coloca la compra. Luego se prepara un plato de embutidos, queso y pan. A Víctor le gusta mucho el chorizo y va muy bien con el queso manchego. Después de comer, se echa una siesta. Esta noche va a ser larga y necesita descansar bien antes de empezar.

Durmió una hora solamente y después de despertarse, se duchó y se vistió. Luego salió de casa para ir a tomar un café con Eliana. La encontró en una cafetería cercana y se sentó a su lado.

Víctor -Hola, buenas tardes, Eliana.-

Eliana -Hola, Víctor.-

Víctor -¿Qué tal te encuentras?-

Eliana -¡Pues, mal, Víctor! No sé qué hacer con lo de Hugo. Obviamente nos estaba siguiendo anoche. El chico está mal de la cabeza. Creo que es capaz de hacer algo peor, ¿sabes? Tengo miedo.-

Víctor -Mira, Eliana. Él habló conmigo y tuvo la oportunidad de hacerme algo pero no lo hizo. Para mí, quiere decir que sólo son palabras y nada más.-

Eliana -Todavía no lo conoces, Víctor. Es un chico rarísimo. Era violento hasta conmigo. Siempre estaba peleando con alguien. Cuando salíamos juntos, ni siquiera podía mirar a otro chico sin que se enfadara con él. Si un chico me miraba demasiado tiempo él quería pegarlo y muchas veces lo hizo.-

Víctor -¿Deberíamos denunciarlo?-

Chapter 24

Once outside of the shop, Victor heads home. It's a nice day again and the sun is shining in a clear blue sky. He's looking forward to starting his job this evening and, of course, a wage would come in handy too.

He arrives home and puts the shopping away. Then, he prepares a plate of cooked meats, cheese and bread. Victor likes chorizo a lot and it goes really well with Manchego cheese. After eating, he has a siesta. This evening is going to be a long one and he needs to have a good rest before starting.

He slept for just an hour and after waking, he had a shower and he got ready. He then left home to go and have a coffee with Eliana. He found her in a nearby cafe and he sat at her side.

Victor "Hello, good afternoon, Eliana."

Eliana "Hello, Victor."

Victor " How are you?"

Eliana "Well, bad, Victor!" I don't know what to do about the Hugo thing. He was obviously following us last night. The guy's got a screw loose. I think he's capable of doing something worse, you know. I'm frightened."

Victor "Look, Eliana. He spoke with me and had the chance to do something to me but he didn't do it. For me, that means that they are just words and nothing more.

Eliana "You still don't know him, Victor. He's a really strange guy. He was even violent with me. He was always fighting with someone. When we used to go out, I couldn't even look at another boy without him getting angry with him. If a boy looked at me for too long he wanted to hit him and many times he did it."

Victor "Should we report him?"

Eliana -Como te dije el otro día, la policía me ha dicho que tendría que pedir una orden de alejamiento e ir al juzgado. No me apetece mucho.-

Víctor -Pues en eso tú sabes mejor que yo. Sin embargo, creo que Hugo me hablaba en serio anoche. Tenemos que tener cuidado. ¿No sería mejor no vernos un rato hasta que se calmen las cosas?-

Eliana -¡Qué va! No pienso cambiar mi vida por él. Mira, tú tienes tu trabajo nuevo esta noche. Tienes suficiente con eso. No te preocupes por ese loco de Hugo. Mira, mañana te invito a comer a mi casa. Vamos a tener una barbacoa en el jardín. Habrá paella y todo tipo de carne. ¿Te apetece?-

Víctor -Sí, mucho. ¿Cuál es la ocasión?-

Eliana -Es el cumpleaños de mi padre. Va a cumplir cincuenta años.-

Víctor -Vale. Pues debería comprarle una tarjeta y un regalo.-

Eliana -¿Una tarjeta? ¿Para qué?

Víctor -Para su cumpleaños. En Inglaterra, en el día de tu cumpleaños, recibes muchas tarjetas de felicitación. ¿Eso no pasa aquí en España?

Eliana -Nunca regalamos tarjetas. Mi madre y yo vamos a comprarle algo a mi padre, pero sólo eso. Lo que pasa en España es que en el día de tu cumpleaños, toda la familia te llama por teléfono para felicitarte. Pasas el día hablando con todo el mundo. Supongo que ésta es nuestra versión de vuestra tarjeta.-

Víctor -De verdad, me parece mucho mejor. Nunca me han gustado mucho las tarjetas. Después de dos o tres días las tiras a la basura. Parece una pérdida de recursos. Prefiero vuestro sistema. Entonces, ¿qué le compro a tu padre?-

Eliana "As I said the other day, the police have said that I would have to ask for a restraining order and go to court. I don't fancy that much."

Victor "Well, in that you know better than I do. However, I think that Hugo was talking seriously last night. We have to be careful. Would it be better not to see each other for a while until things calm down?"

Eliana "No way! I'm not going to change my life for him. Look, you have your new job tonight. You've got enough with that. Don't worry about that idiot Hugo. Look, tomorrow you're invited to my house for lunch. We're going to have a barbeque in the garden. There'll be paella and all kinds of meat. Do you fancy?"

Victor "Yes, I really do. What's the occasion?"

Eliana "It's my father's birthday." He's going to be fifty years old.

Victor "Okay. I'd better buy him a card and a present, then."

Eliana "A card? What for?"

Victor "For his birthday. In England, on your birthday, you get lots of greetings cards. Doesn't that happen here in Spain?"

Eliana "We never give cards. My mother and I are going to buy my father something, but just that. What happens in Spain is that, on your birthday, all the family call you to wish you happy birthday. You spend the day talking with everyone. I suppose that's our version of your card."

Victor "The truth is that it seems a lot better. I've never liked cards much. After two or three days you throw them in the bin. It seems a waste of resources. I prefer your system. So, what shall I buy your father?"

Eliana -No importa si no le compras nada, Víctor. Sé que no tienes tiempo para ir de compras.-

Víctor -Pero dices que vas con tu madre a comprarle algo, ¿verdad?-

Eliana -Sí, nos vamos después de despedirme de ti.-

Víctor -¿Me podrías comprar algo para él? Te doy el dinero. Toma, te doy veinte euros. ¿Le gusta el whisky?-

Eliana -El whisky no, pero sí le gusta el ron. ¿Quieres que le compre una botella de ron de tu parte?-

Víctor -Sí, por favor. Eso sería muy amable.-

Eliana -No hay problema, Víctor. Pues ahora tengo que irme. Mi madre me espera en casa. Y, por cierto, no te preocupes por el Hugo ése. No estoy dispuesta a perder nuestra amistad por él. Me gusta pasar tiempo contigo así que el señor Hugo simplemente tendrá que conformarse.-

Eliana "It doesn't matter if you don't buy him anything, Victor. I know that you don't have time to go shopping."

Victor "But you say that you're going with your Mum to buy him something, right?"

Eliana "Yes, we're going after I leave you."

Victor "Could you buy him something for me? I'll give you the money. Look, I'll give you twenty Euros. Does he like whisky?"

Eliana "Whisky no, but he does like rum. Do you want me to buy him a bottle of rum on your behalf?"

Victor "Yes, please. That would be very nice of you.

Eliana "That's no problem, Victor. Well, I have to go now. My mum is waiting for me at home. And, by the way, don't worry about that Hugo. I'm not willing to lose our friendship because of him. I like spending time with you so Mr Hugo will just have to get used to it."

Lesson 25 The Stem Changing Preterite Past.

In lesson 24 we learnt how to make regular preterite past. (The "I ate tense") You may have noticed, however, that some of the past-tense words appearing in the story don't quite seem to follow this pattern. It's likely that these are what are called the "stem changing" preterite. (And, of course, you've seen a bit of what we call the Imperfect which we will cover in lesson 26.)

Although these are classed as irregular preterite verbs, there's a surprising amount of regularity about them.

Let's look at how they are made.

Firstly, unlike the regular preterite, there is no difference between AR, ER and IR verbs. You do exactly the same for every one of them.

yo	e	nosotros	imos
tú	iste	vosotros	isteis
él		ellos	
ella	o	ellas	ieron
usted		ustedes	

Firstly, notice that none of the endings have accents on them.

Here's an example of how this works with Tener = to have, which is one of these stem changing verbs.

With Tener the stem changes to UV.

yo	tuve	nosotros	tuvimos
tú	tuviste	vosotros	tuvisteis
él		ellos	
ella	tuvo	ellas	tuvieron
usted		ustedes	

Ejemplo:

Ayer tuve un resfriado. = Yesterday I had a cold.

Juan tuvo que ir al hospital. = Juan had to go to the hospital.

.

Another stem changing verb is poner = to put. The stem changes to US.

yo	puse	nosotros	pusimos
tú	pusiste	vosotros	pusisteis
él		ellos	
ella	}puso	ellas	} pusieron
usted		ustedes	

Exemplo:

Puse la llaves en la mesa. = I put the keys on the table.

Pusieron la cámara en el bolso. = They put the camera in the bag.

Here is a list of some of the most common verbs whose stem changes in the preterite:

Andar (To walk)	→ Anduv...	Anduve, anduviste, anduvo...
Estar (To be)	→ Estuv...	Estuve, estuviste, estuvo...
Tener (To have)	→ Tuv...	Tuve, tuviste, tuvo...
Caber (To fit)	→ Cup...	Cupe, cupiste, cupo...
Haber (To have *(done)*	→ Hub...	Hube, hubiste, hubo...
Poder (To be able to)	→ Pud...	Pude, pudiste, pudo...
Poner (To put)	→ Pus...	Puse, pusiste, puso...
Saber (To know)	→ Sup...	Supe, supiste, supo...
Hacer (To do/make)	→ Hic...	Hice, hiciste, hizo...
Querer (To want/Love)	→ Quis...	Quise, quisiste, quiso...
Venir (To come)	→ Vin...	Vine, viniste, vino...

Ahora te toca a ti.

Have a go at making the following sentences:

1, Yesterday I walked through the park.

....

2, We made a tea.

....

3, Did you have a surprise? (tú)(sorpresa)

....

4, They put the cup on the table.

....

5, I couldn't reach. (llegar)

....

6, He came to the house.

....

7, I wanted to go.

....

8, I was there in the morning.

....

9, I put the bag in the car.

....

10, They came at ten.

....

Capítulo 25

Eliana se despidió de Víctor y se fue para su casa. Eran las cuatro de la tarde y le quedaban tres horas antes de empezar su trabajo. Pagó la cuenta y volvió a su piso para arreglarse. A las seis salió de casa y anduvo por las calles estrechas hacia el restaurante. Experimentaba una mezcla de nervios e ilusión. Llegó allí temprano pero decidió entrar y esperar adentro. Guillermo ya estaba allí y lo saludó.

Guillermo   -¡Buenas tardes, Víctor! Llegas temprano. ¿Cómo estás? ¿Nervioso?-

Víctor   -Sí, un poquillo.-

Guillermo   -Tampoco es para tanto. Esta noche trabajas en la barra. Puedes pasar un par de noches allí para hacerte una idea de cómo funciona todo. Luego puedes atender las mesas. ¿Sabes preparar bebidas?-

Víctor   -En eso no tengo experiencia pero seguro que puedo hacerlo. ¿Hay una lista en la carta?-

Guillermo   - Sí. Tómate media hora para ver lo que hay. La mayoría de los clientes son turistas, así que beben mucho, aunque los cocteles no son muy populares. Normalmente piden vino o cerveza. Los camareros te dan los pedidos con el número de la mesa. Tú las traes a la mesa, ¿vale?-

Víctor   -Sí, me queda claro. Espero que pueda hacerlo suficientemente rápido.-

Guillermo   -¡Anda! Es pan comido. Ahora tengo que organizar la cocina. Aquí tienes la carta y allí, en el rincón, está la barra. Vete a familiarizarte con lo que hay.-

Víctor   -Vale, Guillermo.-

Víctor miraba todas las botellas que había

Chapter 25

Eliana said goodbye to Victor and went off home. It was four in the afternoon and there were three hours left before he started his work. He paid the bill and went back to his flat to get ready. At six he left home and walked along the narrow streets toward the restaurant. He was feeling a mix of nerves and excitement. He arrived there early but decided to go in and wait inside. Guillermo was already there and greeted him.

Guillermo   ""Good afternoon, Victor! You're early. How are you? Nervous?"

Victor   "Yes, a little bit."

Guillermo   "It's nothing to worry about. Tonight you're working the bar. You can spend a couple of nights there to get an idea of how everything works. Then you can serve tables. Do you know how to prepare drinks?"

Victor   "I don't have any experience in that but I'm sure I can do it. Is there a list on the menu?"

Guillermo   "Yes. Take half an hour to see what there is. The majority of the customers are tourists, so they drink a lot, although the cocktails aren't very popular. They normally order wine or beer. The waiters give you the orders with the table number. You take them to the tables, okay?"

Victor   "Yes, that's clear. I hope I can do it quickly enough."

Guillermo   "Go on! It's a piece of cake. Now, I've got to organize the kitchen. Here is the menu, the bar is in the corner. Go and get familiar with what's there."

Victor   "Okay, Guillermo."

Victor looked at all the bottles that there was

detrás de la barra. Había muchos tipos de alcohol: whisky, ron, vodka, ginebra, coñac, porto, jerez y una multitud de otras botellas de varios colores. También había tres grifos de cerveza y dos neveras llenas de botellines y botellas de Fanta naranja, Fanta limón, 7up, Sprite etcétera.

Detrás de la barra había una máquina para preparar cafés. Víctor había visto muchas en las cafeterías en Inglaterra pero nunca había usado una. Todo parecía muy confuso.

Guillermo   -¿Sabes tirar una cerveza del grifo?-

Víctor   -No. Nunca lo he hecho. ¿Cómo se hace?-

Guillermo   -Mira. Yo tiro una y luego tú tiras la próxima, ¿vale?-

Víctor   -Vale.-

Guillermo cogió una jarra y la llenó con cerveza. Luego la puso en la barra.

Guillermo   -Así de fácil. Ahora te toca a ti. Hazlo tú.-

Víctor cogió una jarra y empezó a llenarla con cerveza. Todo iba bien hasta llegar a la mitad cuando, de repente, mucha espuma empezó a salir de la jarra y derramarse por el suelo.

Guillermo   -¡Para! ¡Para! ¡Apaga el grifo, ya! La tirabas demasiado rápido, Víctor.-

Víctor   -Lo siento, Guillermo. Es que me ha sorprendido. No esperaba eso.-

Guillermo   -No pasa nada, hombre. Sólo tienes que tirarla con más cuidado. Intenta de nuevo.-

Víctor lo intentó de nuevo y esta vez, le salió perfectamente. Aun así, el incidente había afectado a su confianza. Ya estaba muy nervioso.

behind the bar. There were many kinds of alcohol: whisky, rum, vodka, gin, brandy,port, sherry and a multitude of other various coloured bottles. There were also three beer taps and two fridges filled with beer bottles and bottles of Fanta orange, Fanta lemon, 7up, Sprite etcetera.

Behind the bar there was a coffee making machine. Victor had seen lots of them in cafes in England but he had never used one. Everything seemed very confusing.

Guillermo   "Do you know how to pour a beer from the tap?"

Victor   "No. I've never done it. How do you do it?"

Guillermo   "Look. I'll pour one and then you pour the next one, okay?"

Victor   "Okay."

Guillermo grabbed a pint glass and filled it with lager. Then he put it on the bar.

Guillermo   "As easy as that. Now, it's your turn. You do it."

Victor got a pint glass and started to fill it with lager. Everything was going well until it was half full when, suddenly, a lot of froth started to rise out of the glass and pour onto the floor.

Guillermo   "Stop! Stop! Switch the tap off, now! You were filling it too quickly, Victor."

Victor   "Sorry, Guillermo. It's surprised me. I didn't expect that."

Guillermo   "Don't worry, man. You just have to pourl it more carefully. Try again."

Victor tried it again and this time it went perfectly well. Even so, the incident had affected his confidence. Now he was very nervous.

Guillermo -¿Ves?. Lo puedes hacer perfectamente bien. Mira, esta noche los camareros te van a dar los pedidos de las mesas. Tú pones las bebidas en la barra y ellos las sirven. Si tienes problemas, diles que necesitas ayuda. Si ellos están demasiado ocupados, te ayudo, yo. ¿Vale?

Víctor -Vale, Guillermo. Hago lo que pueda.-

Guillermo "See? You can do it perfectly well. Look, tonight the waiters are going to give you the orders from the tables. You put the drinks on the bar and they will serve them. If you have problems, tell them that you need help. If they are too busy, I'll help you. Okay?"

Victor "Okay, Guillermo. I'll do what I can."

Lesson 26. The Imperfect past. Was...ing, Were...ing and Used to.

Perhaps as you are making your way through the story you have noticed other kinds of things happening to the past tense verbs. Have you noticed verbs with ABA and ÍA on the end? Well, this is what is called the Imperfect Past.

Just as in English, the Spanish language has a past tense which is very descriptive. Unlike the preterite which is used to talk about events or actions that have happened, e.g. "I washed the car". or "I ate some food." the Imperfect past is a past tense whose job it is to describe the background of what happened.

In English, you know this past tense as the one that has this structure:

*I **was** walk**ing** the dog when...*

*We **were** eat**ing** in a nice restaurant...*

*She **was** talk**ing** to the neighbour...*

*My friends **were** say**ing** that...*

In addition to this type of sentence, the Imperfect past is also:

*I **used to** be a policeman.*

*She **used to** work in on a farm.*

*We **used to** eat in that restaurant.*

So, as you have probably noticed, the Imperfect past is found in sentences with WAS ...ING, WERE ...ING and USED TO.

How is it made?

This is probably one of the easiest tenses to form.

AR Verbs.

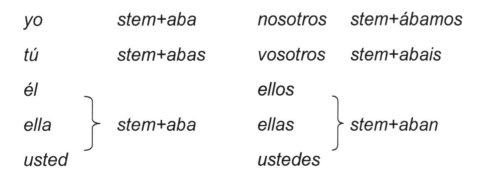

yo	stem+aba	nosotros	stem+ábamos
tú	stem+abas	vosotros	stem+abais
él		ellos	
ella	stem+aba	ellas	stem+aban
usted		ustedes	

ER/IR verbs

yo	*stem+ía*	*nosotros*	*stem+íamos*
tú	*stem+ías*	*vosotros*	*stem+íais*
él		*ellos*	
ella	*stem+ía*	*ellas*	*stem+ían*
usted		*ustedes*	

Here are some examples of Imperfect verb conjugations:

Hablar.

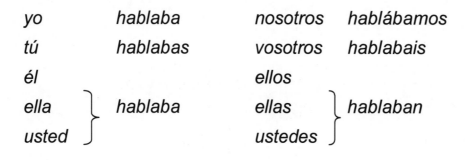

yo	*hablaba*	*nosotros*	*hablábamos*
tú	*hablabas*	*vosotros*	*hablabais*
él		*ellos*	
ella	*hablaba*	*ellas*	*hablaban*
usted		*ustedes*	

Vivir.

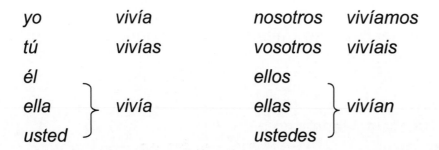

yo	*vivía*	*nosotros*	*vivíamos*
tú	*vivías*	*vosotros*	*vivíais*
él		*ellos*	
ella	*vivía*	*ellas*	*vivían*
usted		*ustedes*	

This is how you might use them in sentences:

Ayer **hablaba** con el vecino. = Yesterday I **was** talk**ing** with the neighbour.

Yo **vivía** en Francia. = I **used to** live in France.

Cuando **vivía** en España **comía** paella. = When I **lived** in Spain I **used to** eat paella.

Siempre **trabajaba** mucho. = I always **used to** work a lot.

Irregular Imperfect Past.

The good news is that there are only three irregular verbs in the imperfect tense!

These are:

SER

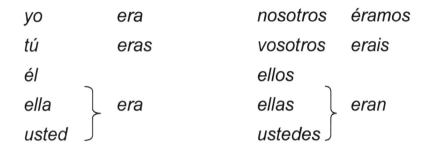

yo	era	nosotros	éramos
tú	eras	vosotros	erais
él		ellos	
ella	era	ellas	eran
usted		ustedes	

IR

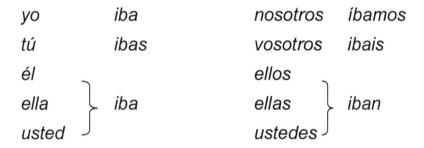

yo	iba	nosotros	íbamos
tú	ibas	vosotros	ibais
él		ellos	
ella	iba	ellas	iban
usted		ustedes	

VER

yo	veía	nosotros	veíamos
tú	veías	vosotros	veíais
él		ellos	
ella	veía	ellas	veían
usted		ustedes	

Ahora te toca a ti.

Have a go at making the following sentences using the Imperfect past.

1, I used to eat meat.

....

2, I was walking along the street. (por la calle)

....

3, We used to watch the television a lot.

....

4, They were talking about politics. (la política)

....

5, Were you going to Spain?

....

6, You all used to come here.

....

7, Pablo was running quickly.

....

8, Leticia used to live in that house.

....

9, I used to be a policeman.

....

10, We were in the park.

....

Capítulo 26

A las siete los clientes empezaron a entrar en el restaurante. Pedían vinos, cervezas y alcohol en abundancia. Víctor intentaba servirlos tan rápido como podía pero le fue difícil. Estaba sudando como nunca. Alrededor de las diez, mientras estaba agachado, cogiendo unas botellas de la nevera, escuchó una voz delante de la barra.

Voz -¡Oiga, camarero! ¿Dónde leches están nuestras bebidas?-

Asustado, Víctor se levantó mientras se preparaba para pedirle perdón. Al otro lado del bar estaba Alfredo con Mercedes y Eliana. Todos se estaban riendo.

Alfredo -¡Qué cara de susto tienes! Estamos de broma, hombre. No te preocupes. Según Guillermo estás trabajando como si hubieras trabajado de camarero toda la vida.-

Víctor -Gracias. De verdad, me asustasteis.-

Eliana -Buenas noches, Víctor.-

Víctor -Hola, Eliana.-

Mercedes -Hola, Víctor, ¡qué profesional pareces! ¿Cómo te apañas en el trabajo?-

Víctor -Bueno, aquí luchando. Creo que he cometido unos cuantos errores ya.-

Alfredo -A ver si puedes ponernos unas bebidas sin cometer un error. ¿Nos pones una jarra, un vino blanco y una Fanta limón?-

Víctor -Claro. ¿Quieres hielo con la Fanta?

Eliana -Sí, por favor.-

Víctor -¿Ya tenéis mesa? Puedo llevaros las bebidas si queréis.-

Chapter 26

At seven the clients started to come into the restaurant. They were ordering wines, beers and alcohol in abundance. Victor tried to serve them as quickly as he could but it was hard for him. He was sweating like never before. Around ten, whilst he was crouched, getting bottles from the fridge, he heard a voice from in front of the bar.

Voice "Hey, waiter! Where the hell are our drinks?"

Shocked, Victor stood up whilst he got ready to apologise. On the other side of the bar was Alfredo with Mercedes and Eliana. They all were laughing.

Alfredo "What a face! We are just joking, man. Don't worry. According to Guillermo you're working as though you've been a waiter all your life."

Victor "Thanks. You really scared me."

Eliana "Good evening, Victor."

Victor "Hello, Eliana."

Mercedes "Hello, Victor, how professional you look! How are you managing the work?

Victor "Well, struggling on. I think I've made a few mistakes already."

Alfredo "Let's see if you can pour us some drinks without making a mistake. Can you give us a pint, a white wine and a Fanta lemon?"

Victor "Sure. Do you want ice with the Fanta?

Eliana "Yes, please."

Victor "Do you have a table yet? I can take the drinks to you if you want."

Mercedes   -No, todavía no. Esperamos a Guillermo. Nos ha prometido la mejor del restaurante.-

Alfredo   -Con nuestra suerte estará al lado de los servicios. Ja ja.-

Eliana   -No seas tonto, papá. Creo que nos va a poner en la terraza. Hace una noche buenísima.-

Víctor les puso las bebidas y todos pasaron unos cinco minutos hablando con él. Estaba muy ocupado así que no podía hablar mucho. Luego, se fueron con Guillermo a su mesa y se despidieron de Víctor. Antes de irse quedaron con él para las doce de la mañana siguiente.

Aunque fue un trabajo duro, a él le gustó su primera noche detrás de la barra. Guillermo parecía contento con su trabajo y le dijo que la noche siguiente iba a trabajar de camarero y atender las mesas. A las dos de la mañana Víctor salió para casa y al llegar, se fue directamente a la cama y se tumbó cansadísimo. En cuestión de segundos estaba durmiendo profundamente.

Mercedes   "No, not yet. We are waiting for Guillermo. He's promised us the best in the restaurant."

Alfredo   "With our luck it'll be next to the toilets. Haha."

Eliana   "Don't be silly, dad. I think he's going to put us on the terrace. It's a lovely night."

Victor served their drinks and they spent five minutes talking with him. He was very busy so they couldn't talk a lot. Then, they went off with Guillermo to their table and they said goodbye to Victor. Before going they agreed to see him at twelve the following morning.

Although it was hard work, he liked his first night behind the bar. Guillermo seemed happy with his work and told him that the following night he was going to work as a waiter and serve the tables. At two in the morning Victor left for home and, once there, went straight to bed and stretched out tiredly. In a matter of seconds he was in a deep sleep.

Lesson 27. Using the Preterite and the Imperfect past together.

The real art to speaking Spanish is being able to tell a story in the past by weaving together both the Preterite and the Imperfect tenses. If you listen carefully, you'll notice that all great story tellers use them both to tell their tale.

Of course, you could simply recount a story using **Preterite** only (The "I ate" tense). However, it would likely be quite boring to the listener and sound like you were reading them a shopping list.

You could also only use the **Imperfect** (The was..ing, were...ing tense) to tell your story. This, too, would be very boring as there'd be no real action.

The ideal, then, is to learn to use them together to describe past events.

Let's look at how you can do this:

Ongoing description interrupted.

Consider this sentence.

"The other day whilst I was eating my evening meal my son arrived from Australia."

"El otro día mientras cenaba yo llegó mi hijo de Australia.

In this example, there are two different past tenses. Can you spot them?

We have the Imperfect "was eating" and the Preterite "arrived".

Here's a pictorial impression of how that sentence works:

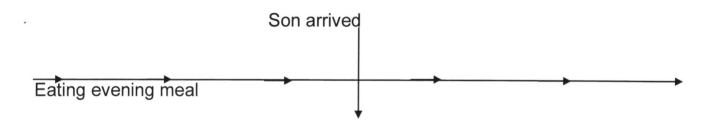

In essence, the Imperfect sets the scene by describing an ongoing activity. The Preterite then comes along and cuts through the activity, providing the action.

Unlike the Preterite, which can only be used sequentially like a shopping list, you can use the Imperfect to overlap multiple activities that were all happening at the same time.

e.g.

This morning whilst cooking the breakfast I was listening to the radio y talking to my son.

Esta mañana, mientras preparaba el desayuno, escuchaba la radio y hablaba con mi hijo.

This morning.

Preparaba el desayuno.

Escuchaba la radio.

Hablaba con mi hijo.

Have a go at translating these sentences into Spanish.

1, Whilst I was cleaning the living room, the phone rang. (limpiar, sonar)

....

2, Miguel was writing an email when the power went off. (escribir, irse la luz)

....

3, Whilst Elizabeth and I were working in the garden it started to rain. (trabajar, empezar)

....

4, This morning, whilst I was watching the television I ate my breakfast. (ver, desayunar)

....

5, He was saying that he was drinking more water. (decir, beber)

....

Capítulo 27

Al día siguiente se levantó a las diez y media de la mañana. Tenía prisa porque la fiesta de Alfredo iba a empezar a las doce. No tenía que comprarle un regalo ya que Eliana lo había comprado el día anterior.

Se duchó y se vistió con prisa y luego desayunó unas tostadas con aceite de oliva y un café sólo. Mientras desayunaba veía la televisión. Todavía le costaba entender todo pero podía hacerse una idea de lo que decían. Estaba muy contento con su español pero sabía que le quedaba mucho más por aprender.

A las once y media salió de casa y se fue directamente a la casa de Eliana. Llegó veinte minutos después. Todos estaban en el jardín y Alfredo estaba encendiendo la barbacoa.

Víctor -Buenos días a todos. Feliz cumpleaños, Alfredo-

Alfredo -Gracias, Víctor. ¿Qué tal tu primera noche en el restaurante?-

Víctor -Pues, bien. Un poco larga y un poco dura pero me gustó mucho.-

Eliana -¿Trabajaste en la barra toda la noche?-

Víctor -Sí, pero Guillermo me ha dicho que esta noche atiendo las mesas. Espero que me salga bien.-

Mercedes -Sin duda, Víctor. Anoche trabajabas como un profesional. Esta noche vas a hacer un buen trabajo, eso lo sé.-

Víctor -Pues eso espero. Necesito el trabajo y me es importante hacerlo bien.-

Eliana -Ya verás, después de dos semanas vas a ser la estrella del restaurante. Ja ja.-

Mercedes -Pues vamos a tomar algo antes de comer. ¿Qué queréis vosotros?-

Chapter 27

The next day he got up at ten-thirty in the morning. He was in a hurry because Alfredo's party was going to start at twelve. He didn't have to buy him a present as Eliana had bought it the day before.

He showered and got ready quickly and then had breakfast, eating some olive oil on toast and a black coffee. Whilst he ate he watched the television. It was still difficult to understand everything but he could get the idea of what they were saying. He was very happy with his Spanish but knew that he had much more to learn.

At eleven-thirty he left home and went straight to Eliana's house. He arrived twenty minutes later. Everyone was in the garden and Alfredo was lighting the barbeque.

Victor "Good morning, everyone. Happy birthday, Alfredo."

Alfredo "Thanks, Victor. How was your first night in the restaurant?"

Victor "Eh, good. A little bit long and a little bit difficult but I liked it a lot."

Eliana "Did you work in the bar all night?"

Victor "Yes, but tonight Guillermo has told me that I'm serving tables. I hope it goes okay."

Mercedes "Without doubt, Victor. Last night you worked like a professional. Tonight you're going to do a good job, that I know."

Victor "Well, I hope so. I need the job and it's important to me to do it well."

Eliana "You'll see, after two weeks you're going to be the star of the restaurant. Haha."

Mercedes "So, we're going to have a drink before we eat. What do you all want?"

Alfredo -Creo que voy a tomarme una cerveza. ¿Y tú, Víctor? ¿Tomas una cerveza conmigo?-

Víctor -Sí, gracias. Me gustaría.-

Eliana -Quiero un vino blanco, mamá.-

Mercedes -Vale. Las preparo yo. Enseguida vuelvo.-

Todos se sentaron en el jardín. De inmediato surgió el tema de Hugo.

Alfredo -¿Qué opinas de Hugo, Víctor? Eliana me dice que te amenazó la otra noche.-

Víctor -No sé qué le pasa, Alfredo. Estaba bastante enfadado conmigo. Hablaba de causarme problemas pero no sé qué tenía en mente. Me parece un poco loco, la verdad.-

Alfredo -Tú no sabes ni la mitad. Mientras salía con Eliana tuvimos unos cuantos problemas con él y sus celos. Es que es una persona muy controladora e intentaba controlar todo lo que hacía Eliana. La pobre lo aguantaba, pero al final tuvo que cortar con él.-

Eliana -Y el problema es que ahora él no quiere reconocerlo. Habla como si todavía fuésemos novios. La verdad es que me tiene loca. No sé qué hacer.-

Alfredo -Yo creo que le hemos dado suficientes oportunidades ya. La próxima vez, voy directamente a la policía y lo denuncio. Quería evitarlo, principalmente por mi hija, pero creo que ya se está pasando tres pueblos.-

Víctor -Creo que ésa es la única cosa que puedes hacer ahora. Y encima, es un chico bastante fornido.-

Eliana -¡Pero bueno! ¿Qué hacemos? Estamos aquí para celebrar tu cumpleaños, papá y no para hablar de tonterías y de gente tonta. Por cierto, ¿cuántos cumples hoy, papá? No me acuerdo bien. ¿Sesenta? Ja ja.-

Alfredo "I think I'm going to have a beer. And you, Victor. Are you having a beer with me?"

Victor "Yes, thanks. I'd like that."

Eliana "I want a white wine, mum."

Mercedes "Okay. I'll prepare them. I'll be right back."

Everyone sat down in the garden. The subject of Hugo came up straight away.

Alfredo "What do you think about Hugo, Victor? Eliana tells me that he threatened you the other night."

Victor "I don't know what's wrong with him. He was quite angry with me. He talked about causing me problems but I don't know what he had in mind. In truth, he seems a bit mad."

Alfredo "You don't know the half. Whilst he was going out with Eliana we had a good few problems with him and his jealousy. He's a very controlling person and he tried to control everything that Eliana did. The poor thing put up with him, but finally she had to finish with him."

Eliana "And the problem is that now he doesn't want to admit it. He talks as though we were still going out together. He really has got me going crazy. I don't know what to do."

Alfredo "I think that we've given him enough opportunities already. The next time, I'm going straight to the police to report him. I wanted to avoid it, mostly because of my daughter, but I think that he's going too far now."

Victor "I think that that's the only thing you can do now. And, what's more, he's a fairly enormous guy."

Eliana "Hey! What are we doing? We are here to celebrate your birthday, dad, and not to talk about silly things and stupid people. By the way, how old are you today, dad? I don't quite recall. Sixty? Haha."

Alfredo   -No seas mala, hija. Ya sabes que hoy cumplo cuarenta y poquitos.-

Eliana   -¡Venga! 'Y poquitos', dices. 'Unos poquitos muchos', diría yo. Pero, de verdad, ¿cómo se siente ser tan mayor?-

Alfredo   ¿Cómo te atreves? Pues, ya verás, hija. Con tu edad piensas que tienes todo el tiempo del mundo y luego, pestañeas tres veces y te salen canas en el pecho.-

Eliana   -¡Jope, papá! Espero que no. Soy mujer. Si me salieran canas en el pecho ¡tendría un problema grande yo!-

Alfredo   -Pues, tú no, hija, pero tú, Víctor, ya verás. Dentro de nada tendrás arrugas saliéndote por todos lados. Ja ja.-

Víctor   -Dios mío. Espero que no, Alfredo. Sólo tengo veinticinco años. Sería un poco temprano ¿verdad?-

Alfredo   -De todas las maneras, tenéis celos de mi madurez y mis rasgos cincelados, ¿a que sí?-

Eliana   -Sí, pero no de tu tripita, papá. Con cada año se hace aun más grande.-

Alfredo   -¿Qué tripa? Bueno, ¿qué se puede hacer? Es que tu madre cocina tan bien.-

Mercedes   -¿Qué decís de mí?-

Eliana   -Papá dice que le haces engordar.-

Mercedes   ¿Quién, yo? ¿Acaso le meto la comida por la boca? No. Creo que la única persona que tiene la culpa de ese estomago es el señor goloso ése.-

Alfredo   -¡Oye! Ésta es mi fiesta de cumpleaños y deberíais tratarme con un poco de respeto. Joer, después de todo esto espero que me hayáis comprado algo bonito.-

Eliana   -Sí, papá. ¡Te hemos comprado una faja! Ja ja ja.-

Alfredo   "Don't be wicked, girl. You know fine well that today I'm forty and a bit."

Eliana   "Come on! 'And a bit', you say. 'A little bit too much', I'd say. But, really, how does it feel to be so old?"

Alfredo   "How dare you? Well, you'll see, girl. At your age you think that you've got all the time in the world and then you blink three times and you've got grey hairs on your chest."

Eliana   "Blinking heck, dad! I hope not. I'm a women. If I got hairs on my chest I'd have a big problem!

Alfredo   "Well, you no, but you, Victor, you'll see. Before long you'll have wrinkles appearing everywhere. Haha.

Victor   "My God. I hope not, Alfredo. I'm just twenty-five years old. It would be a bit early, don't you think?"

Alfredo   "Anyway, you're jealous of my maturity and my chiselled good looks, isn't that right?"

Eliana   "Yes, but not of your little pot belly, dad. With each year it gets bigger and bigger."

Alfredo   "What pot belly? Well, what can you do? It's just that your mother cooks so well."

Mercedes   "What are you saying about me?"

Eliana   "Dad's saying that you make him fat!"

Mercedes   "Who, me? And I suppose I stuff the food in his mouth, do I?" No, I think the only person who is to blame for that stomach is Mr Sweet-tooth here."

Alfredo   "Listen! This is my birthday party and you should treat me with a little bit of respect. Goodness, after all this I hope you've all bought me something nice."

Eliana   "Yes, dad. We've bought you a girdle! Hahaha."

La fiesta fue muy divertida. Durante toda la tarde la familia de Eliana hizo bromas y se rieron mucho. A Víctor, le encantaba estar con ellos. Era una familia feliz y cariñosa y se sentía cómodo cada vez que estaba con ellos. A eso de las cinco les dio las gracias y se despidió de ellos. Tenía que trabajar esa noche y quería echarse una siesta antes de empezar. Había sido un día muy agradable y al tumbarse en casa Víctor se sentía muy feliz y afortunado de haberlos conocido.

The party was great fun. During the entire afternoon Eliana's family made jokes and laughed a lot. Victor loved being with them. It was a happy and loving family and he felt comfortable each time that he was with them. At around five he said thank you and left them. He had to work that evening and wanted to have a siesta before starting. It had been a very pleasant day and as he lay down he felt very happy and fortunate to have met them.

Lesson 28. This, these, that and those.

We are sure that you have seen these words liberally scattered throughout Victor's story. Let's take a look at how they work. Learning how to say "this" and "that" etc. in Spanish is a little challenging because these words are in essence, adjectives whose job it is to describe naming words. This means that they are different in masculine, feminine, singular and plural.

In addition to that, this range of adjectives contains some of the few neuter words that are in the Spanish language. (Neuter words are essentially gender free.)

Let's take a look:

	MASCULINE	FEMININE	NEUTER (no gender)
THIS	ESTE	ESTA	ESTO
THAT	ESE	ESA	ESO
THESE	ESTOS	ESTAS	X
THOSE	ESOS	ESAS	X

Firstly, let's take a look at the neuter words. Why would Spanish speakers need to have words that have no gender? Well, simply because, at times they have to talk about things and they have no idea what they are.

Think of this sentence:

"What is that?"

Because the question has to be asked then it's clear that we don't know what that "that" is. Thus, if we don't know what it is then we can't give it a gender. When that happens, you simply use the neuter.

"¿Qué es eso?"

Also, there are other sentences in which we say "that" or "this" and we aren't referring to anything specific.

"That is what I said." = *"Eso es lo que dije yo."*

"That's all, thanks." = *"Eso es todo, gracias."*

"¿What's this?" = *"¿Qué es esto?"*

"This is crazy!" = *"¡Esto es una tontería!"*

Top tip. *At the beginning it may be a challenge to find the correct word in conversation. However, you can just use the two neuter words until you can find your way around the others.*

The principle list is easy to use once you understand the idea of how they work. Really, the 'these, this, that' words are adjectives or describing words and so, they must agree with the noun or naming word just like in any other case in the Spanish language.

So, if you want to say: "This car." and car is masculine and singular, 'el coche' then you choose the masculine, singular option, which is: ESTE

If you want to say: "These cups." which are feminine and plural, 'las tazas', then you simply choose the feminine, plural option. ESTAS

How to make these work for you.

The way to cement these into your mind is through repetition. Why not start by looking at the furniture in your room now and identify if it is masculine or feminine and singular or plural. Then, give each piece its correct word for THIS. Then do it for THAT, then THESE and finally THOSE. Before you know it you'll be using them without thinking.

Te toca a ti. / It's your turn.

Translate these sentences ensuring you pay attention to the correct genders.

1, These houses are big. (la casa) ....

2, I want this bread. (el pan)...

3, Those cars are red. (el coche)...

4, This is incredible. ....

5, We want that cake. (la tarta) ....

6, What are those? ....

7, These are my books. (el libro) ....

8, Can I have that glass? (el vaso) ....

9, You use these pens. (el bolígrafo) ....

10, Where is that girl? (la chica) ....

Capítulo 28

Un par de horas después, Víctor se levantó y se duchó rápidamente. Luego se vistió y salió de casa para el restaurante. Esa noche iba a atender las mesas por primera vez y se sentía un poco nervioso. Al llegar al restaurante, Guillermo lo saludó calurosamente y le explicó lo que tenía que hacer. Todo parecía un poco complicado pero Víctor entendía el sistema. Pronto los clientes empezaron a llegar y en una hora el restaurante estaba al tope con gente pidiendo comida como locos.

A eso de las diez de la noche, un grupo de chicos jóvenes entraron y se sentaron a una mesa en medio del restaurante. Parecían haber bebido una más de la cuenta. Hacían mucho ruido y todos los clientes los miraban de reojo. Uno de los chicos le gritó a Víctor:

Chico -¡Oye, guiri! ¿Vas a atendernos o qué?-

Víctor miró hacia la mesa y su corazón le dio un vuelco. Allí sentado con cuatro chicos más o menos de su edad estaba Hugo. Respirando profundamente se les acercó.

Víctor-Buenas noches. ¿Qué les traigo?-

Hugo -¡Escuchadle! Cómo habla español el guiri. Ja ja ja. No te preocupes, Víctor. Un día lo hablarás bien. Sigue luchando, hombre.-

Mientras hablaba Hugo, todos los clientes de las mesas de alrededor miraban con interés. Víctor tenía mucha vergüenza pero quería mantenerse profesional.

Víctor -Hugo, éste no es el lugar apropiado para esto. Por favor, chicos, pedid lo que queráis y dejadme hacer mi trabajo.-

Hugo -Sí, por supuesto, Víctor, tienes razón. No querríamos causarte problemas en tu nuevo trabajo. Tráenos cinco jarras de cerveza y unas tapas. Mientras tanto miraremos la carta.-

Chapter 28

A couple of hours later, Victor got up and showered quickly. Then he got dressed and left home for the restaurant. That evening he was going to serve tables for the first time and he felt a little nervous. Arriving at the restaurant, Guillermo greeted him warmly and explained what he had to do. Everything seemed a bit complicated but Victor understood the system. Soon, the customers started to arrive and in an hour the restaurant was filled to the brim with people ordering food like mad.

Around ten at night, a group of young men came in and sat at a table in the middle of the restaurant. They seemed to have drank a few too many. They were making a lot of noise and all the customers were looking at them out of the corner of their eyes. One of the boys shouted at Victor:

Chico "Hey, foreigner! Are you going to serve us or what?"

Victor looked over at the table and his heart missed a beat. There, seated with four young men of about his age was Hugo. Breathing deeply he went over to them."

Victor "Good evening. What can I bring you?"

Hugo "Listen to how the foreigner speaks Spanish! Don't worry, Victor. One day you'll speak it well. Keep working at it, man!"

Whilst Hugo talked, all the customers on the nearby tables looked on with interest. Victor was very embarrassed but wanted to remain professional.

Victor "Hugo, here is not the right place for this. Please, boys, order what you want and let me do my job."

Hugo "Yes, of course, Victor, you're right. We don't want to cause you any problems in your new job. Bring us five pints of lager and some tapas. Meanwhile we'll look at the menu."

Víctor llevó su pedido a la barra y luego pidió tapas para cinco personas de la cocina. No confiaba en Hugo y tenía la sensación de que habría problemas con ellos esa noche. La cocina le dio dos platos de tapas: unas patatas bravas y unos montaditos de queso y jamón. Víctor los llevó a la mesa de Hugo.

Víctor -Aquí tenéis las jarras y las tapas.-

Hugo -Pues has tardado mucho, ¿no? ¿Qué tipo de servicio es éste? Debería quejarme. Y, a ver, ¡ni siquiera está fría la cerveza!-

Hugo se puso de pie y, de forma exagerada empezó a gritar.

Hugo -¡Quiero hablar con el propietario! Este camarero hace un trabajo fatal. La cerveza está caliente y no me sorprende, ya que hemos esperado media hora para que llegaran.-

Víctor -Hugo, por favor, siéntate y cálmate. Sólo he tardado cinco minutos en traeros las cervezas y tú lo sabes.-

Hugo -¿Qué decís, chicos? Éste dice que sólo ha tardado cinco minutos. Creo que no sólo es un camarero incompetente sino que también es un mentiroso. ¡Quiero hablar con el propietario, ahora mismo!-

Dejándolo allí gritando, Víctor se fue a buscar a Guillermo. Lo encontró en la cocina hablando con el cocinero.

Víctor -Guillermo. Lo siento pero tenemos problemas. Un grupo de chicos está armando un lío en el restaurante. Uno dice que quiere hablar contigo porque supuestamente he tardado mucho en llevarles la cerveza y que no está fría.-

Guillermo -¡Dios mío! ¿Qué diablos está pasando? Ya voy.-

Victor took their order to the bar and then ordered tapas for five people from the kitchen. He didn't trust Hugo and had the feeling that there would be problems with them that night. The kitchen gave him two plates of tapas: some potatoes with spicy sauce and some small sandwiches with cheese and ham. Victor took them to Hugo's table.

Victor "Here are the pints and the tapas."

Hugo "Well, you've taken a long time, haven't you? What kind of service is this? I should complain. And, let's see, the beer isn't even cold!"

Hugo stood up and, started to shout exaggeratedly.

Hugo "I want to speak to the owner! This waiter is doing a terrible job. The beer is warm and I'm not surprised as we've waited half an hour for it to arrive."

Victor "Hugo, please, sit down and be calm. I've only taken five minutes bringing you the beers and you know it."

Hugo "What do you say, guys? This one says that he's only taken five minutes. I think that he's not only a useless waiter but a liar too. I want to speak with the owner, right now!"

Leaving him there, shouting, Victor went to look for Guillermo. He found him in the kitchen talking with the cook.

Victor "Guillermo. Sorry but we have problems. A group of young men are creating a scandal in the restaurant. One says that he wants to talk with you because supposedly I've taken too long to serve their beer and that it's not cold."

Guillermo "My God! What the hell's going on? I'm coming."

Guillermo entró en el restaurante. Hugo todavía está gritando y todos los clientes parecen bastantes asustados. Guillermo se acercó a él y lo habló:

Guillermo -Bueno, bueno ¿qué le pasa? Por favor, cálmese. Está asustando a los clientes. Podemos arreglar todo sin tener que gritar. Siéntese, hombre, luego podemos hablar.-

Hugo -No pienso sentarme ni calmarme. Este restaurante es una vergüenza y ese camarerucho, Víctor, debería ser despedido. Ni siquiera sabe servir una buena cerveza.-

Guillermo -Vale, hombre. No pasa nada. No les voy a cobrar por las cervezas. Si no están contentos con el servicio, pues no tienen por qué seguir aquí. Por favor, tengan la amabilidad de salir a la calle. –

Hugo -No te preocupes. Nos vamos. No pienso pasar aquí más tiempo.-

Con ésas, Hugo cogió la mesa con las dos manos y la volcó, arrojando todas las cervezas y tapas al suelo. Al chocar contra las baldosas del suelo, las jarras se rompieron en mil pedazos y la cerveza salpicó a todo el mundo. Luego, con sus amigotes siguiéndolo detrás, salió del restaurante.

Enseguida Guillermo y todos los camareros se pusieron a arreglar las cosas y después de cinco minutos el restaurante estaba una vez más tranquilo y había vuelto la normalidad. Guillermo le pidió a Víctor que viniera a hablar con él a la oficina.

Guillermo -Bueno, Víctor. ¿Qué narices pasó con esos tipos? ¿Por qué estaba tan enfadado ese chico?-

Víctor -Lo conozco, Guillermo. Se llama Hugo. Es el ex novio de Eliana. Nos ha estado amenazando durante los últimos días.

Guillermo entered the restaurant. Hugo was still shouting and all the customers looked quite shocked. Guillermo went up to him and spoke:

Guillermo "Well, well, what's the problem? Please, calm down. You're frightening the customers. We can fix this without having to shout. Sit down, man, then we can talk."

Hugo "I have no intention of sitting down nor being calm. This restaurant is an embarresment and that poor excuse for a waiter, Victor, should be sacked. He doesn't even know how to serve a good beer."

Guillermo "Okay, man. There's no problem. I'm not going to charge you for the beers. If you're not happy with the service, then you don't need to stay here. Please, would you be so kind as to leave."

Hugo "Don't worry. We're going. I don't want to stay here any longer."

With that, Hugo grabbed the table with both hands and flipped it over, scattering all the beer and tapas on the floor. As the glasses hit the tiled floor they shattered into a thousand pieces and the beer splashed everyone. Then, with his friends following on behind, he left the restaurant.

Guillermo and all the waiters immediately got on with tidying everything up and after five minutes the restaurant was calm again and had returned to normality. Guillermo asked Victor to come and talk to him in the office.

Guillermo "So, Victor, what in God's name happened with those guys? Why was that guy so angry?"

Victor "I know him. He's called Hugo. It's Eliana's exboyfriend. He's been threatening us these last few days.

Creo que ha venido específicamente para causarme problemas.-

Guillermo -Ah, ¿fue ése? Alfredo me ha hablado de él aunque no lo conocía de cara. Ya entiendo. Ese chaval tiene problemas, Víctor. Creo que deberías andar con cuidado. No sé qué es capaz de hacer.-

Víctor -Sí, lo sé, Guillermo. De verdad, me da un poco miedo. También, siento mucho lo ocurrido. Puedes tener la confianza de que no hice nada para provocarlo.-

Guillermo -Eso lo sé, Víctor. Nuestra cerveza sale del grifo casi congelada. Tendrías que haber tardado una hora en llegar a la mesa para que estuviera caliente. Ja ja. Ahora, vete a trabajar. Después de cerrar el restaurante te invito a una cerveza, bien fría.-

Víctor volvió a su trabajo. Durante el resto de la noche, pensó en el problema de Hugo. No sabía qué hacer. Parecía que el chico no iba a parar con sus ataques. A las dos y diez el último cliente salió del restaurante y Víctor se sentó con Guillermo a tomar una cerveza.

Guillermo -Bueno, Víctor ¿qué tal el trabajo? ¿Te gusta?-

Víctor -Mucho. Excepto eso de esta noche, claro.-

Guillermo -Me alegro. Pues he visto suficiente para saber que trabajas bien. Entonces, si quieres, tienes un trabajo permanente aquí.-

Víctor -Gracias, Guillermo. Te lo agradezco. No creo que trabaje de camarero para siempre, pero, de momento me gusta mucho.-

Guillermo -¿Y por qué te tiene tanta manía ese Hugo? Es que ¿ahora sales con Eliana?-

I think that he has come specifically to cause trouble for me.

Guillermo "Ah, that was him? Alfredo has talked to me about him, although I didn't know his face. Now I understand. That lad has problems, Victor. I think you should go carefully. I don't know what he's capable of doing."

Victor "Yes, I know. He actually makes me a bit frightened. I'm sorry for what's happened, too, Guillermo. You can be sure that I didn't do anything to provoke him."

Guillermo "I know that, Victor. Our lager comes out of the tap nearly frozen. You would have to have taken an hour to arrive at the table for it to be warm. Ha ha. Now, go and work. After I close the restaurant I'll buy you an ice cold beer."

Victor returned to his work. During the rest of the night he thought about the problem with Hugo. He didn't know what to do. It seemed as though the guy wasn't going to stop his attacks. At ten minutes past two the last client left the restaurant and Victor sat down with Guillermo to have a beer.

Guillermo "Well, Victor, how is the work going? Do you like it?"

Victor "A lot. Except what happened tonight, of course."

Guillermo "I'm pleased. Then I've seen enough to know that you work well. So, if you want to, you have permanent work here."

Victor "Thanks, Guillermo. I'm grateful. I don't think that I'll work as a waiter forever, but, for the moment I like it a lot. "

Guillermo "And why does Hugo dislike you so much? Is it that you are going out with Eliana now?"

Víctor -No. Se lo pedí pero no quería. Ha tenido tantos problemas con Hugo que no quiere meterse en otra relación tan pronto.-

Guillermo -Te gusta, ¿eh? Es una chica majísima. La conozco desde que era un bebé. Dale algo de tiempo, Víctor. Según veo, a ella, le gustas mucho.-

Víctor -No tengo prisa. Puedo esperar. De todas las maneras, salimos mucho y somos muy amigos.-

Guillermo -Muy bien, así empieza la cosa. Pues, nada, ahora voy a cerrar todo e irme a la cama. Te aconsejo que hagas lo mismo.-

Víctor -Gracias, Guillermo. Buenas noches, hasta mañana.-

Guillermo -Buenas noches, hasta mañana.-

Víctor "No. I asked her but she didn't want to. She's had so many problems with Hugo that she doesn't want to get involved in another relationship so soon."

Guillermo "You like her, eh? She's a lovely girl. I've known her since she was a baby. Give her a bit of time, Victor. As far as I can see, she likes you a lot."

Victor "I'm not in a hurry. I can wait. Anyway, we go out a lot and we're great friends."

Guillermo "Very good, that's how it starts. Well, anyway, I'm going to close everything and go to bed. I advise you to do the same."

Victor "Thanks, Guillermo. Good night, see you tomorrow."

Guillermo "Good night, see you tomorrow

Lesson 29. Giving orders with 'The Imperative'. Dar órdenes con el imperativo.

The Spanish language has a special way of telling someone what to do. It's called the 'Imperative' or 'the command tense'. The same exists in English when we say:

"Look!", "Listen! Come here!

In the Spanish language, however, it's used far more frequently. Throughout the first few chapters of the book there have been a number of incidences in which 'the imperative' or 'commands' have been used in conversation. Here are some examples from the story. Did you notice them?

Victor says to the talkative woman: "<u>Disfruta</u> de tus vacaciones." = <u>Enjoy</u> your holidays.

Eliana says to Victor: "<u>Mira,</u> tengo que cenar." = <u>Look</u>, I've got to have dinner.

These examples are of the imperative used in the **TÚ form**. That means they are commands between friends.

Making these commands is easy!

How I do it?

When used in the positive, like "Look!", "Listen!", "Speak!" all you need to do is drop the "S" off the end of your conjugated verb.

Example: *To say, "**You speak**." you would say: "HABLAS".*

*To say, "**Speak!**" you simply say "¡HABLA!"*

*To say, "**You listen**." you would say: "ESCUCHAS".*

*To say, "**Listen!**" you would just say: "¡ESCUCHA!"*

You will also notice that the command is used in the **USTED form** (the polite YOU) in the story. Making the USTED command is different but just as easy. You simply change the ending from **A to E** or from **E to A**.

Example:

*To say "**You speak**." you would say: "(Usted) HABLA"*

*To say "**Speak!**" you just say: "¡HABLE (usted)!"*

*To say "**You listen**" you would say: "(Usted) ESCUCHA".*

*To say "**Listen!**" you just say: "¡ESCUCHE (usted)!"*

¡Ahora te toca a ti!

How would you say to a friend:

1, Look! (mirar)…………………...

2, Listen! (escuchar) ………………...

3, Eat! (comer) ....

4, Drink! (beber) ....

5, Work! (trabajar) ....

Then, how would you say the same to someone who wasn't your friend, using "usted"?

....

....

....

....

....

Capítulo 29

Víctor salió del restaurante y empezó a andar hacia su casa. La noche le había ido bien aparte del problema con Hugo. Víctor no sabía qué hacer con él. Antes, pensaba que sus amenazas eran nada más que palabras sueltas, pero ahora, dudaba que fuera a dejarlo en paz. Mientras andaba pensaba en las opciones que tenía. De repente, de detrás de un camión aparcado apareció Hugo. Ya no estaba con sus amigos y parecía bastante borracho.

Víctor se paró en seco. Pensó en echar a correr pero antes de tener la opción de hacerlo Hugo saltó encima de él y empezó a pegarlo salvajemente. Víctor luchó contra la fuerza de Hugo pero el chico era mucho más grande y fuerte que él y encima, parecía que el alcohol lo había dejado fuera de control.

Los golpes de Hugo le dolían mucho y se sentía bastante mareado. La única cosa que podía hacer era dejarse caer al suelo e intentar protegerse contra los puñetazos que le caían uno tras otro.

La última cosa de la que se dio cuenta fue un golpe fuerte contra su brazo izquierdo seguido por un terrible dolor. Luego perdió la consciencia y todo se volvió negro. Víctor no supo nada más hasta que unas voces familiares lo despertaron de sus sueños.

Chapter 29

Victor left the restaurant and started to walk home. The night had gone well, apart from the problem with Hugo. Victor didn't know what to do with him. Before, he'd thought that his threats were nothing more than just words, but now, he doubted that he was going to leave him in peace. Whilst he was walking he thought about the options he had. Suddenly, from behind a lorry Hugo appeared. He wasn't with his friends now and he looked quite drunk.

Victor froze. He thought about making a run for it but before he had the option of doing so Hugo jumped on top of him and started to savagely hit him. Victor fought against Hugo's strength but the boy was much bigger and stronger than he was and worse still, it seemed as though the alcohol had left him out of control.

Hugo's blows hurt a lot and he felt quite dizzy. The only thing that he could do was to let himself fall to the ground and try to protect himself against the punches that were raining down one after the other.

The last thing that he was aware of was a strong blow against his left arm followed by a terrible pain. Then, he lost consciousness and everything went dark. Victor didn't know any more until some familiar voices woke him from his dreams.

Lesson 30. Buying goods.

In chapter 23 we saw how Victor went shopping in a large hypermarket. Even if you always shop in supermarkets in your Spanish speaking country, there will be times when you have to buy something from a person working at a counter.

Or maybe you like to buy your vegetables fresh from the markets. Whatever the case, it's valuable to have a wide range of vocabulary ready for these occasions.

In markets.

Whilst shopping in markets, if you want to ask how much something is, then all you do is say:

¿A cuánto están los melocotones? (How much are the peaches?)

or

¿A cuánto está la sandía? (How much is the watermelon?)

Saying "I want."

Most English speaking students will have been taught to be very polite when asking for things. We tend to say things like: "Could I have?", "May I have" etc. We also liberally lace each sentence with, "Please" and "Thank you".

Certainly, Spanish speakers from Spain tend to be more direct. They often use:

Quería un..... (literally, "I was wanting a....")

Most Spanish students learn "**quiero/I want**" or even, "**quisiera/I would like**"

However, typically neither are used as much as **Quería**.

The very common Spanish ways to request something are:

¿Me da....?	*Can you give me?*
¿Me pone...?	*Can you put me?*
Póngame.....	*Put me....*

- **Tip.** If you are in Spain don't be tempted to say, "**Sí, por favor**." after every question about what you want.

Spanish people tend to say one, "Gracias", at the end of being served.

Some even find it irritating that we use so many' pleases' and 'thank yous'!

Once you have everything you can ask:

"¿Cuánto es todo?" (How much is everything?)

Or the shop or stall keeper might ask:

"¿Eso es todo?" (Is that all?)

and you can reply:

"Sí, eso es todo." (Yes, that´s all.)

and then, of course...

¡Gracias!

HACER LA COMPRA / DOING THE SHOPPING.

Quiero..., por favor.	*I want…., please.*
¿Me da...?	*Can you give me...?*
¿Me pone...?	*Can you "put me"…?*
¿Tiene…?	*Do you have…?*
¿Cuánto cuesta...?	*How much does ... cost?*
¿Cuánto cuesta?	*How much is it?*
¿Cuánto cuestan?	*How much are <u>they</u>?*
Un paquete de...	*A packet of…*
Un sobre de...	*A sachet of…*
Una caja de...	*A box of…*
Una lata de...	*A tin of…*
Medio kilo de...	*Half a kilo of…*
Un cuarto de kilo de...	*Quarter of a kilo of…*
Gramos	*Grams*

¿Algo más? *Anything else?* ---- **No, nada más, gracias.** *No, that´s all, thanks.*

Open= **abierto/a**   Broken= **roto/a**   Damaged= **Dañado/a**

A replacement= **Un recambio.**   A refund/ Return = **Una devolución.**

Discount = **Un descuento.**   An offer = **Una oferta.**

Handy sentences:

I'd like a refund, please. → **Quería una devolución, por favor.**

Can I have another one? → **¿Me puede dar otro? Éste está**

This one is damaged **dañado.**

Do you have any more? → **¿Tiene más?**

Could you give me more bags, please? → **¿Puede darme más bolsas?**

I haven't brought enough money! → **¡No he traído suficiente dinero!**

Can you take some things off, please? → **¿Podría quitar algunas cosas, por favor?**

Excuse me, I think this is incorrect → **Perdone, creo que esto es incorrecto.**

I think I've been overcharged. → **Creo que me han cobrado de más.**

Are you open tomorrow? → **¿Abren mañana?**

What time do you open/close? → **¿A qué hora abren/ cierran?**

To pay in cash. → **Pagar en efectivo.**

To pay with card. → **Pagar con tarjeta.**

Ahora te toca.

Translate the following sentences:

1, Can you give me a kilo of potatoes, please?..

....

2, How much are the grapes? ....

3, I want to pay in cash. ....

4, How much does this cost? ....

5, No, that's all thanks. ....

Capítulo 30

Eliana -Víctor ¿me oyes? ¿Me puedes escuchar?-

Alfredo -Déjalo, Eliana. Lo ha pasado muy mal. Necesita dormir para recuperarse.-

Eliana -Y ¿si no se despierta? Nunca me lo perdonaría.-

Víctor abrió los ojos y vio la cara de preocupación de Eliana mirándolo. La luz le hacía daño a los ojos y pestañeó tres o cuatro veces.

Eliana -Oh, ¡Dios mío! Estás despierto, Víctor. ¡Gracias a Dios! Me has tenido tan preocupada.-

Mientras hablaba, Eliana lloraba y le besaba la cara a Víctor.

Alfredo -Víctor. ¿Cómo estás, hombre? Me alegro de verte despierto. Nos has tenido preocupadísimos.-

Víctor -Pero, ¿dónde estoy? ¿Qué ha pasado?-

Eliana -¿No te acuerdas? Hugo te atacó y te dejó inconsciente en la calle. Te rompió el brazo, Víctor. Lo siento mucho. Sé que todo eso ha sido mi culpa. Nunca debí haberte involucrado en este lío.-

Víctor -No pasa nada, Eliana. Ese chico está loco. ¿Dónde está ahora?-

Alfredo -Está detenido en la comisaría. Mientras te estaba pegando, pasó un coche patrulla de la policía y lo detuvieron. Has pasado la noche en el hospital, Víctor. Los médicos dicen que estás bien. Tienes el brazo roto pero está arreglado y te han puesto una escayola.-

Víctor -¿Y cuánto tiempo tengo que estar en el hospital?-

Eliana -Dicen que quieren hacer unas pruebas para ver si tienes una concusión,

Chapter 30

Eliana "Victor, do you hear me? Can you hear me?"

Alfredo "Leave him Eliana. He's had a really bad time. He needs to sleep to recover.

Eliana "And what if he doesn't wake up? I'd never forgive myself."

Victor opened his eyes and saw Eliana's worried face looking at him. The light hurt his eyes and he blinked three or four times.

Eliana "Oh, my God! You're awake, Victor. Thank God! You've had me so worried."

Whilst she talked, Eliana was crying and kissing Victor's face.

Alfredo "Victor. How are you, man? I'm happy to see you awake. You've had us really worried."

Victor "But, where am I? What's happened?"

Eliana "Don't you remember? Hugo attacked you and left you unconscious in the street. He broke your arm, Victor. I'm really sorry. I know all this has been my fault. I should have never got you involved in this mess."

Victor "Don't worry, Eliana. That lad is mad. Where is he now?"

Alfredo "He's being detained in the police station. Whilst he was hitting you a patrol car went by and they arrested him. You've spent the night in the hospital, Victor. The doctors say that you are fine. You've got a broken arm but it's fixed and they've put a cast on it."

Victor "And how long have I got to be in hospital?"

Eliana "They say that they want to do some tests to see if you have concussion,

pero si todo está bien, puedes salir hoy mismo.-

Víctor   -¡Mi trabajo! Tengo que trabajar esta noche. Tengo que hablar con Guillermo.-

Alfredo   -No te preocupes, Víctor. Ya lo sabe todo. Dice que el trabajo estará allí para cuando estés listo para empezar de nuevo. Mientras tanto, te quedas con nosotros hasta que te quiten la escayola. Todo esto ha ocurrido por nosotros y por no haber hecho nada antes con ese imbécil de Hugo.-

Eliana   -Espero que no te moleste pero hemos llamado a tus padres para decírselo. Ellos saben que estás bien pero los dos han querido venir directamente. Llegan dentro de un par de horas. Mi padre los recoge del aeropuerto.-

Víctor   -¡Vaya lío! Nunca pensé que Hugo haría algo semejante.-

Eliana   -¡Ni yo! Por eso me siento tan culpable.-

Víctor   -No es tu culpa, Eliana. No tienes por qué sentirlo. Y la policía, ¿qué dice?-

Alfredo   -Un agente de policía espera fuera. Quiere hablar contigo para luego empezar con la denuncia. Según él, ésta no es la primera vez que Hugo ha sido violento. Esta vez podría significar la cárcel.-

En ese momento entró una enfermera y los echó de la habitación. Decía que iba a venir el médico y que tenían que hacer unas pruebas antes de darlo de alta. Eliana y Alfredo salieron de allí y al salir, Alfredo explicó que salía para el aeropuerto de Madrid a por los padres de Víctor y que a lo mejor los vería en casa.

but if everything is okay, you can get out today."

Victor   "My job! I have to work tonight. I have to talk to Guillermo."

Alfredo   "Don't worry, Victor. He already knows everything. He says your job will be there for when you're ready to start again. In the meantime, you'll stay with us until they take off your cast. This has all happened because of us and for not having done anything earlier with that imbecile, Hugo."

Eliana   "I hope you don't mind but we've called your parents to tell them. They know that you're okay but they both wanted to come straight away. They'll arrive in a couple of hours. My father is picking them up from the airport."

Victor   "What a mess! I never thought that Hugo would do something like that."

Eliana   "Me neither. That's why I feel so guilty."

Victor   "It's not your fault, Eliana. You shouldn't feel guilty. And the police, what do they say?"

Alfredo   "A police officer is waiting outside. He wants to talk to so they can start to prosecute. According to him, this isn't the first time that Hugo has been violent. This time it could mean prison."

In that moment a nurse came in and sent them from the room. She told them that the doctor was going to come and that they had to do some test before sending him home. Eliana and Alfredo left and as they went out, Alfredo explained that he was leaving for Madrid airport for Victor's parents and that he would probably see them at home.

Lesson 31. False Friends.

Although many English words are very close to their Spanish equivalent, every now and again, students of Spanish stumble across words that seem to be the same as English and discover to their horror that they mean something totally different.

Here are some of the most common mistakes made.

Nervioso: This can mean 'nervous' but mostly, in Spanish it means agitated or upset. It can also mean excited.

Ejemplo

Ese chico me pone muy nervioso. = That boy gets me very upset / agitated.

Let's look at some more common words.

Realizar: This means to achieve or accomplish something.

Ejemplo

He realizado mi sueño. = I've accomplished my dream.

To say realise in Spanish you use the verb Darse + Cuenta

Ejemplo

Me he dado cuenta de que hoy es su cumpleaños. = I've realised that it's his birthday today.

Asistir: This actually means to Attend and is followed by the preposition A. (Prepositions are the little words that are the glue that joins sentences together)

Ejemplo

Asisto a una reunión de trabajo cada viernes. = I attend a works meeting each Friday.

To say assist in Spanish, you actually use: Ayudar or Atender

Ejemplo

Ayudo con las tareas de casa. = I help with the housework.

¿Le puedo atender? = Can I help/assist you?

Estar constipado: Despite what it looks like, this verb simply means to have a cold.
Ejemplo

Hoy estoy constipado. = Today I have a cold.

To say: Constipated you use Estar estreñido.

Ejemplo
Últimamente he comido mucho queso y ahora estoy estreñido. = Lately I've eaten a lot of cheese and now I'm constipated.

Molestar: This isn't anywhere as strong in Spanish and just means to bother. It's used as an impersonal verb like Gustar.

Ejemplo
¿Sabes?, me molesta mucho tu manera de hablarme. = Do you know what? Your way of talking to me bothers me a lot.

To say, Molest in Spanish you use Acosar sexualmente.

ejemplo
El hombre me ha acosado sexualmente. = The man has molested me.

Note: Let's hope that you'll never have to use this expression. Especially if you're a man!

Acostarse: This is the verb used to say "To go to bed" and has nothing to do with being accosted.

Ejemplo
Pues, creo que me voy a acostar, estoy agotado. = Well, I think I'm going to bed. I'm wiped out.

To say Accosted you can use abordar.
Ejemplo

Un mendigo me abordó en la calle, pidiendo dinero. = A tramp accosted me in the street asking for money.

Note: To be accosted generally means to be greeted in a bold fashion, but it can also mean to be solicited by a prostitute!

Pretender: This verb means to aspire or to try and doesn't mean to pretend. We use the same meaning when we talk about "pretenders to the throne". Basically, someone trying to become king.

ejemplo

¿Qué pretendes decirme con eso? = What are you trying to say with that?

To say, Pretend, you use Fingir.

Ejemplo

Esa persona siempre finge que no nos ve. = That person always pretends not to see us.

Recordar: Despite what it looks like, this verb actually means to remember. It's slightly irregular and the O becomes UE.

Ejemplo
No recuerdo si cerré la puerta o no. = I can't remember if I closed the door or not.

To say Record in Spanish, you use Grabar.

Ejemplo

He grabado toda la serie de Aída. = I've recorded the whole series of Aida.

Remover: In Spain this doesn't mean to remove, but rather, to stir, for example, to stir food in a pan.

Ejemplo

Mientras preparo las paredes mi marido remueve la pintura para que sea de un solo color. = Whilst I prepare the walls my husband stirs the paint so that it's one colour.

To say Remove in Spanish, you use Quitar.

Ejemplo
He quitado la alfombra del salón. = I've taken the rug out of the living room.

Éxito: *This doesn't mean Exit, but rather Success.*
Ejemplo

Últimamente, la mujer ha tenido mucho éxito. = Lately, the woman has had a lot of success.

To say Exit in Spanish, you use Salida.

Ejemplo
Perdone. ¿Dónde está la salida más cercana? = Excuse me. Where is the nearest exit?

Crimen: Rather than any kind of crime, this means serious crime, like murder.

Ejemplo

Hitler cometió muchos crímenes. = Hitler committed many serious crimes.

To say Crime you use Delito.

Ejemplo

El joven ha cometido varios delitos. = The youth has committed various petty crimes.

Sensible: This is not sensible, but rather, Sensitive.

Ejemplo

Es un chico muy sensible. = He's a very sensitive boy.

To say, sensible in Spanish, you use Sensato.

Para ser una chica joven es bastante sensata. = For being a young girl she's quite sensible.

Embarazada: This means pregnant, not embarrassed.

Ejemplo

¡Por fin! Mi mujer está embarazada. = At last, my wife is pregnant!

To say, "I'm embarrassed" you say:

Tengo vergüenza. = Literally: I have shame.

Ahora te toca.

Translate the sentences:

1, I'm going to remove the book. (libro) ....

2, Can you stir the soup, please? (la sopa) ....

3, He is sensible but I am sensitive. ....

4, I'm looking for the exit. (buscar) ....

5, I want to record the concert. ....

6, I attend a Spanish class. ....

7, We assist an old lady. (mujer mayor) ....

8, It's a real bother! ....

Capítulo 31

A Víctor lo sometían a una serie de pruebas y resultó que no tenía una concusión y que podía irse a casa.

Médico   -Bueno, chaval. Parece que ese chico te ha dado una buena paliza. Sin embargo, aparte del brazo roto, no tienes nada grave. Y créeme, podría haber sido mucho peor.

Según el agente de policía que te espera afuera, el chico ese casi mató a otro cuando tenía catorce años. Afortunadamente tú solamente tienes un moratón impresionante en el ojo derecho que va a durar unos días y sin duda, tendrás unos dolores, pero eso se te pasará. Tendrás que volver en una semana para que veamos si el brazo se ha puesto bien pero a partir de ahora mismo, puedes irte para casa.-

Víctor   -Muchísimas gracias. Intentaré no tener que volver pronto.-

Médico   -Eso espero. Cuídate, Víctor. Adiós.-

El médico y la enfermera salieron de la habitación y unos segundos después, entró el policía.

Agente   -Hola, buenos días. Soy el agente Morales. Sólo quiero saber si usted está conforme con denunciar al chico que le atacó anoche-

Víctor   -Si lo denuncio, ¿qué le pasará?-

Agente   -Eso no se lo puedo decir. Todo quedará en las manos del juez. Sin embargo, le recomiendo que lo haga ya que el chico tiene una historia de violencia y durante su entrevista él no mostraba ninguna señal de remordimientos. Una vez denunciado, lo podremos mantener encarcelado hasta el día de su juicio y creo que para usted, ésta es la mejor opción.-

Chapter 31

They gave Victor a series of tests and it turned out that he didn't have concussion and he could go home.

Doctor   "Well, lad. It seems that that guy has given you a good going over. However, apart from the broken arm, you don't have anything serious. And believe me, it could have been much worse.

According to the policeman that's waiting outside, that guy nearly killed someone when he was fourteen. Fortunately you only have an impressive bruise on your right eye that's going to last a few days and, without doubt, you'll suffer from some pain, but that will pass. You'll have to come back in a week so that we can see if the arm has set well but as of right now you can go home."

Victor   "Thanks so much. I'll try not to have to come back soon."

Doctor   "I hope so. Take care, Victor. Goodbye."

The doctor and the nurse left the room and a few seconds later the policeman came in.

Officer   "Hello, good morning. I'm officer Morales. I just want to know if you are okay with charging the boy who attacked you last night."

Victor   "If I report him, what will happen to him?"

Officer   "That I can't tell you. It all rests in the hands of the judge. However, I recommend that you do it given that the lad has a history of violence and that, during his interview he didn't show any signs of regret. Once reported, we can keep him in the cells until his court appearance and I think that, for you, this is the best option."

Víctor -Vale, pues, lo hago por el bien de todos. ¿Qué tengo que hacer?-

Morales le explicó a Víctor el proceso de la denuncia y en cuestión de veinte minutos todo estaba hecho. Mientras salía el policía, entró una enfermera y le confirmó que el médico le había dado de alta y que podía salir en cuanto quisiera. Víctor se vistió y notó las manchas de sangre que había en su ropa. La memoria del ataque le vino de golpe y se sentía muy afortunado de que no hubiese sido peor. En el pasillo fuera de la habitación lo esperaba Eliana. Todavía parecía bastante preocupada.

Eliana -¿Ya, Víctor? ¿Te han dado el alta?-

Víctor -Sí, Eliana. Dicen que puedo irme ya.-

Eliana -¡Qué alivio, Víctor! No sabes lo que pasaba por mi mente durante toda la noche. Los del hospital no nos daban nada de información, solamente decían que te atendían y que estabas cómodo.-

Víctor -Bueno, aparte de sentirme un poco avergonzado por no haber podido defenderme contra ese loco, estoy bien.-

Eliana -Que tú no tienes porqué sentir nada, Víctor. Hugo es un animal, está fuera de control. Y yo debería haber hecho algo antes. Si lo hubiera denunciado antes, esto nunca habría ocurrido. Lo siento mucho, Víctor. Tengo toda la culpa.-

Víctor -No te culpes, Eliana. Tampoco sabías que iba a hacer eso. Nadie tiene la culpa, menos Hugo. Ahora, ¿me invitas a un café? Tengo que comer algo urgentemente.-

Eliana -¡Por supuesto! Aquí mismo hay una cafetería.-

Los dos entraron en la cafetería y pidieron un café y un croissant a la plancha.

Víctor "Okay, then I'll do it for the good of everyone. What do I have to do?"

Morales explained the process of the prosecution to Victor and in twenty minutes or so everything was done. Whilst the policeman was leaving, a nurse came in and confirmed that the doctor had given the okay and that he could leave when he liked. Victor got dressed and saw the blood stains that were on his clothing. The memory of the attack came rushing back and he felt lucky that it hadn't been worse. In the corridor, outside of the room, Eliana was waiting for him. She still seemed very worried.

Eliana "That's it, Victor? They've let you leave?"

Victor "Yes, Eliana. They say that I can go now."

Eliana "What a relief, Victor! You don't know what went through my mind the whole night. The people at the hospital wouldn't give us any information, they just said that they were taking care of you and that you were comfortable."

Victor "Well, apart from feeling a bit embarrassed for not having been able to defend myself against that madman, I'm fine."

Eliana "You don't need to feel anything, Victor. Hugo is an animal, he's out of control. And I should have done something earlier. If I'd reported him beforehand, this would never have happened. I'm really sorry, Victor. It's all my fault."

Victor "Don't blame yourself, Eliana. You didn't know he was going to do that either. No one is to blame, apart from Hugo. Now, are you going to buy me a coffee? I have to eat something urgently."

Eliana "Of course! There's a café right here."

They both go in to the cafe and order a coffee and a toasted croissant.

Eliana -¿Y cómo te sientes ahora? ¿Qué tal el brazo? ¿Te duele?-

Víctor -Doler, no me duele. Pero tengo una molestia en la parte superior.-

Eliana -¡Ay Pobrecito! No te preocupes, te cuido yo.-

Víctor -Bueno, sólo por eso me alegro de que me haya pasado. Ja ja.-

Eliana -No seas tonto, Víctor. Pero sí, mi padre ha dicho que te quedes en nuestra casa hasta que te pongas mejor. Con ese brazo no puedes vivir solo.-

Víctor sabía que sí, se podría apañar bien con un brazo, pero no pensaba decirlo. La idea de vivir en la misma casa que Eliana le venía muy bien. Luego, sin esperarlo, Eliana lo cogió de la mano, lo miró a los ojos y sonrió.

Eliana -Víctor. Hace unos días me pediste que saliera contigo. Te dije que no, porque no quería meterte en problemas con Hugo. Sabía que si fuéramos novios, se pondría aún más pesado. Ahora sé que eso fue un error. La verdad es que te quiero mucho, Víctor. Te he querido desde el principio y me di cuenta de eso anoche cuando pensaba que te iba a perder para siempre. Yo no sé si después de todo, quieres salir conmigo todavía, pero si te parece bien, me encantaría ser tu novia.-

Víctor no podía creer su suerte. También había querido a Eliana desde hacía mucho tiempo. Sin embargo, se le ocurrió vacilarla un poco antes de decirle la verdad.

Víctor -Eliana, de verdad, no sé qué decirte. Después de todos estos problemas creo que debería pensarlo bien. Es que salir contigo podría ser demasiado peligroso.-

Eliana parecía un poco sorprendida. Esquivó su mirada y miró al suelo mientras hablaba.

Eliana "And how do you feel now? How's the arm? Does it hurt?"

Victor "It's not really hurting me. But it's a bit sore at the top."

Eliana "Oh, you poor thing! Don't worry, I'll take care of you."

Victor "Well, just for that I'm happy that it's happened. Haha."

Eliana "Don't be silly, Victor. But anyway, my father has said that you can stay at our house until you get better. With this arm, you can't live alone."

Victor knew that he could manage well enough with one arm, but he wasn't going to say that. The idea of living in the same house as Eliana was very attractive. Then, unexpectedly, Eliana took his hand, looked at him in the eyes and smiled.

Eliana "Victor. Some days ago you asked me if I'd go out with you. I said no, because I didn't want to get you into problems with Hugo. I knew that if we were boyfriend and girlfriend he'd become even worse. Now, I know that I was wrong. The truth is that I love you a lot. I've loved you from start and I realised that last might when I thought that I was going to lose you forever. I don't know if, after all this, you still want to go out with me, but if it seems okay to you, I'd love to be your girlfriend."

Victor couldn't believe his luck. He'd been in love with Eliana for a long time, too. However, he had the idea of having a bit of fun before telling her the truth.

Victor "Eliana, I really don't know what to tell you. After all these problems I think that I should think about it properly. It's just that going out with you could be too dangerous."

Eliana seemed a little bit shocked. She avoided his gaze and looked at the floor whilst he talked.

Eliana -Te entiendo, Víctor. No pasa nada. Sé que has tenido un susto de la leche y no es sorprendente que quieras un poco de tiempo para pensarlo bien.-

Eliana tenía la cara tan penosa que Víctor no pudo seguir con la broma. Tenía que decirle la verdad.

Víctor -Eliana. ¡Que estoy de broma! Claro que sí. Quiero salir contigo más que nada en el mundo. Eso es lo que he querido desde el principio. Te quiero un montón.-

Eliana -¡Víctor! ¡Qué cruel! No sé si quiero pegarte o besarte.-

Víctor -Será mejor que me beses, Eliana. Luego me puedes pegar.-

Eliana lo sonrió y luego se le acercó a la cara. Después de un sólo momento que parecía durar para siempre, se besaron por primera vez. A pesar de sus heridas y del susto de la noche anterior, de repente Víctor notaba una sensación de bienestar que se iba apoderando de todo su cuerpo. Eliana era la chica más bonita del mundo y en ese momento él supo que, sin duda, era la única para él.

Eliana "I understand, Victor. Don't worry. I know that you've had a terrible shock and it's not suprising that you want a little bit of time to think about it."

Eliana looked so sad that Victor couldn't continue with the joke. He had to tell her the truth.

Victor "Eliana. I'm just joking! Yes, of course. I want to go out with you more than anything in the world. That's what I've wanted from the start. I love you so much."

Eliana "Victor! How cruel! I don't know if I want to hit you or kiss you."

Victor "Better that you kiss me, Eliana. Then you can hit me."

Eliana smiled at him and then came close to his face. Then, after a moment that seemed to last forever, they kissed for the first time. In spite of his wounds and the shock from the night before, Victor suddenly noticed a feeling of wellbeing taking over his entire body. Eliana was the most beautiful girl in the world and right at that moment, he knew that, without doubt, she was the only girl for him.

Lesson 32. AI and DEL. The contractions.

How are you doing up to now? Are you enjoying the story?

By this point you must be really getting to grips with basic Spanish structures. Well done to you!

AL and DEL are two very important, although fairly simple joining words (prepositions) that are used very often in Spanish sentences.

Getting them right can make your spoken and written Spanish sound great!

Getting them wrong can cause TOTAL CONFUSION.

AL

"**A**" in Spanish means "TO" and is used liberally throughout the Spanish language.

Although **A** can be linked with most words without consequence, there is one situation in which a little rule must be followed.

When **A**= TO joins up with **EL** = THE, the result, "A EL" is not allowed.

Probably this is because it sounds clumsy to pronounce.

Instead what happens is that the "E" is dropped and the "A" joins directly with the "L" to make "AL" which translates as "TO THE".

Note: This only happens when A and EL are joined. When we link A with LA, LOS, or LAS, nothing changes.

IR A = To go to

IR often has **A** bolted on to it when talking about present or future events.

It breaks down like this: (Even though you probably know it by heart now!)

yo **voy a**	nosotros **vamos a**
tú **vas a**	vosotros **vais a**
él/ella **va a**	ellos/ellas **van a**

Let's look at some sentences using this structure.

Vamos AL cine. = We are going to the cinema.

Ellos van AL centro = They are going to the town centre.

Vais AL parque = You all are going to the park.

However, when feminine or plural destinations are used nothing changes:

Vamos A LA playa. = We're going to the beach.

¿Vas A LAS dunas? = Are you going to the dunes?

Él va A LOS estadios. = He's going to the stadiums.

Have you noticed that it's only when A and EL come together that they join up into AL?

Very Interesting Note:

When using IR A to talk about the future, you can form the sentence:

GOING TO GO.

All you have to do is this:

Voy a ir a.... = I'm going to go to...

Mañana, voy a ir al gimnasio. = Tomorrow I'm going to go to the gym.

¿Vas a ir a la fiesta, tú? = Are you going to go to the party?

Vamos a ir a la casa de mis padres. = We are going to go to my parents house.

Let's take a look at how these AL works with Trabajar.

The verb TO WORK is **TRABAJAR**.

Thus, if you want to say:

I work

then you simply say:

(yo) TRABAJO

"Trabajo" also means:

I AM WORKING

Your place of work is:

"EL TRABAJO"

This is a naming word, that's why it has the "EL" at the beginning.

Therefore, If you want to say:

"I'm going to my place of work."

You say:

(Me) Voy AL trabajo.

and if you want to say:

"I'm going to work." (To do some work)

you say:

(Me) Voy a trabajar.

Your place of work is always "El Trabajo" yet, you can go to do some work in any place.

Ejemplo.

Mañana, voy a trabajar en el jardín. = Tomorrow, I'm going to work in the garden.

Voy a trabajar con mi hermana en su casa. = I'm going to work with my brother in his house.

JUGAR

Another verb that uses the preposition (Glue word) A is **JUGAR** = To play.

This is how it breaks down

*yo **juego a***	*nosotros **jugamos a***
*tú **juegas a***	*vosotros **jugáis a***
*él/ella **juega a***	*ellos/ellas **juegan a***

With this verb, as with all of them, the same rule applies when A joins with EL.

As it happens, most games and sports tend to be masculine singular, thus the AL rule is used most frequently with this verb.

ejemplo.

Juego al golf.

Juego al fútbol.

Juego al baloncesto (basketball)

DEL

When "DE" is joined to "EL" in Spanish, the same thing happens as with AL. The two join together to make DEL.

Let's look at the verb **VENIR** = To come.

This is how it breaks down.

yo **vengo**	nosotros **venimos**
tú **vienes**	vosotros **venís**
él/ella **viene**	ellos/ellas **vienen**

Venir normally has the preposition DE, which kind of makes sense in English too. We also say, "To come from".

Here are some examples:

Vengo del sur. = I'm (coming) from the south.

Vienen del chalet de sus padres. = They are coming from their parents' villa.

¿Venís del supermercado? = Are you coming from the supermarket?

Clearly, when DE is joined to LOS/LAS/LA then nothing changes.

Él viene de la casa de su novia. = He is coming from his girlfriend's house.

Vienen de las discotecas. = They are coming from the nightclubs.

DEPENDER

Another verb that uses DE is "depender".

In English we say:

It depends ON...

In Spanish they say:

Depende DE... (It depends OF)

Ejemplo:

No sé si voy mañana. Depende del tiempo. = I don't know if I'm going tomorrow. It depends on the weather.

Mi felicidad depende de muchas cosas. = My happiness depends on many things.

Todo depende de ti. = It all depends on you.

Beware:

*Depende **EN**...is prohibited!!*

Ahora te toca. Translate the following story.

My Hobbies.

I'm a very active person. I do many sports. I play football, basketball and rugby.

On Saturdays I go to to the park to play football with my friends. At twelve, I come from the park and I go to the sports centre. There, I play basketball for a couple of hours.

On Sundays I normally go to play rugby in the morning. It depends on the weather. If not, a friend comes to my house and we play on the Playstation during the morning.

On Sunday afternoons, I don't play anything. I go to the pub and have a couple of beers with friends.

....
....
....
....
....
....
....
....
....

Key. Active = activo   Sports Centre = El Polideportivo

for (duration of time) = durante   If not = Si no   Playstation = La play(station)

Pub = el Pub (el bar)

Capítulo 32

Terminaron el desayuno y se fueron directamente a la casa de Eliana. Al llegar a la puerta se oyó que pitaba un coche. Los dos se giraron y vieron a Alfredo llegando con los padres de Víctor. Bajaron del coche y se acercaron a Víctor.

Padre -¡Víctor, hijo! ¿Qué tal estás? ¿En qué líos te has estado metiendo?-

Madre -¡Hijo mío! ¿Qué tal te encuentras? Vaya moratón que tienes en el ojo. ¿Te duele?-

Víctor -No, mamá. No me duele nada. Estoy bien. Sólo he experimentado un poco de la hospitalidad española. Ja ja.-

Alfredo -¿Y qué pasó con la denuncia? ¿Qué han hecho con el Hugo ése?-

Eliana -Se queda en la cárcel hasta el juico.-

Víctor -Y con un poco de suerte, se queda allí después también.-

Alfredo -Eso espero, hombre. Pues, ¿qué hacemos en la calle? ¡Que entremos a tomar algo! –

Todos entraron en casa donde Mercedes había preparado una comida magnífica. Después de la comida la madre de Víctor lo cogió de brazo y lo llevó a otro cuarto para hablar con él a solas.

Madre -Víctor. Qué susto nos has dado. Tu padre y yo pensamos que deberías venir para casa. Seguro que puedes coger un trabajo con la misma compañía. Lo dejaste bien con ellos.-

Víctor -No tienes porqué preocuparte, mamá. A pesar de lo que parece, estoy muy bien aquí. El problema con Hugo ya se ha arreglado. Lo más importante es que tengo

Chapter 32

They finished breakfast and went straight to Eliana's house. As they arrived at the door they heard a car honking its horn. They both turned and saw Alfredo arriving with Victor's parents. They got out of the car and came up to Victor.

Father "Victor, son! How are you? What sort have mess have you been getting yourself into?"

Mother "Son! How are you feeling? That's some bruise you've got on your eye. Are you in pain?"

Victor "No mum. It doesn't hurt at all. I'm fine. I've just been experiencing a little bit of Spanish hospitality. Haha."

Alfredo "And what's happened with the prosecution? What have they done with Hugo?"

Eliana "He's staying in prison until the court case."

Victor "And with a bit of luck, he'll stay there afterwards, too."

Alfredo I hope so, man. So, what are we doing in the street? Let's go in and have something to drink!"

Everyone goes in to the house where Mercedes had prepared a magnificent meal. After eating, Victor's mother grabbed his arm and took him to another room so they could talk alone.

Mother "Victor. What a shock you've given us. Your father and I think that you should come home. I'm sure you can get a job with the same company. You left things well with them."

Victor "You don't have to worry, mum. Despite what it may seem, I'm really fine here. The problem with Hugo is fixed now. The most important thing is that I've got

mi casa, mi trabajo y mi novia aquí. De verdad estoy muy contento, mamá.-

Madre -¿Novia, Víctor?-

Víctor -Sí. Eliana y yo somos novios.-

Madre -¿Cuándo ocurrió eso, Víctor?-

Víctor -Esta mañana, mamá. Estoy muy feliz. Eliana me ha gustado desde el principio.-

Madre -Pues, me alegro por ti, Víctor. Sólo queremos lo mejor para ti. Acuérdate que siempre que quieras, estaremos allí y siempre tendrás tu habitación. Pero también tienes que vivir tu vida y si esa vida tiene que estar aquí en España, pues que así sea.-

Víctor -Gracias, mamá. Bueno, deberíamos volver al salón. Van a pensar que estamos tramando algo.-

Los dos volvieron al salón y todos se sentaron a tomar un café. Mientras tomaban el café hablaban sobre lo ocurrido.

Mercedes -Bueno, le hemos dicho a Víctor que se quede con nosotros hasta que se ponga mejor del brazo. Todos nos sentimos muy culpables por lo que ha pasado.-

Madre -Os lo agradecemos mucho. Por lo menos sabemos que estará bien cuidado aquí.-

Alfredo -También está la cuestión del trabajo y el piso. He estado pensando sobre todo eso. Sé que sería imposible que trabajara Víctor de camarero por lo menos durante los próximos meses. Sin embargo, no quiere decir que no pueda trabajar. Así que, si quiere, hay un trabajo en la oficina. Será de hacer el papeleo y cosas así, pero por lo menos puede seguir trabajando y ganando un poco de dinero, y más importante, pagándome el alquiler. Ja ja. ¿Qué te parece, Víctor?-

my house, my job and my girlfriend here. I truly am very happy, mum."

Mother "Girlfriend, Victor?"

Victor "Yes. Eliana and I are going out together."

Mother "When did that happen, Victor?"

Victor "This morning, mum. I'm really happy. I've liked Eliana since the beginning."

Mother "Then, I'm happy for you, Victor. We just want the best for you. Remember that, whenever you want, we'll be there and you'll always have your room. But you've got to live your life too, and if that life has to be here in Spain, then so be it."

Victor "Thanks, mum. Well, we better return to the living room. They're going to think that we're plotting something."

They both returned to the living room and sat down to have a coffee. Whilst they drank their coffee they talked about what had happened.

Mercedes "So, we've said to Victor that he can stay with us until his arm gets better. We all feel very guilty for what's happened."

Mother "We're very grateful. At least we know that he'll be well looked after here."

Alfredo "There's also the question of work and the flat. I've been thinking about all that. I know that it would be impossible for Victor to work as a waiter for at least six months. However, that doesn't mean that he can't work. So, if he wants, there's a job at the office. It'll be paperwork and things like that, but at least he can continue to work and to earn a bit of money, and more importantly, pay me his rent. Haha. What do you think, Victor?"

Víctor -Me parece fantásticamente bien. ¡Eres muy amable, Alfredo! ¿Cuándo empiezo?-

Alfredo -Mañana por la mañana si quieres.-

Eliana -Venga, papá. Acaba de salir del hospital. Dale cuartelillo. El pobre debería tener, por lo menos, una semana de recuperación antes de empezar. ¿No te parece?-

Alfredo -Bueno, Eliana. Supongo que podría tener una semana para que se vaya ese moratón. No quiero que mis clientes piensen que doy empleo a gamberos. Ja ja.-

Eliana -Pues así se queda. Está semana no tengo estudios así que podemos pasar la semana con tus padres, si quieres, viendo los lugares de interés.-

Víctor -Qué buena idea, Eliana.-

Eliana -Y para que lo sepáis, mamá, papá, Víctor y yo ya somos novios. Víctor me pidió que saliéramos antes pero no quería por lo de Hugo y eso. Ahora que ya no está en medio de todo, le he dicho que sí.-

Alfredo -Bueno, Víctor. Tú no pierdes el tiempo, ¿eh? Ja ja. De todas las maneras, felicidades a vosotros dos.-

Mercedes -Me alegro por vosotros. Eres un buen chico, Víctor. Seguro que serás muy bueno para Eliana.-

Eliana -Joer, mamá. Y yo para él, ¿eh? Soy buena chica también ¿sabes?-

Mercedes -Tienes razón, Eliana. Entonces Víctor, ¡qué suerte tienes! Ja ja-

Pero Víctor ya lo sabía. Ya tenía todo: la chica más guapa del mundo, un buen trabajo nuevo, una familia nueva, su propia casa y para tener todo esto sólo le ha costado una buena paliza y un brazo roto. En su opinión,

Victor "That seems fantastic, Alfredo. Your very kind! When do I start?"

Alfredo "Tomorrow morning, if you want."

Eliana "Come on, dad. He's just come out of hospital. Give him a chance. The poor thing should have, at least, a week to recuperate before starting. Don't you think?"

Alfredo "Well, Eliana. I suppose he could have a week to let his bruise disappear. I don't want my clients thinking that I give jobs to trouble makers. Haha."

Eliana "Well that's sorted. This week I haven't got to study so we can spend the week with your parents, if you want, looking at some places of interest."

Victor "What a good idea, Eliana."

Eliana "And so that you know, mum, dad, Victor is my boyfriend now. Victor asked me out before but I didn't want to because of Hugo and that. Now that he's not in the middle of everything, I've said yes."

Alfredo "Well, Victor. You don't waste any time, do you? Haha. Anyway, congratulations to the pair of you."

Mercedes "I'm happy for you both. You're a good lad, Victor. I'm sure that you'll be good for Eliana."

Eliana "Goodness, mum. And me for him, eh? I'm a good girl, too, you know!"

Mercedes "You're right, Eliana. So, Victor, you lucky thing! Haha."

But Victor already knew it. Now he had everything: the most beautiful girl in the world, a great new job, a new family, his own house and, to get all of that, he just had to be beaten up and have his arm broken. In his opinion,

todo había valido la pena. Había venido a España para tener una aventura y eso es lo que había encontrado. Mientras escuchaba a su familia hablando animadamente entre sí, se pellizcó ligeramente en la pierna para asegurarse de que no estuviera soñando. Afortunadamente, le dolió suficiente para mostrarle que lo que tenía era verdaderamente suyo. Una vez seguro, empezó a sonreír como nunca en la vida.

it had all been worth it. He'd come to Spain to have an adventure and that was what he had found. Whilst he listened to his family talking happily to each other, he pinched himself lightly on the leg to be sure that he wasn't dreaming. Fortunately, it hurt enough to tell him that what he had was truly his. Now that he was sure, he began to smile like he'd never smiled before in his life.

¡Felicidades! How to move on from here.

Well done for having completed what has been a massive leap forward for your Spanish. We really hope that this has been an interesting learning experience for you.

Of course, there is so much more for you to know and we will be bringing you the next steps in the following books in this series. And, of course, Victor is sure to have many more thrilling adventures in the future.

Across the years we have learnt that learning is rarely a one time event and so, now that you've reached the end, probably the best place to start is right back at the beginning.

Now that you have a bigger picture in your mind and a greater understanding of the Spanish language you are sure to see many new things as you repeat the chapters again.

As we suggested at the beginning, to make it more challenging you can aim to translate from English to Spanish this time around.

Also, read out loud rather than in your head. Just this one small change is guaranteed to create a masssive improvement to your spoken Spanish.

If, however, you feel that you are ready to move on to something more challenging, then, do so. However, you can continue to listen to the audio book whilst you do other things, keeping everything fresh in your mind and reinforcing all that you have gained from having worked through this book.

Come and visit us at www.lightspeedspanish.co.uk or join us on our Facebook page. There you can put into practice all that you've learnt up to now in some lively discussions with interesting people.

Para terminar, we would like to say a big, GRACIAS, to you for choosing to improve your Spanish with us and we hope to be of service to you in the future.

Hasta pronto,

Gordon y Cynthia ☺

Appendix 1

Now for the 'Nitty Gritty'

One of the greatest challenges for students of the Spanish language has been in knowing how to **break down** Spanish verbs, or, as it is known, to **conjugate**. In fact, many people have given up learning Spanish because they couldn't get over what seemed like an impossible hurdle.

Yet, it really is quite simple once you've got a handle on how verbs work! Easy or not, we have found that many people have a terrible fear of the dreaded word:

GRAMMAR!

Perhaps this is because of their traumatic school days, maybe they had a horrible teacher or worse still, an incompetent teacher. However, the truth is that each of us use incredibly complex grammar every time we open our mouth to speak.

That means that **you are already an expert!** All that's missing is for you to learn the names of the structures you already use every day, with the greatest of ease.

What's so important about grammar anyway?

If you could imagine that language was a physical body then the words or vocabulary would make up the flesh or all the soft parts. The grammar, however, would be the skeleton or better put, the strength. For, just as everything hangs on the skeleton, your entire language hangs on the grammar you use.

Imagine a body without the bones! It would be a floppy mess. Likewise, Spanish without grammar can be messy too.

Don't believe anyone that tells you otherwise.

First things first.

The first things you should learn are what are called the personal pronouns or what you know as the:

I, you, he, she words.

They are the following:

Singular		Plural	
I	= Yo	We	= Nosotros/as
You	= Tú	You all	= Vosotros/as
He	= Él	They	= Ellos
She	= Ella	They	= Ellas
You	= Usted*	You all	= Ustedes*

Unlike English, the above words are not used every time that a Spanish person talks about themselves or someone else. The reason for that is because Spanish verb conjugation is quite different to English.

*Usted and Ustedes are the polite "You" in Spanish. In mainland Spain, they are used less and less these days. For beginners, it's okay to be aware that they exist without worrying too much about them for the moment.

However, if you will be using your Spanish in South America or in the USA, then you will need to pay attention to them from the beginning.

Note: The "Vosotros" form in the list above isn't normally used in Latin America. Instead they tend to use the "Ustedes" (you all) version for all groups whether they are talking informally or formally.

Action: Look as we compare a Spanish and English conjugation and see what differences and similarities you notice.

We'll use the verb TO EAT:

	English	_Spanish_
_I_	Eat	Como
You	Eat	Comes
He/She/You	Eats	Come
_We_	Eat	Comemos
You all	Eat	Coméis
They/You all	Eat	Comen

Did you notice that the English conjugation of the actual verb was the same each time except in He/She?

Yet, in Spanish, every person has their own special conjugation.

It's for this reason that, if you wanted to say: "I eat" in Spanish, you don't necessarily have to say "**Yo como**". You can just say "**Como**" and any Spanish speaking person would know that you were saying "I eat".

Of course, you can't do that in English, can you?

If you just said, "**eat**", people would wonder who you were talking about!

Recommendation. Even though the Spanish don't use **Yo, Tú, Él,** etc. as much as in English, for example, we recommend that to begin with you use them all the time, until you get to know them. After that, you can begin to use them as an emphasis, just as Spanish speakers do.

e.g. To a Spanish speaker, the sentence:

"Yo como mucho pescado."

sounds like this:

"I eat a lot of fish, me!"

However, without the **"Yo"**, it would be simply:

"I eat a lot of fish."

So remember: Once you've learned them off by heart, use them sparingly. ☺

Breaking down verbs or Conjugation.

And now let's look at how we break the verbs down and an easy way to remember the different endings.

As you probably noticed, when a Spanish verb is conjugated, each person is given their own ending and this helps to identify who it is we're talking about.

All we need to do is have a system that will ensure we remember what ending goes with what person.

And that's easy!

First let's look at the three different types of Spanish verbs that exist.

1. Verbs that end with **AR**

2. Verbs that end with **ER**

3. Verbs that end with **IR**

Some examples would be:

>Hablar   to Talk

>Comer   to Eat

>Vivir   to Live

The first thing to do when you break down a verb is to take it down to its stem. To do that all you do is just take off the *AR, ER, or IR.*

Using the three examples mentioned above, that would give us:

Habl

Com

Viv

Here comes the clever part. ☺

We choose the ending according to the person that we are talking about.

So, how do we know what ending to add?

To know how to do this, you only need to learn a few simple memory triggers.

These are:

I or Me = Yo.

Action. Take your finger and draw a big **O** on your chest. This lets you know that when you are talking about yourself in Spanish, your conjugated verb will (99% of the time) have an **O** on the end.

e.g.

I talk	Habl**O**
I eat	Com**O**
I live	Viv**O**

You (1 person) = Tú.

Action. When I'm talking to you, **remember that** you are one of my **friendSSSSS** and, because you are one of my **friendSSSSS,** I'm going to put an **S** on the end.

So, when you are talking to one person, you put an **S** on the end of the stem......

BUT WAIT A COTTON PICKING MINUTE!!

Before you add the **S** you must also **put the vowel back**. (On all except the YO/I.)

e.g.

You talk	Habla**S**
You eat	Come**S**

(**IR** verbs are a bit special, we'll explain that later.)

He/She/You formal = Él/Ella/Ustedes.

Action. When you're talking about He, She or You formal , well, they're not your friends any more, they're just He, She or You (not my friend)! So, you **DROP THE S** off, because they aren't your friends. (Or at least just for the sake of this exercise.)

e.g.

He/She/(You formal) talks   HablA

He/She/(You formal) eats   ComE

Note: In the English conjugation, this is the only one that changes. We ADD an S!! In Spanish we take it off!

We = Nosotros.

Action. Imagine that **we** are all covered in **MOSS**. And because we are all covered in **MOSS**, we are going to add **MOS** onto the end of the stem.

e.g.

We talk   HablaMOS

We eat   ComeMOS

You All = Vosotros.

Action. Imagine that **you all** are covered in **IS**. ☺ (Whatever that means! Some students add an extra letter to make it more memorable, lol.) And so, because you all are covered in **IS,** I'm going to add **IS** onto the end of the stem.

e.g.

You all talk	Habl**áiS**
You all eat	Com**éiS**

They/You all formal = Ellos/Ellas/Ustedes.

Action. Imagine that **they** are at the e**N**d of the conjugation and because they are at the e**N**d, we are going to put an **N** at the e**N**d of the stem.

e.g.

They talk	Habla**N**
They eat	Come**N**
You all eat	Come**N** (formal)

Now, run through this twice more. Do it until you can remember the ending for each person. Then, test yourself out.

Person		What ending?
I.	YO	?
YOU.	TÚ	?
HE/SHE/YOU FORMAL.	ÉL/ELLA/USTED	?
WE.	NOSOTROS	?
YOU ALL.	VOSOTROS	?
THEY/YOU ALL FORMAL.	ELLOS/ELLAS/USTEDES	?

The special IR verbs.

As we said, the **IR** verbs are special and they are special because they are **under-cover** verbs. They **pretend** to be **ER** verbs except *outside of the boot.*

"What the.......?" we hear you say.

Let's show you what we mean:

The Spanish Boot.

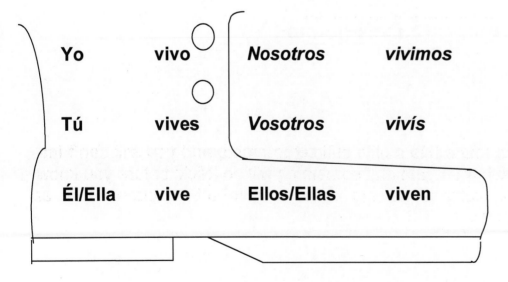

Yo	vivo	*Nosotros*	*vivimos*
Tú	vives	*Vosotros*	*vivís*
Él/Ella	vive	Ellos/Ellas	viven

All Spanish verbs are what we call "Boot verbs". That means that, no matter how irregular or weird they are, they will always behave perfectly normally outside of the boot.

Notice how the above **IR** verb pretends to be an **ER** verb except when it falls outside of the boot. Then, it goes back to normal.

This is the case for **ALL** Spanish verbs.

So, there we have the basic Spanish verb conjugation. Let's see how much you've retained in that fantastic mind of yours.

Test Yourself.

1. I eat. ....

2. They live. ....

3. We talk. ....

4. You live. ....

5. You all eat. ....

6. I drink beer. (Beber cerveza) ....

7. We listen to music. (Escuchar música) ....

8. They write letters. (Escribir cartas) ....

9. He makes bread. (Hacer pan) ....

10. She runs. (Correr) ....

The answers are below.

How did you do? If you've found this a little difficult to grasp, and you still can't imagine how it works, just review it again and something will go 'click' before you know it! You can also listen or watch us talking about this subject on our website at www.lightspeedspanish.co.uk

Search for the lesson:

Beginners Spanish Podcast 5 - Conjugating Spanish Verbs.

ANSWERS.

1. Yo como.

2. Ellos viven.

3. Nosotros hablamos.

4. Tú vives.

5. Vosotros coméis.

6. Yo bebo cerveza.

7. Nosotros escuchamos música.

8. Ellos escriben cartas.

9. Él hace pan.

10. Ella corre.

Answers to all the lessons.

Lesson 1.

1, *El perro.*
2, *La casa.*
3, *Las mesas.*
4, *Los chicos.*
5, *Un gato.*
6, *Una vaca.*
7, *Unas chaquetas.*
8, *Unos vasos.*
9, *Un gorro y una bufanda.*
10, *Unos bolsos y unos abrigos.*

Lesson 2.

1, *Los chicos*
2, *Las mesas*
3, *Las sillas*
4, *Las oficinas*
5, *Los manteles*
6, *Los móviles*
7, *Los platos*
8, *Los trenes*
9, *Las copas*
10, *Los portátiles*

Lesson 3.

Adjective	Ser	Estar
Feliz (happy)	*( )*	*(*)*
Confundido (confused)	*( )*	*(*)*
Rubio (blond)	*(*)*	*( )*
Duro (hard)	*(*)*	*( )*
Cansado (tired)	*( )*	*(*)*
Inglés (English)	*(*)*	*( )*

Lesson 4

1, La chica es alta y delgada.

2, El chico pequeño y tímido.

3, Los coches grandes, negros y azules.

4, Las mujeres altas y guapas.

5, Una silla ancha, marrón y cómoda.

Lesson 5

1, Se levanta.

2, Nos duchamos.

3, Se preparan un café.

4, Nos peinamos el pelo.

5, Me lavo/cepillo los dientes.

Lesson 6

1. Es MI coche. (my)

2. Son VUESTROS amigos. (your/vostros)

3. SU casa es grande. (their)

4. Son NUESTRAS manzanas. (our)

5. ¿ Éste es SU perro? (your/usted)

6. ¿Cuándo es TU cumpleaños? (your/tú)

7. SUS plátanos están verdes. (their)

8. Te presento a MIS hijos. (my)

9. Tú tienes NUESTRAS entradas. (our)

10. Éste es TU cuaderno (your/tu) y estos son MIS libros. (my)

Lesson 7

1, (Yo) Voy a España.

2, (Nosotros)Vamos a comer un sándwich.

3, (Ellos) Van a llegar pronto.

4, (Vosotros) Vais al banco.

5, (Tú) Vas a ser un profesor.

6, (Yo) Voy a comer patatas fritas.

7, (Él) Va a tomar un café.

8, (Ellos) Van a hablar.

9, (Ella) Va a la casa de su amigo/a.

10, (Nosotros) Vamos a la playa.

Lesson 8
1, He hablado con el hombre.
2, Tengo un coche rápido.
3,¿Has   comido?
4, ¿Tenéis un momento?
5, Han escrito un libro.
6, ¿Ha frito patatas fritas usted?
7, ¿Has visto mi coche?
8, He puesto el café en la mesa.
9, Hemos visto la televisión.
10, ¿Han bebido un té ustedes?

Lesson 9
*1. Los chicos **están** en la clase.*
*2. Yo **soy** profesor de matemáticas.*
*3. Vivo en Inglaterra pero **estoy** en Francia.*
*4. Mi padre **es** español y mi madre **es** inglesa.*
*5. Ellos **son** hombres y hoy **están** muy felices.*
*6. Yo **soy** Marco y **estoy** en el centro de la ciudad.*
*7. Nosotros **estamos** de vacaciones en Australia. (on holiday)*
*8. Ellos **están** vivos, pero ellas **están** muertas.*
*9. Mi amigo **está** borracho.*
*10 Mi hermana **es** muy inteligente.*

Lesson 10
1, Frecuentemente
2, Ligeramente
3, Recientemente
4, Suavemente
5, Afortunadamente

Lesson 11
1, ¿Hay una iglesia por aquí?
2, ¿Está la iglesia por aquí?
3, Hay un hombre en la calle.
4, El hombre está en la calle.
5, ¿Está aquí la gente?
6, ¿Hay gente aquí?
7, Los perros están aquí.
8, Hay perros aquí.
9, El banco está aquí.
10, Hay un banco aquí.

Lesson 12

A capital letter is used to show where the accent would be normally:
Estación = estAcion   Árbol = arbOl   Ratón = rAton
Sillón = sIllon   Sartén = sArten   Bolígrafo = boligrAfo
Televisión = televIsion   Fotografía = fotogrAfia   Cajón = cAjon

Lesson 13

1, Veo A mi amigo.
2, Veo - mi casa.
3, Tengo A mi amigo aquí conmigo.
4, Tengo - muchos amigos.
5, Busco A Jorge.
6, Busco A mi perro.
7, Busco - un fontanero.
8, Hay - cuatro personas en el salón.
9, Están – las cuatro personas en el salón.
10, Busco A tu hermano.

Lesson 14

1, We are frightened. = Tenemos miedo.
2, They are hungry. = Tienen hambre.
3, Pedro is ashamed. = Pedro tiene vergüenza.
4, I'm thirsty. = Tengo sed.
5, You, normally, are in a hurry. = Normalmente tienes prisa.
6, Are you tired? (Formal) = ¿Tiene sueño, usted?
7, I have to work tomorrow. = Tengo que trabajar mañana.
8, They have to eat now. = Tienen que comer ahora.
9, We have to be there, soon. = Tenemos que estar allí pronto.
10, I have to sleep. I'm tired. = Tengo que dormir. Tengo sueño.

Lesson 15

1, It's sunny and hot today. = Hace sol y calor hoy.
2, It rains a lot in England. = Llueve mucho en Inglaterra.
3, It's raining in England. = Llueve/ está lloviendo en Inglaterra.
4, It's stifling because it's not windy. = Hace bochorno porque no hace viento.
5, There's frost on the cars. = Hay escarcha en los coches.

Lesson 16

1, Estoy comiendo pescado.
2, El lunes como con amigos.
3, Pablo está corriendo.
4, Mañana trabajo en la oficina.
5, Ella está trabajando en la oficina hoy.
6, Estoy pensando en ir(me) a España.
7, Estamos escuchando la música.
8, Están luchando en la calle.
9, Salimos el viernes.
10, Él escribe un libro.

Lesson 17

1, Son las tres menos cuarto.
2, Son las dos y diez.
3, Es la una y quince/ cuarto.
4, Son las once menos veinticinco.
5, Son las siete menos diez.
6, Son las cinco y veintitrés.
7, Son las doce menos tres. / Faltan tres para las doce.
8, Es la una y media.
9, Son las siete menos quince/cuarto.
10, Son las nueve.
11, Voy a llegar a las tres.
12, ¿A qué hora vienen?
13, Vamos a estar allí a las nueve y cuarto.
14, ¿A qué hora comes? (or come/coméis/comen)
15, Él va a llamar a medianoche.

Lesson 18

*1.-Margarita **sabe** hablar francés.*
*2.-¿Tú **conoces** a Julio Iglesias?*
*3.-Disculpe, ¿usted **sabe** donde está la biblioteca?*
*4.-Nosotros **sabemos** nadar muy bien.*
*5.-Ellos **conocen** al doctor Ramírez.*
*6-7.-Nosotros **sabemos** quién es el presidente de los Estados Unidos, pero no lo **conocemos** personalmente.*
*8.-Ella es una estudiante nueva, y no **conoce** bien la universidad.*
*9. ¿**Conoces** (tú) la ciudad de Madrid?*
*10.-Ella **sabe** muy bien todos los verbos nuevos.*
*11. ¿A qué deportes **sabes** (tú) jugar bien?*
*12. ¿**Conocen** tus compañeros a tus abuelos?*

Lesson 19
1. Me gustan los perros.
2. ¿Te gustan los animales?
3. No nos gusta esta casa.
4. A Samantha le gusta el té.
5. A Raúl y a Elsa les gusta ir al teatro.
6. Me gusta el helado de chocolate. ¿Y a ti?
7. ¿A Peter le gusta el francés?
8. Me gusta leer y escribir.
9. A mi hermana no le gusta la tarta.
10. No me gustan los bichos. ¿Y a ti?
11. ¡Me gustan!
12. No me gusta.

Lesson 20
1. ¿Dónde vives? Vivo en ……………
2. ¿De dónde eres? Soy de …………………
3. ¿En qué trabajas? Soy…………………..Trabajo de/en/para……………….
4. ¿Tienes familia? Sí, tengo ……….. hijos. Estoy casado/a, soltero/a, divorciado/a
5. ¿Tienes pasatiempos? Sí, juego al………….. Leo, hago ejercicio, escucho la música, escribo novelas….etc.
6. ¿Qué te gusta hacer? Me gusta…………………..
Now, translate these answers.
7. I live in France. = Vivo en Francia.
8. I'm from Spain. = Soy de España.
9. I'm a carpenter. = Soy carpintero.
10. I have three sisters. = Tengo tres hermanas.
11. I like to go out with friends. = Me gusta salir con amigos.
12. I like to read novels. = Me gusta leer novelas.

Lesson 21

¡Perdone! ¿Me trae más pan y una botella de vino tinto, por favor?
También, ¿me trae un café con leche y la cuenta por favor?
Hola, buenas tardes. ¿Me pone una cerveza y un ginebra con tónica (gin tonic), por favor?
Perdone, ¿me pone otra cerveza y un agua, por favor?

Lesson 22

1, Siga todo recto/derecho hasta la glorieta/rotonda.
2, Luego, doble a la izquierda y siga hasta los semáforos.
3, Después, tome/coja la tercera calle a la derecha.
4, Al final de la calle, doble a la izquierda.
5, Siga todo recto/derecho hasta los semáforos y pare. Allí está a la izquierda.

Lesson 23

1. Mil doscientos treinta y cuatro. = 1.234
2. Trescientos sesenta y siete. = 367
3. Cuatrocientos sesenta y cinco. = 465
4. Quinientos setenta y nueve. = 579
5. Cinco mil, setecientos cuarenta y tres. = 5.743
6. Veinticuatro mil, novecientos noventa y nueve. = 24.999
7. Trescientos sesenta y dos mil, setecientos cincuenta y seis. = 362.756
8. Ochenta y dos. = 82
9. Tres millones, cuatrocientos noventa y seis mil, ochocientos veintiuno. = 3.496.821
10. Siete mil, trescientos veintiséis. = 7.326

Lesson 24

1, Caminamos por el parque.
2, Pedí una hamburguesa.
3, Entraron en la casa.
4, Jugasteis/jugaron ustedes en la nieve.
5, Escuchaste la música.

Lesson 25

1,Ayer aduve por el parque.
2, Hicimos un té.
3, ¿Tuviste una sorpresa?
4, Pusieron la taza en la mesa.
5, No pude llegar.
6, Vino a la casa.
7, Quise ir(me).
8, Estuve allí por/en la mañana.
9, Puse el bolso/la bolsa en el coche.
10, Vinieron a la diez.

Lesson 26

1, I used to eat meat. = Comía carne.

2, I was walking along the street. (por la calle)= Andaba por la calle.

3, We used to watch the television a lot.= Veíamos/Mirábamos la televisión mucho.

4, They were talking about politics. (la política) = Hablaban de la política.

5, Were you going to Spain? = ¿Ibas a España?

6, You all used to come here. = Veníais aquí.

7, Pablo was running quickly. = Pablo corría rápidamente.

8, Leticia used to live in that house. = Leticia vivía es esa casa.

9, I used to be a policeman. = Yo era policía.

10, We were in the park. = Estábamos en el parque.

Lesson 27

1, Mientras limpiaba el salón sonó el teléfono.

2, Miguel escribía un email cuando se fue la luz.

3, Mientras Elizabeth y yo trabajábamos en el jardín empezó a llover.

4, Esta mañana, mientras veía la televisión desayunaba/desayuné.

5, Decía que bebía más agua.

Lesson 28

1, Estas casa son grandes.

2, Quiero este pan.

3, Esos coches son rojos.

4, Esto es increíble.

5, Queremos esa tarta.

6, ¿Estos qué son?

7, Estos son mis libros.

8, Puedo tener ese vaso.

9, Usas estos bolígrafos.

10, ¿Dónde está esa chica?

Lesson 29

1, ¡Mira!

2, ¡Escucha!

3, ¡Come!

4, ¡Bebe!

5, ¡Trabaja!

With usted.

1, ¡Mire!

2, ¡Escuche!

3, ¡Coma!

4, ¡Beba!

5, ¡Trabaje!

Lesson 30

1, ¿Me da un kilo de patatas, por favor?
2, ¿A cuánto están las uvas?
3, Quiero pagar en efectivo.
4, ¿Cuánto cuesta esto?
5, No, eso es todo, gracias.

Lesson 31

1, Voy a quitar el libro.
2, ¿Puedes remover la sopa, por favor?
3, Él es sensato pero yo soy sensible.
4, Busco la salida. (If you added 'por' you didn't need to as 'buscar' is to 'look for'.
5, Quiero grabar el concierto.
6, Asisto a una clase de español.
7, Atendemos a una mujer mayor.
8, ¡Molesta mucho! (Es una molestia)

Lesson 32

Yo soy una persona muy activa. Hago muchos deportes. Juego al fútbol, al baloncesto y al rugby.

Los sábados voy al parque a jugar al fútbol con mis amigos. A las doce, vengo del parque y voy al centro deportivo. Allí, juego al baloncesto durante un par de horas.

Los domingos, normalmente voy a jugar al rugby por la mañana. Depende del tiempo. Si no, un amigo viene a mi casa y jugamos a la Playstation durante la mañana. Los domingos por la tarde, no juego a nada. Voy al bar y tomo un par de cervezas con mis amigos.

Index of expressions and idioms used in the story.

So far, in the lessons linked to each chapter, you've been concentrating on grammar and vocabulary. Now, it's time to take a look at the many expressions that you've come across in the story.

Some of them make sense when you look at the translation in English, and yet others don't really seem to translate at all.

We'll aim to help you understand them a little better. Once you can use these expressions correctly, your Spanish will be at a very high level. So, here we go.

We've put them into alphabetical order for you, so you can use this as a reference in the future.

Alguna vez.

This is the Spanish speaker's way of saying, 'ever' or 'once'.

e.g.

¿Alguna vez has probado pulpo? = Have you ever tried octopus?

¿Alguna vez has comido sesos de cordero? = Have you ever eaten lamb's brains?

A medias.

When you want to say, "to go halves" when paying for food or something similar, this is what you say.

"Vamos a pagar a medias, ¿vale? = We're going to go halves, okay?

Hacerlo a medias. = Share the work.

A que...

This is the second part of the expression: "Apuesto a que..." = "I bet that it's...". However, Spanish speakers just use the 'a que' part for speed which translates pretty much as "isn't it".

e.g. ¡A que está riquísima la comida! = Isn't the food delicious!

Ir/Salir/Venir a tomar algo.

If you hear this once, you hear it a thousand times in mainland Spain. It means to have something to eat and / or to drink. It's a virtual anthem in Spain, where going out is one of their favourite pastimes.

e.g.

¡Oye! ¿Quieres salir a tomar algo conmigo mañana por la tarde?= Hey! Do you want to come out for a drink with me tomorrow evening?

Anda.

This is the verb, 'to walk'. It's used often at the beginning of sentences, often as a way of showing surprise. It's similar to the English version; 'Get out of here!'

¡Anda! Qué bien. = Get away! How nice.

Aquí, luchando.

This means literally, 'Here, fighting.' and is used in a similar way to the English expression, 'Struggling on.' or, 'Getting by.'

e.g.

¿Cómo estás estos días? ...Bueno, aquí, luchando. = How are you these days? Well, struggling on.

Aquí tienes.

This is an interesting expression which means "Here you have it/them." or more like English, "Here you are." This is used when someone is handing something to another person. Notice that there is no "it/them" in the expression. (Lit: Here you have.)

Armar un lío.

This is to cause a fuss or to cause trouble. 'Un lío' is a mess.

e.g.

Vaya lío que has armado, Jorge. = What a mess you've made, Jorge.

Bueno.

In its conventional sense, this means "good". However, it's also used at the beginning of sentences and means "well" or "then".

e.g.   Bueno, no sé. = Well, I don't know.

Caerte bien.

This is a great expression which is used to say that you like/get on well with someone, or not, as the case may be.

Literally you say, "They fall well on me." or "They fall badly on me."

e.g.   Me cae muy bien, Jorge. = I like/get on well with Jorge.

Esa chica me cae muy mal. = I really don't get on well with that girl.

You can use it as a question.

¿Te caen bien los padres de tu novia?= Do you like/get on with your girlfriends parents?

Notice how the verb CAER behaves like GUSTAR.

Claro que no/sí.

This is the way to say "of course" or "of course not".

e.g. P. ¿Puedo entrar? R. Claro que sí. = Q. Can I come in? A. Of course.

You don't need to say, "que sí" and can simply say, "¡claro!" which means "of course" even on its own.

Conformarse con.

A nice little verb that allows you to say, "I'll be happy with" or "I'll make do with."

e.g.

Esta noche me conformo con una buena peli y comida para llevar. = Tonight I'll be happy with a good film and a take-away.

Costarte.

To say, "It's hard for me." you can use this expression. Literally, you are saying, "it costs me".

e.g. "Me cuesta mucho hablar con él. = It's hard for me to talk to him.

Cumplir años.

Unlike in English where we say, 'He's going to be 16 next week.' Spanish speakers often use the verb 'cumplir', which means 'to accomplish'.

e.g.

Este año va a cumplir 70 años. = This year, he's going to be 70 years old.

Y el sábado que viene, cumplo 16. = And this Saturday, I'll be 16.

"Darle un beso" compared to "Besarlo/la"

Because of the way that many Spanish speakers greet one another, which is with a kiss on either cheek, they have ways of differentiating between a kiss on the lips between a couple and a kiss as a greeting.

To greet with the customary kisses on the cheeks is:

Darle un beso a alguien.

e.g. Le di un beso a mi tía cuando la vi. = I gave my aunty a kiss when I saw her.

To kiss someone in a romantic, girfriend/boyfriend way is:

Besar a alguien.

e.g. De repente la besó apasionadamente. = Suddenly, he kissed her passionately.

Darse cuenta.

This expression literally translates as "to give oneself account" and means "to realise" something.

e.g. Me doy cuenta de eso. = I realise that.

No sé si se da cuenta del problema. = I don't know if he realises the problem.

It works like all reflexive verbs.

Dar cosa.

This is a strange expression which translates like: "To make you feel funny/strange/weird/yukky/horrible."

Literally it means to "give thing". It's used like Gustar in many respects.

e.g. No me gusta el pulpo. Me da cosa verlo en el plato. = I don't like octopus. It makes me feel yukky seeing it on the plate.

Dar de alta / baja

This is a very interesting expression used in a number of contexts. It means to be connected, cut off, to be signed on the sick, to be signed off the sick along with many other situations.

The best way to remember it is that 'dar de alta' means going back to normality, or back in a working state.

'Dar de baja' is being out of service.

¿Tienes internet? No, todavía no me han dado de alta. = Have you got internet? No, they still haven't connected me.

¿Qué te pasa? El médico me ha dado un mes de baja. = What's wrong with you? The doctor has put me on the sick for a month.

Dar miedo.

To say you are frightened, you can say "Tengo miedo". However, another way is to say: "It gives me fear."

e.g. La montaña rusa me da mucho miedo. = I'm frightened of the rollercoaster.

Dársete bien/mal.

This is an expression which is used to say whether you are good at something or bad at something. It has an interesting structure. Take a look at some examples:

Se me da bien cantar.= I'm good at singing.

Se me dan bien los idiomas. = I'm good at languages.

Se le da bien hablar en público. = He's good at speaking in public.

Note: This works rather like Gustar in as much as you either use DA for single things you are good at or DAN for plural things we are good at.

The only thing that changes are the pronouns. ME, TE, LE, NOS, OS, LES.

Denunciar.

In Spain, this word is used a lot. It refers to the right that everyone has to report someone to the police for, basically, anything. Once "denounced", the police are obliged to make an official visit to that person and warn them.

¡Qué ruido! Voy a denunciarlo mañana. = What a noise! I'm going to report him tomorrow.

De prueba.

This is used to say: "on trial", when you have just started a job, for example.

Empiezo el lunes pero estoy de prueba un mes. = I start on Monday but I´m on trial for a month.

De repente.

When something happens suddenly, then this is the expression to use.

e.g. Estaba leyendo en casa, yo, cuando, de repente, sonó el teléfono.

= I was reading at home when suddenly the phone rang.

De retraso.

When something arrives late, then you can say:

El tren llega con una hora de retraso. = The train is running one hour late.

De sobra.

This means, in essence, extra or surplus.

Tenemos tiempo de sobra. = We have time to spare.

Lo sé de sobra. = I know only too well.

De todas formas.

You can use this expression to say: "Anyway".

e.g. De todas formas no quería ir. = I didn't want to go anyway.

De una vez.

This is the Spanish way of saying: "once and for all" or "finally".

e.g. "Quiero tenerlo en la mano de una vez." = I want to have it in my hand once and for all."

Dormilón.

This is the word that Spanish speakers use to say "sleepyhead".

e.g. ¡Despiértate ahora!¡Qué dormilón eres! = Wake up now! What a sleepyhead you are!

Echarse un amigo.

Although this expression means to "find a friend", the verb "Echarse" and "Echar" for the matter is one of the most flexible in the Spanish language. There are literally hundreds of expressions that use it. The pure meaning of "Echar" is "to pour on". Thus the expression above literally means "to pour oneself a friend". Why don't you pop "expressions with echar" into Google and have a look. You'll be amazed.

Echarse una siesta.

The meaning is simple enough: "To have a siesta." Like the above expression, this uses 'echarse' in a way that reallly doesn't translate well into English. This is how it's used:

Creo que me voy a echar una siesta, estoy muy cansado. = I think I'm going to have a siesta. I'm really tired.

En absoluto.

As strange as this may seem, this expression actually means "absolutely NOT!"

Many students think it means the exact opposite and go around answering people's requests to go for a coffee with "Absolutely NOT!". Lol.

e.g.   P. ¿Te gusta el vino rosado? R. ¡En absoluto!

        Q. Do you like rosé wine?   A. Absolutely not!

En pleno/a...

If you want to say "in the middle of something" then this is the expression to use.

e.g. Llegaron en plena noche. = The arrived in the middle of the night.

En punto.

This is used when talking about time and means "on the dot".

e.g. Pues, te veo a las doce en punto. = So, I'll see you at twelve on the dot.

¡Eres un crack!

A nice Spanglish expression which means that you, or another person, are very good at what they do. It comes from the English word 'crack' as in; a crack marksman.

e.g.

Oye, te vi ayer en la cancha. Hombre, ¡eres un crack! = Hey, I saw you on the tennis court yesterday. You're an expert, man!

Estar de broma.

To say, "I'm joking" then this is the phrase to use. Broma is a joke, but not one that you might tell to someone. That's "un chiste". Broma is more like when you joke with someone, or poke fun at them.

e.g.

No lo tomes tan en serio, estoy de broma. = Don't take it so seriously, I'm joking.

Estar en marcha.

This just means "to be running" when referring to a motor or machine.

e.g.

El coche todavía está en marcha. = The car's still running.

Estar listo.

This means "to be ready".

Estoy listo para salir. = I'm ready to leave.

However, if you use it with Ser, then it changes its meaning to "to be clever".

Es un chico muy listo. = He's a very clever boy.

Estar mal de la cabeza.

When you want to say that someone is 'crazy in the head', then this is the one.

¿Qué me dices? ¿Estás mal de la cabeza o qué? = What are you saying? Are you crazy in the head or something?

Clearly, 'crazy in the head' could be substituted for other expressions that mean the same in English, like: Off your trolley. A looney. Two sandwiches short of a picnic. Etc.

Estrechar la mano.

This means to shake someone's hand. It sounds like, "stretch out the hand".

Al conocerle, le estrechó la mano. = When meeting him, he shook his hand.

(La) Faena.

This word derives from bullfighting and it is the battle between the man and the bull. However, it is used quite often to describe a busy situation.

Bueno, la faena empieza a las cuatro. = Well, the busy time starts at four.

Hasta.

Although this means 'until' or 'to' in its normal use, it can also mean 'even' like in 'even me'.

e.g. Ha hablado mal con todo el mundo, hasta conmigo. = He's talked badly with everyone, even me.

Guiri.

This is the name that the Spanish from mainland Spain give to white foreigners. It can be used in a negative way and tends to describe the people who come to Spain to get drunk and tanned and who shout at Spanish barman things like, "Dos cervezas en plástico vasos." (We only have ourselves to blame lol.)

Habérmelo dicho.

This is one of the famous Spanish sentences that has an important piece missing from it.

It's very common for Spanish speakers to say things that are partial, assuming that everyone can silently add the missing piece in their mind. For students of the language, this is a problem!

This expression means, "You should have told me it." and in its entirety is, "Deberías habérmelo dicho."

However, for speed, they've shortened it down to the following:

¡Mamá, necesito ir al baño! ¡Jope, niño! Habérmelo dicho antes de salir de casa.

Mum, I need the bathroom! Goodness, boy! You should have told me before leaving the house.

Hablar por los codos.

This literally translates as "to talk through the elbows". It's used to describe a talkative person.

e.g. Joer! Elizabeth habla por los codos.= Goodness! Elizabeth is a chatterbox/gobby.

Hacer falta.

This is another way to say "to need" and is quite common.

e.g. Hacen falta tres más. = Three more are needed.

Sólo hace falta la conclusión. = It just needs the conclusion.

Hacer transbordo.

This means to change trains.

e.g. Tienes que hacer transbordo en Madrid. = You have to change trains in Madrid.

Leches.

This is a very 'light' swear word (not even a swear word, really) in mainland Spain. It is like saying: 'For God's sake.'

You can simply say it on its own as an expression of frustration or add it to a sentence as an intensifier.

e.g.

¿Dónde leches he puesto mis llaves? = Where have I put my keys, for God's sake?

Llevar.

This verb has many uses but the one we want to mention here is its use when "taking someone somewhere."

There is a temptation to use "tomar" when saying "I'm going to take my mum to the hospital." Spanish speakers tend to use "llevar" which is more like "to carry".

e.g. Si quieres ir al aeropuerto, yo te llevo. = If you want to go to the airport, I'll take you.

Me gustaría.

This is "I like" in what is known as the conditional form. Simply stated, it's the 'would' version of the verb. It means, 'I would like'.

e.g.   Me gustaría una cerveza. = I would like a beer.

Me toca.

A very interesting verb, this is used in a number of situations, like winning the lottery, for example. It means, "It's my turn / go." Or " I need / it's about time."

Here are some examples:

Me toca comer algo. = I need to / It's about time I ate something.

Oye, te toca. = Hey, it's your turn. (Playing cards)

La semana pasada me tocó la lotería. = I won the lottery last week.

Menos mal.

This is a way of saying: """It's a good job that…"

e.g. Menos mal que llegaste antes de la tormenta. = It's a good job you arrived before the storm.

Narices.

Always mentioned in the plural in this context, it's a 'light' way of saying, 'What the hell?'

No sé qué narices hace por aquí ese chico. = I don't know what the hell that boy is doing around here.

No es para tanto.

When you want to say something along the lines of, "It's no big deal." then this is the phrase to use.

e.g. Mira, no te preocupes. No es para tanto. = Look. Don't worry. It's no big deal.

No sólo… sino también.

For those who might remember the Cook and Moore show, "Not Only but Also", this is what it was called in Spanish.

This often catches students out as in English we tend to use "but" in sentences such as:

Not only that **but** this.

In this sentence in Spanish, the **"not only"** is **"no sólo"** and the **"but"** is **"sino"** and NOT "pero".

So that sentence would be:

No sólo eso **sino** esto también.

Here are some more examples:

No sólo es bueno, sino también es amable. = He's not only good, but he's kind too.

No sólo hablan francés, sino también hablan chino. = They not only speak French, but they speak Chinese, too.

'Solo' is also used on its own and means 'rather' in the following context.

No hice la tarea ese día sino la hice durante el fin de semana. = I didn't do the homework that day but rather I did it at the weekend.

Pan comido.

When you want to say 'It's easy', with an expression like, 'it's a piece of cake', then this is what you use.

e.g. Tengo un exámen mañana…¡Anda! Será pan comido! = I have an exam tomorrow... Go on! It'll be a piece of cake.

Parecerte bien.

To ask someone if they approve of something you can use this expression. Be aware, however, that it's also used in lots of other ways.

e.g.

¿Te parece bien? = Does that seem okay to you?

¿Qué te parece? = How does that seem to you?

Me parece bien. = It seems good/okay to me.

Para nada.

This means "no way" or "not at all".

e.g. ¿y tú hablas con él?- ¿Yo? ¡Para nada! = And do you talk to him? – Me? No way!

Para ser.

This is a way of making a comparison and it works like "For being..." in English.

Para ser español, no tienes mucho acento. = For being Spanish you don't have a lot of accent.

Pasarse.

This verb means to go too far.

e.g.

Te has pasado con él, ¿no te parece? = Don't you think you've gone too far with him?

Also, when going too far, 'tres pueblos' are often mentioned. It's like saying that you went so far that you went three towns too far.

e.g.

Te pasaste tres pueblos cuando me dijiste eso. = You went way too far when you said that to me.

Por adelantado.

This is how you say "in advance". For example, when a payment has to be made in advance.

e.g.

    Tienes que pagar un mes por adelantado = You have to pay a month in hand.

Por un tubo.

This is the expression you can use to say things like: "By the millions." Or : "In their droves."

e.g. En Benidorm vas a ver bares por un tubo.= In Benidorm, you're going to see bars in their millions.

¿Qué echan?

Echar is a widely used verb, as you may well be discovering. However, in this instance, it's used to ask and to talk about "what's on" whether it's the television or the cinema.

e.g. ¿Qué echan esta tarde en el cine? Echan una peli de Almodóvar. = What's on this evening in the cinema? They're putting an Almodovar film on.

¡Qué guay!

This is "How cool!" and it's pronounced a bit like the letters "K Y".

¡Qué ilusión!

Ilusión is excitement in the Spanish speaking world. Thus, when you say, "Qué ilusion" you are saying, "How exciting". (Not to be confused with the false friend, "excitación", which is another kind of excited!)

¡Qué impresionante!

Here's another that starts with "Qué". This means "how impressive". In fact, you can make this sentence work by adding any adjective with "Qué".

e.g. ¡Qué increíble! = How incredible!   ¡Qué triste! = How sad! etc.

¿Qué lleva?

When you want to ask what a certain food has in it you use this verb.

e.g. ¿Qué lleva la salsa? Lleva almendras. = What does the sauce have in it? It has almonds.

¿Que pasa?

This is one of the most popular greetings in Spain which means, "What's happening? It is also used to specifically ask what is going on.

e.g.   Hola, ¿qué pasa tío? = Hi, what's happening, mate?

¿Qué pasa, cariño?¿Por qué lloras? = What's wrong, darling? Why are you crying?

¡Qué va!

When you want to say "No way!", this is the right expression for you. It literally translates as " What goes!" but is understood as "No way, Not likely, Not on your Nelly." ☺

Quedar.

Knowing how to talk about meeting up with people is always a challenge. Lots of students use encontrarse which is okay to use, but isn't what most Spanish speakers use. They prefer the verb, "quedar".

e.g.   *Hoy he quedado con un amigo para las doce. =*

  I've agreed to meet with a friend at twelve.

It's normally used with "con".

e.g.   *No puedo ir hoy porque he quedado con mi hermana. =*

  I can't go today because I have agreed to meet up with my sister.

or with "para"

  Quedamos para la una. = We agreed to meet for one o'clock.

Quedarse claro.

This is how you can say that something is or isn't clear to you. It works like Gustar with the Indirect Object Pronouns. (The furniture remover's list.)

¡No sales este viernes! ¿Te queda claro? = You are not going out on Friday. Is that clear?

Si, me queda claro. = Yes, that's clear.

Quedarse grande/pequeño.

When you are trying on clothing or shoes, this is the expression to use to say, "It's too big, or too small."

It works in a similar way to Gustar, so if you are talking about 1 item, you use 'queda' and two or more items, 'quedan'.

e.g. Los zapatos me quedan un poco pequeños. = The shoes are a little small for me.

La chaqueta me queda grande. = The jacket is big for me.

The same verb is used to say if something 'suits you, sir!'

Este vestido te queda muy bonito. = That dress is lovely on you.

El traje te queda muy feo. = The suit looks absolutely horrible on you.

Rumbo a...

This just means "on the way to..." and can be used like this:

Estoy en rumbo a tu casa. = I'm on the way to your house. Or

Lo voy a hacer rumbo a casa. = I'm going to do it on the way home.

Sabe a.

To say that a food tastes of something you say: "Sabe a..."

e.g.   Este helado sabe a limón. = This ice-cream tastes of lemon.

Tu comida sabe a gloria. = Your food tastes wonderfully.

Salir bien.

This is what you use to say that things "turn out well".

No te preocupes. Siempre todo sale bien. = Don't worry, everything always turns out well.

Sin embargo.

To say, "however", or, "nevertheless" then this is one expression you can use.

Iba a llegar temprano, sin embargo, no pasó. = He was going to arrive early, however, it didn't happen.

Soy un paquete.

Translating literally as "I'm a packet", this means something like, "I'm a mess." or "I'm no good/clumsy".

Te invito.

In Spain, this is a very common expression. It means "to pay". When people are having a drink together, it's very common for one of them to say: "Te invito yo" or "Os invito yo" = I'm paying.

It's rare for people to pay separately. Everyone takes their turn, of course, so it's like a big round, each one paying the entire session.

Tener ganas de…

Basically, this is used to say "looking forward to…".

e.g. Tengo ganas de ir de vacaciones. = I'm looking forward to going on holiday.

Note: After the DE you can simply add a verb in infinitive.

e.g. Tengo ganas de ver a Simón. = I'm looking forward to seeing Simon.

Tener cara de pocos amigos.

Literally, this means to have a face of someone with few friends. The actual meaning is to "look extremely unhappy". Or more colloquially, "to have a face like a smacked arse."

Tener mucha ilusión.

This expression literally means, "to have a lot of excitement." or in more normal words, "to be really excited" about something. Many students make the mistake of using the verb "excitar" for excited. This is what's called a false friend as, although it means excited in Spanish too, it's a very different kind of excitement. (The kind we have when we want to make babies!)

Tener nervios en el estómago.

Very similar to English, this is how you can say that you have "butterflies in your tummy" or "a nervous stomach".

Tengo un examen mañana y tengo nervios en el estómago. = I've got an exam tomorrow and I have butterflies.

Tener pinta.

This means to "have the look of" and can be used for both positive and negative descriptions.

e.g. Ese hombre tiene pinta de ser alemán. = That man has the look of being German.

Tener su encanto.

This is like the English expression, "to have its charm".

e.g. *Bueno, el lugar no es bonito pero tiene su encanto.* = Well, the place isn't pretty but it has its charm.

Tras.

This is the "after" we use in sentences like, "Day after day." or, "One after the other".

e.g. *¡Qué ocupado estoy! He tenido trabajo tras trabajo hoy.* = I'm so busy! I've had job after job today.

Un poco mucho.

This may seem like an oxymoron (a contradiction in itself) but it really makes sense. It means, "a bit much", which is something we say in English.

e.g.

Le has echado un poco mucho, ¿no?." = You have added a bit much, haven't you?

Valerte.

"Vale" is used a lot in Spain to say: "okay". However, it comes from the verb 'valer' which means 'to be worth'. In this sense it's used as a question to see if you are okay with something:

Vengo mañana a las tres. ¿Eso te vale? = I'll come at three tomorrow, is that okay for you?

¡Vaya!

You will see this expression everywhere. It translates as "What a…!".

e.g.

¡Vaya vida! = What a life!

Sometimes it's used with the word "más" which translates as "very".

e.g. *¡Vaya hombre más extraño!* = What a very strange man!

Vivir una aventura.

This is translated as "to have an adventure" although the real translation is "to live an adventure". The reason for this is that if we had written the direct translation, "tener una aventura" it would have meant: "to have an affair!".

Vivir la cultura.

The English equivalent of this saying is "to immerse yourself in the culture" of a country.

e.g. Me gusta el sol de España pero me importa más vivir la cultura. = I like Spain's sun but it's more important for me to immerse myself in the culture.

Vuelo con escala.

When you need to take a connecting flight, your flight is called: "Un vuelo con escala". Escalar means to scale, for example, "to scale a mountain". So you could recall it by thinking of climbing from one flight to the next.

Ya es el colmo.

"Colmar" means to fill to the brim. "El colmo" is the brim of a glass. This expression is used to say: "That's the limit!" or "That's enough!"

Vocabulary Builder.

Here you have the list of all the words that we give you in the vocabulary building audio. You can use this list as a reference as well as a way to test your memory. Simply cover the Spanish to check if you have the word captured in your imagination. Then, cover the English to check that you know them the other way around, too. It's important to be able to recall the words from English to Spanish and from Spanish to English.

Note: This entire list is also available in video format in Youtube.

Just go to Lighspeedspanish in Youtube and look in our Playlist.

Nouns and Adjectives

Word	Meaning	How to remember it:
aburrido	boring	A boring read
aceptable	acceptable	No help needed here
afueras	outskirts	If you're going to 'swear' go afuera
ahora	now	Hora hour. Ahora = To the hour =now
algo	something	'I'll go' for something
allí	there	Imagine a E over there
alojamiento (el)	lodgings	You have to put 'a lock' on your lodgings
amable	friendly	He's very amiable
amigo (el)	friend	Friends go with me
andén (el)	platform	You **and en** your ticket on the platform
angloparlante (el)	English-speaking	Anglo-Saxons talking English
año (el)	year	Just like the English word, 'annual'
antes	before	My uncles always arrive before my aunties
antiguo	old	So old, it's an antique
apodo (el)	nickname	open a pea pod and inside is your nickname
apuntes (los)	notes	Imagine punting on a lake and whilst taking notes
aquí	here	Imagine a key at your feet. Right here

Word	Meaning	How to remember it:
arrendador (el)	landlord	You knock on the 'door' to collect the 'rent'
así	like this/that	I see it like this
aventura (la)	adventure	The same thing....with no D
avión (el)	aeroplane	Imagine drinking a big EVIAN in an AVIÓN
banco (el)	bank	same
básico	basic	No help needed here
bebida (la)	drink	A baby drinks milk
bien	well	I've 'been' well
billete (el)	ticket/bill/note	You get the bill for the ticket
bolígrafo (el)	pen	A 'ball' point pen that draws graphs
bueno	good	I know you will be good, but when?
brazo (el)	arm	Imagine your arm is made of brass
cajón (el)	drawer	Open the draw to see a car horn
camarero (el)	waiter	Waiter comes to table on a camel
camisa (la)	shirt	Assistant says, 'Come ere sir, and buy this shirt'
cansado	tired	The can's had a hard day
capítulo (el)	chapter	Cap the chapter with a title
cara (la)	face	Imagine a big carrot sticking out of someone's face
casa (la)	house	Imagine your home as a big castle
casi	nearly	Casa house...Casi...nearly a house
centro (el)	town centre	Put an O on the end
chico (el)	boy	Boys can be cheeky
cine (el)	cinema	The same word, shotened
ciudad (la)	city	See you Dad. I'm off to the city.
clase (la)	class	You are in the class A
cocina (la)	kitchen	(LA accent) The cook have you seen her?
cola (la)	queue/line	A long line of colas waiting to go in the m/c
comida (la)	food	'Come ere dear' and eat your food

Word		Meaning	How to remember it:
con		with	In a prison with a con. Café con leche.
contigo		with you	I'll have a tea with you
concidencia (la)		coincidence	It's a coincidence you're 'ere'
contento		happy	Happy and content
cuaderno	(el)	notepad	It's in the shape of a quadrant
dependiente (el)		shop assistant	We depend on them to serve us
depósito (el)		deposit	No help needed here
derecha (a la)		right (to the)	Reach out to your right
desde		since	From dis day forward, I've been learning Spanish
después		after/later	I'll put my dress on later
detalles		details	Tie a string around the details
detrás		behind	You take out de trash behind the house
día (el)		day	How are you today, dear?
dinero (el)		money	Robert Dinero has lots of money
dirección	(la)	address	In what direction is this address?
disponible		available	I've got available a disposable income
dormitorio (el)		bedroom	school dormitory
duda	(la)	doubt	I doubt he'll 'do dat'
duro		hard	It's hard and durable
entrevista	(la)	interview	You have to enter into the entrevista
España		Spain	Imagine a big spanner unwinding Spain
español		Spanish	Spaniels running all over España
estancia	(la)	a stay	I'm going to stay and 'stand ere'
estación	(la)	station	I'm looking for "a station"
estudiante	(el)	student	a student
feliz		happy	Felix the cat was always happy
fenomenal		Phenomenal	No help needed
gente	(la)	people	Imagine gentry, all dressed up in their finery

Word	Meaning	How to remember it:
gracias (las)	thanks	Thanks for telling me I have a grassy ass.
hambre (el)	hunger	I'm so hungry I could eat a whole HAM
hasta	until/up until	I asked her until she said NO
hay	there is/are	Ay! There is a stone in my shoe
hermano (el)	brother	My brother is a 'hairy man'
hija (la)	daughter	A cowboy shouting for his daughter: Yeeha!
hispanohablante	Spanishspeaking	Hispanics talking Spanish
historia (la)	history/story	Talking about history is telling his story
hombre (el)	man	One brave man
hora (la)	hour/time	Very similar
hoy	today	Oy! I want it today!
ilusión (la)	excitement	It's not real excitement, it's just an illusion
información (la)	information	You don't need any help here! ☺
Inglaterra	England	Imagine a map of England and your tear it
inglés (el)	English	In England they drink sherry "in gless"
instituto (el)	college	The institute of languages
interesante	interesting	I´ve an interesting aunty
interior (el)	inland/interior	The interior of a country
intermedio	intermediate	No help needed
internet	the internet	The same word, without the word 'the'
investigación (la)	investigation	It's the same!
Izquierda (a la)	left (to the)	This key 'ere dear. In my left hand
jamón (el)	ham	Do you want some ham on your sandwich?
jarra (la)	large glass/pitcher	Drinking from a jar
largo	long	Not only is it large but it's long, too.
lejos	far (away)	Lagos is very Lejos from here
lleno	full	Japan is full of Yen / Lleno

Word	Meaning	How to remember it:
luego	then/later	The loo we go later, later to the loo
maleta (la)	suitcase	I put ma letter in my suitcase
mañana (el)	tomorrow	I'm seeing a man tomorrow
manera (la)	way	You can learn it this way, or in this manner
maravilla (la)	wonderfully	You've got a wonderfully 'marvellous' villa
más	more	We need more people in Sunday mass
mayoría (la)	majority	The majority 'ere
medio	half	It's medium. Not big, not small
mejor	best	The majorly best one
mensaje (el)	message	It's a message only for men
mes (el)	month	What a mess this month has been!
mesa (la)	table	Look at the mess on this table!
miedo (el)	fear	I'm in fear of my 'hair do'
mucho	a lot	How much money have you got? A lot!
mundo (el)	world	The world, like the **moon** is made of **dough**
muy	very	'Muy' house is very big
negocio (el)	business	You have to negotiate a lot in business
nervios (los)	nerves (nervous)	I'm nervious, oh, oh, oh.
nivel (el)	level	Tie a 'knee bell' at knee level
noche (la)	night	Every night you put a notch on the bedpost
norte (el)	north	They say people from the north are naughty
noticias (las	news	The news gives you the notices
novio (el)	boyfriend	Boyfriend called Nobby
nuevo	new	If you break a spiders web, they make a new web
oferta (la)	offer	'Ta' for the offer
oficina (la)	office	You work 'IN A' office
ojos (los)	eyes	If someone poked you in the eye, you'd say "oh ho!"
opción (la)	option	No help needed here.

Word	Meaning	How to remember it:
opinión (la)	opinion	No help needed here
ordenador (el)	computer	helps put things in order (imagine a door on it)
padres (los)	parents	Imagine your parents as priests
página (la)	page	There's a 'page in a' book
país (el)	country	Imagine a map and each country is a pie
pan (el)	bread	Bread is made in a pan!
pantalones (los)	trousers/pants	Pantaloons
par (un)	a pair	Just the I missing
parecido	similar	Similar to Paris
parte (la)	part	Have a party in that part of town
pasillo (el)	aisle	It's like a passage
pequeño	small (size)	Imagine a little bird 'pecking' at the window
pero	but	I won't have an apple but I'll have a pear
persona (la)	person	Ahh, a person
piso (el)	flat/apartment	Imagine scattering peas all over your flat
plan (el)	plan	No help needed here
plato (el)	plate	Plate in the shape of an O
poco	little	Imagine poking a little O with a stick.
primero	first	The prime one
privado	private	No help needed here
profesor (el)	teacher	Imagine a professor with a mortar board & cape
pronto	soon	Want printing soon? use prontaprint
puerta (la)	door	Imagine a pear on the door with a W in it.
pues	well/then	Big button....pwess it well then
punto (el)	dot	A little point
queso (el)	cheese	Imagine cheese coming in a big case
rato (un)	a little while	A little rat here for a little while

Word	Meaning	How to remember it:
reservado	reserved	No help here
sala de chat (la)	chat-room	Imagine everyone in the chat room eating salad
saludos	greetings	greetings from the 'loo 2'
segundo	second	Just put an O on the end
seguro	sure	You can have the security to be sure
sensato	sensible	So sensible, he 'sat' down.
siempre	always	You always **see em pray** in a church
sin	without	It's a sin to go without
sitio (el)	site/place	sitting in a site
solo	alone	I'm going solo
sólo	only	The only difference is the accent
sorprendido	suprised	Someone suprises you with a saw
suerte	luck	I 'swear to' you, I'm lucky
también	also	I also have a tambourine
tanto	as/so much	Why have you got so much tan on your toe
tapa (la)	snack with drink	Prawn tapping the plate "Eat me"
tarde (la)	late/afternoon	Arriving in the afternoon is tardy and late
tiempo (el)	time/weather	It's about time this weather got better!
tienda(la)	shop	Pop your head in and ask "any tea in der?"
todavía	still (not)	This toad I have ere is very still.
todo	everything	We have everything on our TODO list
trabajo (el)	work/job	You can't smoke tobacco in el trabajo
transferencia (la)	transference	You can make the transference here
tren (el)	train	Sounds the same
vacaciones (las)	holidays	Just like our word 'vacacions'
viaje (el)	journey	I'm going on a journey VIA the north
vale	fine, okay	Okay, I'm off to the ballet.
verano (el)	summer	In summer you can go 'bare bummed'

Word	Meaning	How to remember it:
verdad (la)	true/the truth	The truth is that dad's bare. Bear dad.
vez (la)	time(1 time)	1 time I knew a girl called Beth
vuelta (la)	a turn	My belt turn once around my body
vuelo (el)	a flight	A yellow plane with V for Virgin
zona (la)	area	Imagine pointing out a zone on a map

Verbs

Word	Meaning	How to remember it:
abrir	to open	the 'breeze' opens the door
acostarse	to go to bed	Imagine getting acosted on the way to bed
aguantar	to put up with	You can stand it if you 'want to'
alegrarse	to be happy	I'm very happy with a leg.
alquilar	to rent	A big key for the rented car
aparecer	to appear	A parrot appears.
aprender	to learn	Apprentices learn
arreglar	to fix/sort out	Regulate something.
ayudar	to help	'Ah! you der' help, please
bajar	to go down	Imagine going down the stairs on your back
buscar	to look for	I'm looking for a bus or car
cargarse	to load	to load with cars
cenar	to dine	If you don't have dinner you'll get 'thinner'
chatear	to chat (Internet)	Chatting into someone's ear
comenzar	to start	To comence something
comer	to eat	Come ere and eat
comprar	to buy	When I buy I make comparisons
contar	to recount a story	I simply can't tell you the story.

Word	Meaning	How to remember it:
contestar	to answer	You can contest an argument by answering back
costar	to cost	A coffee costs a lot in Costa coffee
decidir	to decide	I 'decide here'
decir	to say	I tell you there be death ere.
dormirse	to fall asleep	Shut the 'door' so I can fall asleep
encantar	to adore	I'm enchanted by it
encender	to switch on/light	Encendiary device
encontrar	to find	You encounter what you are looking for
entender	to understand	I'm going to understand in 7, in 8, in 9, in 10 there.
entrar	to enter	Not much help needed here
escribir	to write	Get a scribe to write for you
esperar	to hope/wait	Imagine waiting with **this pear**
estar	to be	I want to be "A star"
faltar	to be lacking	There's a fault, something's missing
gustar	to be pleasing	Like something with 'gusto'
hablar	to talk	blah blah
hacer	to do/make	hAcer make computers
ir	to go	Go by ear
llamar	to call	Phone made of 'Jam'
llegar	to arrive	You arrive in 'your car'
mandar	to send	Send a man
mejorar	to get better	It's majorly better
meterse	to get involved	I'm sticking my nose in by a meter.
mirar	to watch/look	Look at yourself in the mirror
mudarse	to move	Move yourself to a mud hut
necesitar	to need	It's a necessity to know this verb
organizar	to organize	The same
pagar	to pay	To pay and then bag

Word	Meaning	How to remember it:
parecer	to seem	That parrot seems a little sad
pasar	to pass/spend	Passing time
pensar	to think	Think with a pen
picar	to press	Imagine picking at a keyboard button
poder	to be able	Harry Potter is very powerful
poner	to put	I want you to 'put there' the thing
preferir	to prefer	I prefer to be 'ere'
preocuparse	to worry onself	You are preoccupied with worries
preguntar	to ask	Ask if she is pregnant
preparar	to prepare	The same
reservar	to reserve	No help needed here
respirar	to breathe	To breath with a respirator
saber	to know (things)	I know that saber tooth tigers existed
sacar	to take out	Taking things out of a sack
seguir	to follow	You follow one 'gear' with another 'gear'
sentarse	to sit	You sit on your 'arse'
sentirse	to feel(emotions)	You sense a tear
ser	to be	Someone is going to be knighted
significar	to mean	What is the significance of that
tener	to have	I have a tenner (ten).
tomar	to take	Take a tomahawk
trabajar	to work	You aren't allowed tobacco in work
traer	to bring	The waiter brings the drinks on a tray
venir	to come	'Ben' comes 'ere' each day
ver	to watch/see	Imagine watching bare bummed footballers
viajar	to travel	I'm going to travel via car
vivir	to live	'Viva Las Vegas'- long live Spain
volver	to return	You return in a Volvo car

10612043R00143

Printed in Great Britain
by Amazon.co.uk, Ltd.,
Marston Gate.